PRAISE FOR
TURN TO STONE

"*Turn to Stone* marks the arrival of a brave, feminist, seeking, and essential voice in nonfiction. Read this book and be forever changed."

—Emily Rapp Black, *New York Times* bestselling author
of *The Still Point of the Turning World* and *Sanctuary*

"With prose that seems magic, Emily Meg Weinstein captures the inmost, almost-inexpressible experiences of climbing: those moments of transmutation, high above the ground, of stone into light, air into freedom, body into song."

—Katie Ives, author of *Imaginary Peaks: The Riesenstein Hoax
and Other Mountain Dreams*

"How should we live? Emily Meg Weinstein bravely sets out to answer this question in *Turn to Stone*. Eschewing tired pop-psychology platitudes, Weinstein shares with insight and humor the tale of a path not commonly taken, an honest and clear-eyed story to read while the world burns around us."

—Kerry Cohen, author of *Crazy for You* and *Loose Girl*

"*Turn to Stone* may be a book about what Emily gave to climbing and what climbing gave to her, but it is also about what she gives us, and that is a hell of a lot. As a writer, an athlete, and an explorer of peaks and valleys both internal and external, Emily helps us face what scares us most and find the courage to become the people we are meant to be. Her voice is vulnerable, authentic, and wickedly funny. This book will be a fixture in every Sprinter van, Subaru, and beat-up backpack from Joshua Tree to the Adirondacks and beyond."

—Laurel Braitman, *New York Times* bestselling author
of *Animal Madness* and *What Looks Like Bravery*

TURN
TO
STONE

A Memoir

EMILY MEG WEINSTEIN

SIMON ELEMENT

New York   Amsterdam/Antwerp   London
Toronto   Sydney/Melbourne   New Delhi

SIMON ELEMENT

An Imprint of Simon & Schuster, LLC
1230 Avenue of the Americas
New York, NY 10020

"Birmigham" quoted on page 1 by Shovels and Rope
"Sinnerman" quoted on page 1 by Nina Simone
"Psalm 40" quoted on page 187 by Katie Ford printed with permission of Katie Ford

Names and identifying characteristics have been changed to preserve anonymity. Some dialogue has been recreated.

First Simon Element hardcover edition September 2025

SIMON ELEMENT is a trademark of Simon & Schuster, LLC

Simon & Schuster strongly believes in freedom of expression and stands against censorship in all its forms. For more information, visit BooksBelong.com.

For information about special discounts for bulk purchases, please contact Simon & Schuster Special Sales at 1-866-506-1949 or business@simonandschuster.com.

The Simon & Schuster Speakers Bureau can bring authors to your live event. For more information or to book an event, contact the Simon & Schuster Speakers Bureau at 1-866-248-3049 or visit our website at www.simonspeakers.com.

Interior design by Laura Levatino

Manufactured in the United States of America

10 9 8 7 6 5 4 3 2 1

Library of Congress Cataloging-in-Publication Data has been applied for.

ISBN 978-1-6680-4785-9
ISBN 978-1-6680-4787-3 (ebook)

For M & M

PETRIFICATION (NOUN)

1. a state of extreme fear

2. the process by which organic matter is turned to stone

CONTENTS

TURN TO STONE

PROLOGUE

I WAS A HUNDRED FEET ABOVE THE GROUND, clinging. In the distance, Joshua trees saluted the golden hour's infinity with their cheerful punk spikes and victorious fringed limbs, but all I could see was a faint rose tinge on the granite wall inches from my face.

The rope connecting me to my climbing partner below dangled from my harness like a wet noodle. It would only go taut and hold me if I fell, but first, I'd fall a distance—much farther than I wanted to fall. When I looked down at my feet to find the next foothold, the wind blew my hair into my eyes and mouth.

"Help me," I whispered, or more like prayed.

A voice spoke inside my head. Not God's—mine.

No one is coming to save you, it said. *You got yourself into this, and you must get yourself out. There is no God. There is only gravity, dirt, rock, and sky.*

The crack was within sight, but not within reach. The crack would make me safe. I could put my hands in the crack, and they would stay there. I could jam my toes in the crack and stand up on my feet. I could put a metal piece of protective gear in the crack, and make sure it was stuck there, and clip the rope knotted between my belly and groin to it. Then, if I fell, I would not fall so far.

But until I got there, all there was to hold on to was a slight vertical bump, like a doorjamb. It was like trying to hold yourself on a wall by pinching the edges of a piece of molding.

I couldn't hold on much longer. My rubber-shod toes were pressed on little nubs the size of chicken nuggets. (If I were a better climber, the bumps would be no wider than dimes.) Soon, my legs would start to shake and my fingers would start to slip.

I could not stay where I was. I had to make a move.

I looked longingly at the crack above. The voices of my mentors told me what to do.

"Place your feet *with intention*," said Glenn, with his Deadhead pony-tail and Lennon glasses and sinews never obscured by sleeves.

"Make a *plan* for your feet," said Flora, in her kind and measured scientist voice.

"Just hold on!" chuckled Fred, in his SoCal drawl, miming with his huge, strong fingers. "You'd be surprised how much your *body* wants to live."

Sometimes, when I climbed, I heard other voices—like my last real boyfriend's, a pathological liar who had threatened to decapitate me—so I pulled on the rock with the strength of someone who could kill him first.

Now, clinging on, things people had said to me no longer mattered. What was true and what was not no longer mattered. Love and trust did not matter, marriage and babies did not matter. All that mattered was just holding on.

I didn't need a ring or a house or even a van. I was closer to forty than thirty, but at this exact moment, I didn't need to figure out how to finally achieve everything that had thus far eluded me, nor make peace with not having and maybe never getting anything my heart desired. This was the one place in the world where sorrow and shame couldn't reach me. All I needed, and all I wanted, was to claw myself six feet higher and jam my hand in the crack.

There, was my only thought. *Now.*

My mind was quiet while my brain calculated. Then it told my body: *Go.*

I breathed in and reached up. I breathed out and placed my foot with intention. Each time my fingers grasped a new bump or dent or wrinkle or edge, I thought only: *Yes.*

Then I arrived. It was just a broken place, with space inside its darkness.

I sank my fingers into the crack until they locked in place. I twisted my foot into it, until the whole toe was jammed, unfurled myself, and stood tall. I grabbed a piece of metal protective gear from my harness, slotted it into the crack, pulled up the rope from between my legs, and attached myself to the wall.

I tugged on the piece. It was good. I was safe.

I pressed my cheek against the rock's scratchy face, looking back over my shoulder at all the things I climbed to escape—the compendium of lonely weekends and holidays, the persistent longing for love and sex and safety and babies that was only getting louder and harder to bear, the bad mess I always made of it all. Just then, the sun fell below the horizon. I hugged the rock with my one free arm and wept.

I never let any man see me cry, but I could let the rock see. The rock wasn't human. It couldn't love me. I didn't have to try to make it. I didn't even have to let it. I didn't have to be afraid of what it might do to me, in the name of love. Everything that happened here was something I had done, myself.

Things would get better now, they had to. Eventually, even the terse descriptions in climbing guidebooks always said, "The difficulties ease."

"Emily?" shouted my belayer, holding the rope down below. "Everything all right?"

"Fine!" I shouted back. "Climbing!"

I took a ragged breath, inhaling the cold, clean scent of the wall.

Then I charged up the crack in perfect rhythm, karate-chopping one hand and then the other, twisting one foot, then the other, until I was almost vertically walking. "Swimming up stone," I'd once heard it called.

I kept climbing until I didn't need to use my hands anymore. The rock flattened out and became something like ground beneath my feet. I howled with joy and relief, then looked for a place to build an anchor.

Down on the ground, it was hard to connect, hard to attach, hard to untangle, hard to let go. But up here, I understood.

"Make it good," Fred always said, about the colorful metal protective gear I had to place correctly in the rock myself, the only thing that would catch me if I fell. Up here, I could make it good.

There was blood on my hands, but I felt no pain. I built a bomber anchor just like I'd been taught and clipped my belay device to it, threading it with the rope that would hold my partner's life, just as moments ago, they had held mine. Checking everything twice, I yelled down, "On belay!" and watched the setting sun paint the desert sky, grinning through my tears as I pulled up the rope I had hung.

PART I

RUN FOR
YOUR LIFE

Rock of ages, cleave for me
Let me hide myself in thee
—Shovels and Rope

But the rock cried out
I can't hide you, the rock cried out
—Nina Simone

1

Run for Your Life

Well, I'd rather see you dead, little girl
Than to be with another man
        —Lennon and McCartney, "Run for Your Life"

HE ONLY SAID IT ONCE, at an Egon Schiele retrospective on the Upper East Side.

He was wearing his camel coat. We stood in front of each painting for a long time, holding hands and telling stories, and I thought: *This is why this is good.*

I was mesmerized by a huge canvas called *Lovers Man and Woman.* A couple, nude, in bed. The man on his back, staring at the viewer. The woman on her elbows and knees, head tucked under, hips raised, feet flexed, pale back long and bony. The man's outstretched arm snaked through the woman's folded ones. Though the woman's face was hidden, her posture conveyed anguish, while the man's expression was challenging, poised, collected.

"Why does she look so sad," I wondered, "when he looks so satisfied?"

"Maybe he cheated on her," Robbie said.

"Maybe she cheated on him," I said.

There was a change in the weather, his eyes, the room.

Still holding my hand, Robbie said, matter-of-factly, "If you ever suck another man's cock, and kiss me with that mouth, I'll cut your head off."

My brain knew it was bad, but not what to do or say. If I said something, we might have a fight, and those were always bad.

It didn't sound like a joke, but maybe he doesn't really *mean* it. Did the Beatles really mean it, in the song? Sometimes Robbie, like Lennon, called me "little girl," as a joke, or a term of endearment. Maybe threatening to cut my head off was a similar metaphor, or figure of speech.

Not long after Robbie told me the specific circumstances under which he would decapitate me, we spent a perfect winter afternoon at the art museum in New Haven, where he kept an apartment that was empty save for a bed, a recliner, and a flat-screen TV.

We made out on the benches in the empty galleries. We saw a pink neon spiral inside which blue neon letters said, THE TRUE ARTIST HELPS THE WORLD BY REVEALING MYSTIC TRUTHS.

IT WAS MOSTLY LOCALS at the horse race on the beach in Oaxaca, five months earlier, in August 2008, but there was another pair of American travelers, two guys about our age. Like my college best friend, Leila, and I, one blond, one dark-haired.

The dark-haired one, Robbie, had blue eyes and thick, tan calves. *Like tree trunks*, I thought, finally getting the simile. The blond one had a map of the whole world tattooed on his back. They told us they were going to import mezcal to the States, that it was going to be the next tequila.

The mezcal, the pride of Oaxaca, was everywhere—in bars in shapely glass bottles, on the dusty shelves of the little tiendas, in plastic water bottles with hand-painted cacti on them.

After the horse race, Robbie and his friend and Leila and I drank mezcal at a bar right on the beach, steps from our respective cabanas, until, hours later, it was only Robbie and me, our bare feet touching in the sand.

He was some kind of business guy, he said. Finance. I said something about capitalism, and he said something that made me laugh. Then he said, "You have a beautiful mind."

His cabana wasn't as fancy as ours. Our sheets were new and smooth and his were old and pilled. Our fan was on the ceiling and made of wood, and his was plastic, rattling on the cement floor. This did not matter, because we did not sleep.

I was so relieved. It had been two years since my last actual relationship, with a guilty Catholic and quiet alcoholic with whom I had guilty, quiet, Catholic sex, after I drank one or two beers in the six-pack and he finished the rest that same night, in an apartment upstairs from his grandmother's, outside which a single pair of granny underwear flapped frequently on the clothesline like a damp flag of surrender. Then the sex with various randos that was often worse than no sex at all. Then a long drought.

Before, in my early twenties, there had been a beautiful boy who stripped down to his boxer briefs each week after yoga class, climbed into my bed, and never touched me. Then, in my mid-twenties, there was an expatriate ex-Marine hippie-hermit on a walled farm in Peru who ravaged me like the world was ending for three straight days before waking up on the fourth to tell me that he'd had "a really intense dream" and didn't want me to get my heart broken. He said I should stay until the end of the week, but only to watch David Lynch movies and rip bong hits. Then came the guilty Catholic alcoholic, the randos, the drought.

From these experiences, I amassed a Pandora's box of fears about my own desires for sex and love. I feared not having sex for a long time. I feared having sex I liked a lot that suddenly got taken away with zero explanation, or came and went, like mysterious weather, according to no pattern I could prepare for without remaining in a constant state of desire with no expectation of it ever being satisfied. I feared someone I wanted body and soul telling me what a fun friend I was, and how important it was that we stayed "in each other's lives" because of our "great conversations." I feared someone I desired turning their back on me and curling into the fetal position in my own bed, or theirs—literally overnight, in the middle of what I had naively thought could be a love affair, or maybe even love itself, and unilaterally deciding it was "just friendship" instead. I feared being wanted by someone boring and messed-up and quietly alcoholic in a way that felt more like a mucky, sucking need than any kind of mutual desire, and the only way to not be alone was to give in and pretend, which was the only thing even more lonely. Being wanted by someone I didn't want was even more gutting than not being wanted at all, because my unmet desire had at least been real, if only to me, while the numb absence of feeling was like an empty room in myself.

The sandy, sleepless night in the cabana soothed these fears. Or obliterated them.

The next day, Robbie and I exchanged numbers while Leila glowered from a waiting cab. Then Leila and I took his recommendation and went up to a town in the misty mountains, where the locals would sell you magic mushrooms fresh from the mist, and the family that rented the cabins came to build and light your fire for you while they took effect.

It was all just as he described. Leila and I stayed up all night, and I burned a recent bestseller, page by page, because I was sure I could write a better one. Leila briefly believed she had lost her engagement ring, but then remembered she had left it at home, in New York.

BACK IN NEW YORK, a few weeks later, Robbie called.

It was the final Friday of September 2008. I had just turned twenty-nine.

He named a café on Park Avenue in the twenties, a part of Manhattan I never went to. When I got there, he was wearing a blue shirt with a white collar, already finishing a drink.

He ordered a $300 bottle of champagne and paid for it with three hundred-dollar bills. We drank it and talked, and it was just like Mexico. His eyes were so blue.

The hundred-dollar bills gave me pause, but they went with the shirt. He had a jacket, too. It wasn't from a thrift store, like the ironic suits of the struggling artists in my ironic Brooklyn neighborhood. Robbie's jacket was a finance jacket, new and expensive. There were no tears in the pale pink lining, only a label.

It was still light when we went out on the street to smoke. Robbie lit a cigarette, and we passed it back and forth. With one hand, he threw the butt on the ground and ground it out with his dress shoe. With the other, he hailed a taxi and opened the door.

"Where do you live?" he asked, standing before the yellow taxi in his blue shirt with the white collar.

In the cab, he pulled me astride him. He tasted like cigarettes and smelled like the beach. Crossing the East River, as we squeaked on the vinyl, I saw the bright steel beams of the Williamsburg Bridge speeding by, flashing red.

It was four days before Robbie called another taxi and left my apartment. That first weekend, and for all the months after, we slept and woke and fucked and fought at all hours. We lived beyond time and did not always eat food. That first weekend, we were so in our own world that we didn't even notice that the stock market crashed.

Right away, Robbie said he wanted to be my boyfriend. He said he loved me. He said he was a direct descendent of a European revolutionary I'd never heard of, which was actually why his dad had had something to do with the bauxite mines in Jamaica, which was why Robbie sometimes spoke in a Jamaican accent that reminded me of the false patois of the highly problematic Sacha Baron Cohen character Ali G.

At the end of that first week in October, something happened at Robbie's job because of the stock market crash. He worked at Citigroup, he'd said. Or maybe Citibank. Chase? One of the banks. He called me, drunk, from a pay phone. His cell phone had been shut off, he said, because of work.

He hadn't lost his job, but he was going to work in London now. He was going to fly there every two weeks. He'd already been going once a month, but now he was going to be relocated to the London office, and they would give him his new phone.

He didn't have a cell phone for the whole rest of the time I knew him. I could only call him on the landline at his condo in New Haven, where, he said, he was also attending the low-residency executive MBA program at Yale. When he was in London, he called from numbers that showed up with the country code 44.

My junior year of college, I studied abroad at Oxford. I knew the country code for England. It really is 44.

THE FIRST TIME HE CAME BACK FROM LONDON, Robbie called me from a pay phone and asked me to meet him at Penn Station.

At Penn Station, he said we needed to go to Grand Central, to get oysters at the Oyster Bar. Even though it would have been only a short walk, Robbie insisted on a taxi from Penn to Grand Central, and paid with a crumpled bill.

At the Oyster Bar, we ate oysters and drank martinis. I drank one and a half martinis, which was the most I could drink without puking, and Robbie drank two and a half, then ordered another.

The check came. It was well over a hundred dollars. I waited for Robbie to pull out his hundreds, but he told me something was going on with his money, with his bank, with his card, because of the financial crisis and the new job in London.

He asked if I could cover it. He said he'd pay me back. As soon as things got sorted out in London.

I had only recently gotten my first credit card. It had JetBlue miles.

This is good, I thought, throwing it down. *Miles.*

QUITE QUICKLY, despite the condo in New Haven, Robbie was basically living with me, when he wasn't in school for a weekend or in London for a week or two at a time, working at Citigroup. Or Citibank.

We went to art museums and walked in the park. We had sex for hours at all hours and then lay on my velvet couch in silky bathrobes, reading philosophy aloud to each other and then had sex again on the velvet couch in the silky bathrobes.

"Anytime," Robbie said.

That part was true. He'd have me anytime, and I had never had that.

THERE WERE OTHER REASONS why it was good. He was an amazing cook, a magician. He could make a delicious meal out of anything. If there was a can of sardines in the cabinet and a single, slimy scallion in the fridge, somehow, with condiments and spices, Robbie made something delicious. Later, when nothing made sense, I would wonder if I let it not make sense for so long because he made things that did not make sense—like a can of sardines and one slimy scallion—taste so delicious.

One night, I came home from my day job tutoring kids all over the city, and Robbie had made two pots of soup. One was dark purple—he'd found a can of black beans. The other was light and creamy—he did something with coconut milk. He put them in bowls in the shape of a yin-yang. He put a dot of the dark in the light, a dot of the light in the dark. He didn't touch his, just waited, watching me, as I tasted.

"How is it, baby?" he asked, tenderly.

"It's the most delicious thing I've ever tasted," I said, and I was telling the truth.

BY THE END OF OCTOBER, the problem with Robbie's credit card had not been resolved. Every meal we ate and every drink he drank went on my credit card. Miles and miles.

Robbie wanted to go to Bermuda for Thanksgiving. Robbie wanted me to get an IUD.

He bought plane tickets with his frequent-flier miles. I made an appointment at Planned Parenthood.

Robbie wanted to buy expensive knives to give to Leila and Simon for their wedding gift in June. That, I didn't do. June seemed far away.

THE NIGHT OBAMA WAS ELECTED, we were at his place in New Haven, having a fight. I wanted to go out and watch the victory speech in a crowd, but the fight went on too long, though I didn't understand how it started.

Suddenly, for reasons unknowable, he would be very angry—maybe screaming, maybe crying. He always said it was something I did, or said, but then the next time, when I tried not to do or say that thing, it was something else.

When the worst of it passed, I could hear the people outside, shouting and honking their horns, but Robbie didn't want to go out. He didn't want me to go out, either. He said I'd get raped. It sounded more like a threat than a concern. So I watched the speech on my phone in the condo bathroom, listening to Barack Obama's kind, sane voice echoing off the marble walls.

AS NOVEMBER DARKENED and things got weirder, I'd think of Bermuda, and decide to figure it all out after that. I hated everything about Bermuda from the moment we arrived. The water was not warm. It was like a subtropical Britain, Union Jacks everywhere. White people being rich and Black people still working for them. Every other building in the colonizer town was a bank, and I hated every moment I spent hanging, terrified, on to the back of the motorbike Robbie insisted on renting and drove too fast.

I was homesick for my family in a way I hadn't been since kindergarten. My parents fretted, as usual, about how to contact me while I was in Bermuda, and, once there, for the first time I felt scared by the fact that they couldn't reach me instead of liberated, as I usually did by travel. I felt bizarrely disappeared, like I'd never come back from the Bermuda Triangle.

Robbie brought hash, cleverly packed into emptied-out vitamin capsules, and it was surprisingly strong. I hated hash anyway, but Bermuda made me hate hash more, and the hash made me hate Bermuda more.

We broke the headboard of the bed in the dark, cheap room he rented us. It was a cheesy, eighties pastel curve. I looked at the broken plastic and thought, *I want to go home.*

When we arrived at the airport to do just that, there was a misunderstanding. Robbie had not, as promised, bought round-trip tickets with his frequent-flier miles. His miles had bought one-way tickets, the ones that got us there. Robbie insisted otherwise, but I couldn't make him look up the email in his phone because he had no phone. I couldn't make him look up the email in my phone because we were in Bermuda, and I had no phone service.

But it's no big deal, baby, he said. *I'll pay you back, I promise.* Besides, he frequently reminded me, we were going to get married one day and would be very rich.

In order to leave Bermuda, I had to pay for our tickets. On the Sunday of Thanksgiving weekend. At the counter.

As they swiped my card, I didn't feel the usual queasiness that struck as the tally of Robbie's expenditures rose. I'd have given literally anything to leave Bermuda.

BY DECEMBER, we were fighting all the time, but we still had sex all the time, and when this was over, was I really ready for another long drought, and did I really want to be dateless, yet again, at Leila's wedding in June?

Also, the money. I had to get him to give it back first.

One night, we had a fight about whether our future kids should go to boarding school in Switzerland. Another night, he told me that my writing was "like an emerald covered in moss," and for some reason that made me cry, and for some reason that made him yell. Another night, we put up water for tea and then started having sex and didn't hear the kettle whistle. All the water boiled away, and the teapot my mother had bought for me was melted and charred and smoldering, almost on fire. I opened the kitchen window and threw it, sizzling, into a pile of snow.

I went right online and ordered a new teapot, even though I owed a lot of money on my credit card already. I couldn't not have the teapot. I'd loved it so much. The teapot arrived two days later, and I placed it on the stove. It was just like the old teapot, but a little too new. It was not the same teapot. Or maybe I was not the same person.

When he got in a mood, I just tried to give him what he needed. That's what I learned, in all earlier iterations of intimacy—that having "trauma" meant needing "support," and getting "support" meant "sharing your feelings," and if that meant screaming or crying, then later, we could "repair," which meant that I apologized for whatever I did to cause the screaming and the crying, and then tried my very best not to do it again. Sometimes Robbie even noticed me trying, and he whispered into my hair, "Get to know me. I've had a crazy life."

IT WASN'T THE THING HE SAID at the Egon Schiele exhibit on the Upper East Side, when he casually told me he'd decapitate me. It was the night a few weeks later, in February, when, riding the subway back to Brooklyn from the Upper West Side, I decided to hop off at Penn Station and take an affordably off-peak Amtrak train to New Haven, instead of going home to Brooklyn first and taking the cheaper, grosser bus the next day, as planned.

When I called Robbie's landline from the train to tell him I was coming, he started yelling at me that I couldn't come, I just couldn't come, he couldn't tell me why, but I couldn't come there, *not tonight, please don't.* The whiplash of the way he yelled "DO NOT COME HERE," and then pleaded, tearfully, "Please, baby, please don't come," turned me around.

I got off the Amtrak train somewhere in southern Connecticut, crossed the platform, bought a different ticket, and took another train back to Penn Station. Rather than go through the subway turnstile to take the A train to Fourteenth Street to get the L home to Brooklyn, I walked through the familiar tunnels to the Long Island Rail Road and took another, very late train to the very last stop—Port Washington.

13

I always told people that I didn't grow up there, just "adolesced." I always told people that it was East Egg, where Daisy lived in *The Great Gatsby*.

The station was so quiet, and the air so sweet, late at night coming back from the city. I crossed the parking lot to Deluxe Taxi and climbed into an idling Cadillac reeking comfortingly of air freshener. I charged the ride to my father's business account and signed for it on triplicate carbon paper on a little clipboard with a ballpoint pen. Then I let myself into the house with the key under the mat, and crawled into my childhood bed.

I BROKE UP WITH ROBBIE over Google Chat from my parents' house. He called me a bitch.

When I got back to my apartment in Brooklyn to change the locks, Robbie had left me a suicide note under the doormat. It said he had jumped off the Williamsburg Bridge, called me a bitch again, and said that he loved me.

When I worried he was dead, my parents encouraged me to call their couples therapist, who told me, very calmly, "That man is a pathological liar, and he is manipulating you."

Then my mom sent me to another therapist, who had me tap on my upper lip while repeating the words "I am safe."

My parents came to Brooklyn and packed up all of Robbie's clothes in two cardboard cartons so I didn't have to get near enough to smell them. My dad was so swift with the tape dispenser; it was just like I was leaving for college again. They helped me pay off the credit card debt, and I felt so fucking privileged—and so fucking stupid.

"At least it's not rehab," I mumbled.

"Or legal fees!" said my mom. "Could be worse!"

Eventually, they told me they'd gotten rid of the boxes. The camel coat. The blazer with the pale pink lining. The blue shirt with the white collar. Were they in a landfill? At Goodwill?

Put it out of your mind, they said. And I began to.

I slowly went back to being myself. And then I went looking for someone else to become.

2

Yosemite

THE SWEETNESS OF MY BROTHER'S FACE was always the first thing I noticed when I hadn't seen him for a while. Now he was lean, and very tan, as he pulled up to meet me outside the Medford, Oregon, airport, the nearest one to the river we'd raft. Aptly named Noah, he'd become a boatman—a whitewater river-rafting guide.

There was nothing sharp or pointy about him, just a gentle solidity. His hair was the same color as mine, dark brown, his olive skin also an exact match. The only difference in our coloring was that he had brown eyes, like our mom, and I had green ones, like our dad.

When we were kids in Queens, we played astronauts and went to the moon. We did ballet routines, and I made him point his toes while I lifted and twirled him. We danced to Bruce Springsteen and Billy Joel, hurled ourselves and each other at piles of couch pillows, hacked paths through a backyard dirt mound overgrown with weeds so we could play commando, explorer, spy.

He was four years younger, but we'd always functioned as equals. When I got older and read books all the time, he made me a special room in one of his living-room tents of blankets and chairs.

"Here, Emily," he'd said, when he was maybe five or six. "You can *read* in here."

Now that the bad thing had happened, he'd made me another safe place to go. This time, it was a river.

"Let's go get you cleaned up!" he said in a faux-Jersey accent, patting my face with an open hand. Sometimes we spoke to each other in dialogue from *The Sopranos*.

On the drive, he explained all the things I could do to help get ready for the trip—come to the supermarket, count out the life vests, move heavy stuff. And there was one more thing.

"So I'm kind of hooking up with one of the other guides," my brother said, "and her dad and brother are coming on this trip. They're pretty religious—like Christian fundamentalists or something—so try not to say anything crazy about Jesus or God."

"Like what?" I asked.

"Like, 'Fuck God,' or 'Fuck Jesus,' or 'I'm gonna fuck Jesus.'"

"What makes you think I would say something like that?"

"Because," my brother laughed, "you say stuff like that *all the time*."

WHEN JAMES SHOOK MY HAND at the pre-trip meeting by a motel pool in Grants Pass, Oregon, he wore a sneer and no shirt. He had a blond ponytail and a natural squint.

James and his father had driven up from California that day. I'd always imagined extremely religious Christian people as either Puritans, far-right, obviously closeted Republicans, or creepy priests. But James's dad had a kind, open face. When he said, "It's nice to meet you," it sounded true.

I stayed with the guides at the guide house that night, woke up at dawn the next morning, and rode in the trucks that pulled the trailers full of rafts and metal boxes full of gear down to the put-in, while we all drank coffee out of stainless steel mugs with carabiner handles.

The guides were all younger than I was—my brother, at twenty-six, was one of the oldest. They wore an unofficial uniform that was different from the head-to-toe black of the punks back in Brooklyn. Board shorts with stripes and flowers, sunglasses on fabric strings. They all had the same sandals, the same baseball caps with the name of the rafting company on them. Their hair was variegated with different colors, as if they'd dyed it, but the streaks were all from the sun. Their tans and their muscles were like accessories.

They weren't exactly punk—they wore nothing as impractical as chains or studs—but they all had necklaces, some kind of tooth or stone or metal spike on a leather cord. After they finished rigging their boats, they looped colorful ropes around their waists and clasped them with metal carabiners. These would be used to right a boat, my brother said, if one flipped over on a rock and were pinned there by the current.

He'd told me what to buy—sandals called Chacos, board shorts, a rain jacket. I'd bought it all in black, at the Patagonia and EMS stores in SoHo.

"Here," my brother said. "Got you some Chums." That's what the sunglass strings were called. Even the Chums were black. He pushed the earpieces of my sunglasses through the little cloth tubes, and placed them, gently, over my head. Then he laughed at my all-black outfit. "You look like Johnny Cash about to go rafting."

"I prefer 'wilderness ninja,'" I sniffed.

The boys all had names like Tanner and Taylor and Tyler and Skyler, something that sounded like Brandon but was maybe spelled with different vowels. The girls were strong and freckled and impossibly confident. It seemed like there were multiple Kellys, of multiple genders, with multiple spellings. They all called me "Noah's sister," which made me feel proud and protected.

"Hey, Noah's sister!"

"So, you're Noah's sister?"

They ran all over the slippery gray rocks at the riverbank, building a water world.

Someone gave me a pump and told me to inflate the thwarts—the tubes in the middle of the raft you could sit on. I bounced up and down, watching the gray rubber strain as it filled with air.

A guide came over and said, "That's good, Noah's sister!" then twisted the valve and let out a short hiss. "It'll expand in the heat, so not all the way."

There was so much to know just about water and air. It could really take your mind off the people problems.

The guests arrived, and my brother gave a safety talk that made them all laugh. He explained how you could drown in the shallows, if your foot got caught and the force of the river held you face down, so always keep your feet up. Rattlesnakes are more afraid of you. Here's how you know if the portable toilet is occupied. We zipped up our life jackets and got in the boats.

In the very first rapid, a paying guest flipped her inflatable kayak and swam the whole thing, choking on water by the time she got pulled from the froth. She didn't want to get back in the kayak, and none of the other guests wanted to take her place.

The guides were about to deflate the inflatable kayak when James volunteered. He paddled right up to my brother's boat.

"Come on," said James, looking at me, again not wearing a shirt, but that grin bordering on sneer. The inflatable kayak had two seats. I looked at my brother.

"Go," he said. "You'll have fun. That last rapid was the biggest one today."

"Okay," I said. I exchanged my boat paddle with one blade for the kayak kind, with two.

James sat in the back of the boat and steered. I sat in the front, where all I had to do was paddle. We started swapping adventure stories. I was pretty proud of the time I had tagged along on tour in Europe with an anarchist punk band, but James, though seven years younger, had already done more, even wilder things—hitchhiked to Alaska, hopped freight trains, rock climbed in Yosemite.

James told me he wasn't a Christian fundamentalist, like the rest of his family. He was the black sheep. He hated his mother, he thought he might have ADHD, and he smoked cigarettes, but his dad didn't know.

I told him all about my life in New York—everything except Robbie. It was hard to know how to bring up, in casual conversation, the recent ex-boyfriend who'd turned out to be a pathological liar, stolen several thousand dollars, threatened to kill me, and then faked his own suicide, so I stuck to my best stories—my travels in Central and South America, my punk rock–adjacent days, the funny things the kids I tutored for a living said, my cool Brooklyn apartment next to the Italian pastry shop where they gave me free espresso.

"I bet you and your New York friends just sit around drinking espresso and talking about movies," James said, and I laughed and confessed that that was kind of exactly what we did.

I'd never really thought about the colors of rivers. Or the way the whitewater smelled different from the flat. The water was green, in the places it wasn't white. As the river wound its way to the sea, it went around bend after bend, revealing different versions of the same vista—the two wooded slopes on either side, intersecting at changing angles.

When we pulled into camp, James said, "Tomorrow morning, you come with me."

WE CAMPED ON SANDY BEACHES on the edge of a pine forest. My brother showed me how to pick a good, even place to sleep. He gave me one of the deluxe waterproof camping mattresses that the guides used.

It never rained. I'd brought no tent. I arranged my things, each night, on rock furniture. At night, I didn't read books. Instead, I looked at the stars and listened to the river.

James and I had many adventures and long conversations together in our inflatable kayak. One afternoon, we speedboated ahead of the rest of the trip with one of the guides, to score a choice campsite. We spent the afternoon alone in the sun, eating pie with a serving spoon, eating cold leftover ribs from the cooler with our hands, jumping off a fifty-foot rock that scared me, though I wanted to impress James. We stayed up late by the fire talking and drinking beer, snuck away to smoke cigarettes in the woods.

"Rock climbing is better," said James, as we paddled the river. "No paying customers, and you can smoke weed whenever you want."

On the last night of the trip, James mentioned that he kind of had a girlfriend.

"Call me if you're ever in California," he said at the end of the trip, still shirtless.

He was like all the guys I had ever liked—hot and mean, weirdly vacillating between a confessional intimacy and a confusing aloofness. I felt pulled toward him and pushed away at the same time. It was like magnetism, but also like the way magnets floated on an invisible cushion of resistance when you tried to stick like to like. As a kid, I'd practiced overriding it, forcing the red and silver sides together, so I could feel the force that would pop them apart again when I let go. Then I'd flip them around and put them near each other the way they were naturally attracted, and watch them close the distance until they stuck.

After what happened with Robbie, I'd begun to wonder whether I'd ever be able to trust my own desire again, trust that force that pulled on me, like magnetism, or the current of a river. The river could suck you down, choke you, leave you sputtering, but it could also take you for a glorious ride. How would I ever know if I were properly aligned with any force of nature? How would I know whether any person, or any feeling, was good or safe or right or real?

But James was a real person, with a real name. His dad had been there, and his sister. They were real people, too. We'd done dangerous things like jump off the big rock and swim through some of the smaller rapids, but we'd stayed safe.

Maybe not all danger was mortal. Maybe not all attraction was fatal. Maybe this force I felt could lead me somewhere I wanted—maybe even needed—to go.

"TAKE MY CAR," my brother said, when we got back. "It's just sitting here at the guide house. Go have adventures. See the West."

So I changed my ticket back to New York and instead spent the Fourth of July on Leila's parents' yacht in Seattle. Then I changed my ticket again, so I could try to sneak into a hippie fair in Oregon, which I did sneak into—and then promptly out of, as soon as I met a guy with a house in town. Someone at the fair told me about hot springs, and then someone at the hot springs told me about a bluegrass show at an inn in a ghost town on the coast of far Northern California.

Everything in the West was new, and different from New York. Forests and trees, not concrete and steel. Pickup trucks and country roads, not trains and bridges and taxis. Creeks and swimming holes and a big, cold ocean with foggy, rocky beaches that were nothing like the warm, wide, sandy ones back East. Hippies who grew their own weed and delivered their own babies, instead of metrosexual lawyers and pale, cynical musicians. Here, the musicians farmed.

I changed my ticket home three times, not wanting to go back to New York, back to the place where Robbie had told me he would kill me, and I hadn't made him leave.

It was almost September. Soon, I'd have to start my day job, tutoring, again. I was broke, but I was always broke. And now, I was broken—or maybe always had been, and always would be.

ONE MORE EXPERIENCE, I thought, dialing the number. One more adventure. Just to make sure I wasn't the same person anymore.

James answered.

"It's Emily," I said. "From the river."

"Come to Yosemite with me," he offered immediately. "Tonight."

"But I'm in Oregon," I said. "It's already six."

"Then you can be here by midnight. You can sleep in my tree house. Start driving."

He directed me to an unfamiliar suburbia, where he lived with his parents, attended community college, worked at some carpentry job.

When I got there, it was well after midnight. James's estimation of my driving time had been based on the average ground speed of a twenty-two-year-old male, rather than a twenty-nine-year-old woman who'd failed her road test on the first try, totaled the family station wagon six months later, and then lived, carless, in New York, for almost a decade.

He still wasn't wearing a shirt.

He held me to his bare skin and squeezed. It was my first experience of what I later came to call "the California hug." Our whole bodies were pressed together, chakra to chakra, from sternum to pelvis. He was a head taller than I was, so even my ears were encircled in his arms, which slowly tightened, like a cozy vise, until I felt my entire body go limp in the most pleasing way. Just when I thought he couldn't squeeze any harder, or I couldn't melt any more, he inhaled deeply, causing me to do the same, then groaned with satisfaction as he exhaled, slowly releasing me. It was like sex yoga, or something similarly Californian. I felt my heart and breath quicken, but also a dizziness, a queasiness, a sense of approaching the top of a roller coaster but never coming down, and also like I was flying, had been punched, or might faint.

"Took you long enough," said James. "I drank a Mountain Dew."

I slept in the tree house. James did not. It stayed hot at night, wherever this suburbia was.

In the morning, I went in the house. It was fancy in an understated way I'd never seen before. On Long Island, the trappings of wealth were shiny and ostentatious. Huge bar mitzvah pictures gaudily framed, leather lounge chairs the same pantherish black as the eternally brand-new luxury SUVs in the driveways.

But James's house had nature wealth. A coffee table made out of a giant burnished tree stump, woven wall hangings in quiet colors, big, framed photographs of waterfalls, a pile of smooth antlers in a glazed ceramic tray.

His parents made us coffee. Then they asked if I wanted to come to church with them. I didn't explain about being Jewish. I just said, "Uh—"

They asked James, separately, if he wanted to go to church. We were going to Yosemite, he said, not church.

"Be safe," they shrugged.

Then his mother added, almost as an afterthought, "Try not to do anything to get this nice girl killed."

I tried to imagine what my own parents would say if I told them I was going to Yosemite. First, they might find out about some impending natural disaster or approaching weather pattern. They would ask if I knew about it. They might call an authority—forest-fire department, state troopers—and *get more information*. They would attempt to convey this information, call me repeatedly, leave multiple voicemails, then send emails about the voicemails. I would receive a separate email— *Subject: Your travel insurance policy*. They might suggest that I speak to a doctor they were currently seeing on a quarterly basis who ordered extensive and expensive blood work and supervised draconian elimination diets, or that I research possible endemic diseases in the region. My mother might give, or overnight express me, a baggie. Inside the baggie would be other baggies, insulated with paper towels. There might be iodine pills in there, if my parents determined that my proposed adventure were in the fallout zone of a nuclear power plant. They might, as they soon would, during the Fukushima disaster in 2011, call me frantically, until they reached me on a street in San Francisco, and tell me that they needed to fly me away from the West Coast because it was too close to Japan. Mom was on the other line with Delta right now—when could I be at the airport? I would look around at all the people on the street in San Francisco, who were drinking their lattes and not being evacuated to Long Island. They might find a report of the most recent accident that had occurred in Yosemite—maybe the limb of a big, old tree had fallen on the tent of a Boy Scout. Did I know about this? Was I going to the area where this had occurred? If I were going to a different area, did they have the same kinds of trees there? Did I get the email about the travel insurance policy? Could I estimate the total cost of my trip so my mother could email that to the travel insurance company? Who was I going with? Could they have their phone number? How about their parents' phone numbers, just in case?

I was well over eighteen. I was almost thirty. It didn't matter. If they lived long enough, they'd be calling me at the senior center from the residential care facility to remind me not to sit too close to the holographic television because of the electromagnetic field.

They were almost as afraid of electromagnetism as they were of radioactivity. One summer, dropping me off at camp, they'd noticed that the top bunk I'd chosen was right under the cabin's smoke alarm. My mom had read that there was radioactive material in some smoke alarms, so my parents immediately called the camp and asked to speak directly to Forrest, the maintenance man, who was the shirtless object of many a teenaged crush, including mine. They convinced Forrest to enter my bunk while it was empty, climb up on my bed, and move the smoke alarm.

"Forrest was so nice about it," they said proudly, when they told me of this caper, after they picked me up that summer. "He said he completely understood."

I was mortified. Forrest had talked to my parents? Forrest had been on my bed?

"But where did he move it?" I sputtered.

"Over some other girl's bed," my mother said triumphantly.

But if it was dangerous to sleep under the smoke alarm, why had they made it so the *other* kid slept under the smoke alarm?

"Look," my dad said. "There're regulations. But we care about *you*. We love *you*."

They were good at making phone calls. If they knew about James and our trip to Yosemite and decided they needed to reach me to tell me about some risk they'd assessed, they would find a way to call James's parents. And then his parents would find out what people did to cope with the unknown when they didn't have Jesus.

But my parents didn't know where I was. They didn't know who James was. They could find out, but it would take some time. I had a window here, to get somewhere they couldn't find me, or even call me.

In my mind, I was an outlaw. I was Nancy, on the run with a rotating cast of Sids. But I was no Alexandra Supertramp. I was Alexandra Portnoy—a female version of the protagonist of a Philip Roth book, if Philip Roth had been able to imagine female subjectivity.

I was always on the run from one single entity. It was not the law, from which my white privilege almost entirely shielded me, giving me plenty of space to act like the permanent teenager I felt like I would always be. It was the Weinsteins. I was on the run from the Weinsteins.

But I also was one. It was confusing, running from something that was also inside of me. It was also impossible.

That was part of what I'd been chasing, with the scary boyfriend, why I'd allowed him so far into my life, why I'd gone so far into his weird world. It was the feeling of getting away, disappearing—even if where I disappeared *to* wasn't necessarily a good place, or was even the actual Bermuda Triangle.

My family was full of love, but it was also sometimes full of fear— threats and dangers that weren't always entirely real. Sometimes, after my parents panicked about a thing that wasn't even a real thing, it felt perversely, deliciously good to walk up to the edge of a danger that was *definitely* real.

ONCE HIS PARENTS WERE GONE, James jumped up from the kitchen island and began raiding their pantry. He threw things in shopping bags—granola bars, tortilla chips. We put the shopping bags in my borrowed Subaru. He went into the garage, grabbed a plastic tub, stuffed its contents into a backpack, and put that in the Subaru, too. He climbed up in the tree house, took the Therm-a-Rest and sleeping bag I'd slept on, and added those. This whole process took less than ten minutes.

"If you have a thing about real shitters," he said, "go now. You might not see another one for a while."

In the bathroom, they had those towels only Christian people have. Jews could have nice towels, too, but only Christian people had *these* kinds of towels, with seasonally appropriate embroidery, or ribbons sewn across them. Maybe it was the towels, or maybe it was the potpourri, but James and I were different. Probably because of our different Gods, even though we had agreed, on the river trip, that neither of us believed in God, only nature. But we still came from the different cultures of our different Gods, and the towels were proof.

"That took you forever," James said when I got back. I didn't know how to explain that the Christian towels had made me nervous.

We drove across the hot Central Valley. We bought fruit from a stand and beer from a store. James steered with his knees while he rolled cigarettes and joints, never swerving. When I asked to stop and pee, he pulled over and pointed at the side of the road. When we left the bigger highway for the smaller one, he clutched a beer between his thighs and opened it with his cigarette lighter, handed it to me, and opened another for himself.

During the one stretch of our road trip I drove, people honked at me on the highway. Due to my lack of driving experience, people honked every time I tried to change lanes. I would honk back, then give them the finger. That was what all the grown-ups had done back in Queens.

"Ya fucking moron!" my mom, or my best friend's mom, Susan Saperstein, would yell, almost affectionately. Then we would go back to singing our songs, or listening to far-left public radio about Iran-Contra, or wheat allergies, long before everyone knew the truth about gluten.

Here in California, driving on what they called a "freeway" instead of a "highway," someone honked. I honked back and flipped the bird.

"Fucking moron!" I yelled.

"What's with the road rage?" asked James. "That guy was trying to let you in."

"Oh," I said. "He honked."

"That's because you speed up and slow down incoherently."

"I get scared I'm going to hit someone in my blind spot."

"Then check your blind spot."

"I get scared someone is going to cut me off."

"They might be trying to let you in!"

"Oh."

James, rolling a joint, rolled his eyes. "Maybe you'll drive better when you're high."

"So what do I do when someone honks to let me in?"

"You give them *the peace sign*," said James. "To say 'thank you.' Like this." He demonstrated with one hand as he lit the joint with the other.

"Yeah, well," I said, "in *England*, where I studied abroad at *Oxford*, two fingers turned the *other* way *also* means 'fuck you.'"

"This is California," said James. "Here, it means 'peace.'"

That was my first clue that things could be different, out here. Maybe everything could mean something different. Maybe even I could be different.

WE GOT TO YOSEMITE VALLEY in the early afternoon. It was before the drought, and the trees were all green. James drove around the traffic-clogged loop road while I gawked. He told me what everything was called, but they were just words—falls, points, peaks, domes.

Everywhere were people fitting the landscape into the frames of their devices, pointing them at the waterfalls, then at Half Dome.

James was angry at the tourists. I'd heard the same rants from archaeologist friends on my travels in Peru; gringos who referred to other white people as gringos. James called the tourists names—"touron" and "flatlander." I didn't understand why he was so angry, since we'd escaped nearly all the tourists by simply walking into a meadow. If the meadow had been in Central Park, it would be patchworked with blankets.

James said he liked slacklining—walking, like a tightrope walker, on a flat piece of nylon webbing strung between two trees or rocks or mountains—better than rock climbing now, and besides, his ex-girlfriend still had his rope. He rigged up a slackline over a bit of river he pointed at and called the Merced. The slackline was three fingers wide. He winched it taut between two trees, then walked on it back and forth, with his hands in the air. Then he held my hand while I tried, letting go gradually, like I was a kid on a bike without training wheels.

I had to hop off before it crossed the water, but I could take a few steps on my own.

"Watch out for that little bit of death there," James said, pointing at a tangle of sharp branches on the bank.

"You're so good at this!" he complimented me. "Graceful."

He put some beers in the river, weighed them down with rocks. We'd done this on the rafting trip, too. It was a warm summer day, somehow different from a summer day back East. It wasn't as humid; I didn't get as sweaty. The grass in the meadow was gold instead of green. Only the river was wet. There was no dirt, only sand. Even the sand was made of tiny rocks the same color as the giant walls that formed the Valley.

We sat and drank beers and took turns on the slackline all afternoon in the meadow. James rolled cigarettes, and I stole a drag for every three of his. We couldn't smoke weed unless we hid, James said, or the rangers would catch us. The tobacco kept my mouth wet, sharpened me against the beer blur. The two together reminded me of Robbie.

He was right. It was like being on the river, but without the paying guests. Those *tourons*.

We sat in the meadow, looking up at the big stone wall.

"That's El Capitan," he said. "I'm going to climb it one day."

"I'm going to write a book one day," I told him.

"I'm sure you are," he smiled. "That will be your El Cap."

Looking around at the Valley, I realized I had seen it all before, though only in black and white. The Ansel Adams print, of Half Dome, on the walls of different doctors' offices. At the therapist, where I'd gone to talk about Robbie, and the orthodontist on Central Park South, who had tightened my braces until tears ran into my ears.

Now my mouth hung open, gaping at its size.

"It's three thousand feet," said James.

I calculated. That was three hundred ten-foot stories, many times the height of my four-story Brooklyn apartment building, taller than my grandparents' forty-story Upper East Side condo, and all the sky-scrapers in New York.

I didn't look at it and think, *I need to climb to the top of that thing.* I didn't really understand that that was even possible. I just liked being near it, and looking up.

I felt almost nonexistent, wearing little clothing in this golden field, looking up at this golden rock in the golden hour with this golden boy in his golden state. Less painfully human, more like an animal.

I could smell him. Not just with my nose. With some other, deeper part of me.

I felt a little afraid of James, of what he might decide we should do next, but not afraid of what he would do *to* me. If he got me killed, as his own mother had somewhat ominously suggested back in suburbia, it would probably be an accident. He wouldn't *actually* try to kill me, the way Robbie had threatened to. We'd just disappear into the wilderness, or the river, or be eaten by animals, or one day become trees. We'd already had an adventure, a good one, a safe one, with our families, even. He thought I was a beautiful girl who deserved to see beautiful things. He was beautiful to me, and the intoxicated feeling that hit me in the solar plexus every time I saw or smelled him never entirely ebbed.

The air temperature cooled, just slightly, as the sun slowly lowered. I moved closer to the warmth emanating from his body.

"We need a place to camp!" announced James, jumping to his feet.

We drove to a parking lot. "This is Camp 4," he said.

"That sign says FULL," I read.

"We'll see about that."

He grabbed the Therm-a-Rest from the back of the car and stuck it under his arm, wadded up the sleeping bag and jammed it into the same armpit. With his other hand, he grabbed a full six-pack from the floorboard and handed it to me.

"You go first," he said. "Pretty girl. Nonthreatening."

Pretty girl. "Beautiful women want to be told they are smart," I'd read once. "Smart women want to be told they are beautiful." I had always known I was smart, but I had never been sure I was pretty enough. Maybe if someone thought I was pretty enough, they would treat me like I mattered.

He looked at me seriously and said, "Here we go."

We strode through the campground, which was crowded with picnic tables and bear boxes and tents and families and small groups of mostly punk-hippie hybrid guys throwing metal things around on tabletops and tarps. At the far end, there were big tent cabins like the ones at my sleepaway camp in Connecticut, and some slacklines stretched between trees. Tall pines shaded the campground and covered the ground in fragrant needles.

We came to a young couple making dinner alone in a campsite.

"Cool if we camp here?" James asked them. Without waiting for an answer, he threw down the sleeping bag and Therm-a-Rest.

"Have a beer," he said.

I put the six-pack on the picnic table, and James opened two with his lighter.

"I'm James," he said, then nodded at me. "She's Emily."

We were poaching a campsite, but I felt like we were robbing a bank.

We didn't eat dinner. I had little appetite, full from drinking beer all day. James opened a can of sardines, and we passed it back and forth, sharing a single plastic fork. Then he led me through the boulders and into the woods until we got to a little cave.

"Safety cave," James announced.

We crawled inside and he rolled us a spliff.

"Are they really watching?" I asked.

"Oh yeah," he said, blowing smoke. "This land is federal, so they're federal agents. Those fuckers hide in the bushes and wear night-vision goggles."

People just lived here, he told me. In this park, in these caves. In these mountains, in towns with bluegrass bars. In their cars, on the road forever, like in books about men on boats, or men in boots. They lived here, and climbing these mountains was their life.

It was getting dark. "I didn't really sleep last night," said James. "I'm tired."

We went back to the campground, and he grabbed the Therm-a-Rest and the sleeping bag and dragged them a short distance to the edge of the campsite, away from the other tents. There was a sign that read, NO CAMPING BEYOND THIS POINT.

"They really mean that," he said.

Even though the campground was crowded, in the national park, there were no lights besides fires and flashlights. We didn't exactly have privacy, but we were in darkness.

I sat down on the Therm-a-Rest and kicked off my Chacos. James pulled the sleeping bag, unzipped, around his shoulders, like a cape. He spread his arms wide, until the cape was a tent.

Kissing him felt like being devoured, like trying to eat something before it ate you first.

"You know what they say about camping," said James, as we wriggled out of our few clothes, panting and scratching like animals.

"No, what?" I said.

"It's fucking intense. Get it?"

"I get it. Fucking in tents."

It was. It was fucking intense.

THE NEXT MORNING, he decided that I also had to see Tuolumne. We drove out of the Valley and uphill for a long time.

We passed a lake. "Tenaya," he said. We stopped at the edge of a big meadow—bigger than the one from the day before.

"This is Tuolumne Meadows," he said. I'd never seen a place quite like it. The air had been like this in the Andes, in Peru—thin and clear and harder to breathe—but Peru's mountains were brown. This world was green, with wildflowers and flowing water and gray-white domes of rock everywhere, each with its own name.

We crossed the road and walked into the woods and came to a place where the river was more like a waterfall, frothing over rocks. We dunked ourselves in the frigid shallows. An older European woman nearby whooped and yelped at the cold.

"She sounds like you," said James. The night before, in the dirt, he'd covered my mouth with his and swallowed all my noise.

He led me to some other part of the forest where there weren't any people. We took off our few clothes. James looked critically around the clearing, balled up our clothes into a pile, and placed it on top of a rock. "For your head," he said.

It was fucking intense in the light of day, too.

ON THE OTHER SIDE OF THE MOUNTAINS, he showed me a big blue lake (Mono), and a Mobil gas station, where, he said cryptically, "a lot of big missions" began. We stopped in on a friend of his in town, drank beers and walked on the slackline again, stayed for dinner—meat, grilled expertly by shirtless males—until it was dark. Suddenly, he announced he had to work the next morning.

"Aren't we really far away from the Bay?"

"Not so far," he said. "I've done it in five. We just have to make it by eight tomorrow morning. Or ten, if I call my boss."

We drove back up the highway with the mountains on one side and the flat desert on the other, turned at the important gas station and filled up with gas, then shot past the little stone booth at the park entrance, now empty and locked.

35

He pulled over by the meadow. "Let's go see it," he said, "in the dark."

We went out into the meadow. I was on top this time. I could see so many stars. I made all the noise I wanted.

We got in the car. "Let's drive naked," he said. "To keep us awake."

I'd never been naked in a car before, with my seat belt on. James didn't wear his. He turned up the heat and opened the windows and drove with his knees.

He pulled over again and we tumbled out of the car, onto the hood. The hood was hot. We were on the side of the road, in the gravel. The asphalt was smoother. We rolled over and over. By the time we finished, we were lying on the yellow line.

We lay there for a moment, adjacent and breathing, as if we were in a bed and not the middle of a highway. Then he leapt upright and stuck his hand out and pulled me up so hard I jumped.

We went back to the car on the side of the road. Under my bare feet, the pavement still held some of the warmth of the day.

I reached into the car for my clothes. The dashboard said it was 1:00 a.m. and fifty-four degrees. With no warning, a car came speeding around a bend in the road, zooming over the spot where we'd just been entangled. In some parallel universe, our bodies were smeared across the blacktop. We looked at each other, the wide whites of our eyes just visible by the light from inside the car, the fingernail moon, the stars in the sky.

When Robbie had called from hotel rooms he claimed were in London, there was some kind of tile that made his voice echo, but who knew what it was made of, or where it really was?

Though James seemed dangerous in his way, the rocks were the rocks, the road was the road, the world was the world. I'd wanted to do another dangerous thing with a dangerous guy, but prove that it could turn out okay.

"Close one," James said evenly. "That could've been bad."

Then he was peeing near the rear bumper, stretching his arms luxuriantly above his head. I crouched by the front one, feeling like the most alive animal, who belonged to the mountains and wasn't yet roadkill.

This, I thought, pulling my shorts over my scraped-up thighs. *This.*

Then I had another thought, which came from nowhere: *I am finally free. They don't know where I am. They can't get to me here.*

"So, that's everything," said James, getting back into the car. "Here we go."

That was as close as I ever came to death in the mountains, before I even climbed one—the night I almost met my end, naked on the yellow line in the middle of Tioga Road. Instead of the end, it was the beginning.

After I peeled myself off the pavement, alive, I stopped looking for new and creative ways to get fucked-up or killed. After that, I began looking for new ways to live.

3

Joshua Tree

"**O**NE OF YOU GIRLS want to give this a try?"

The shirtless man shook the end of the rope at us. Leila nodded at me to go first. I put on the harness and tied my shoes, and Glenn, the tall one, made a loop with the end of the rope.

"The alien," he said, "gets strangled, and then you stab him in the eye."

He handed me the rope with the neat squiggle in it. "Figure eight follow through," he said. "That's the eight. Follow it through."

All three of them watched as I threaded the rope through the loops in the harness at my groin and belly button, then followed the figure eight.

"Trust the gear," Glenn continued. "Trust the rope. Trust the system. You are safe."

"I'm gonna give you the girlfriend belay," grinned the younger one, holding the other end of the rope at his crotch. "Nice and tight."

He yanked on the rope, and it pulled me to the wall.

FOR MOST OF MY LIFE, I'd thought Joshua Tree was the title of a U2 album. But it turned out it was also a place, in the desert east of Los Angeles.

It was the first spring after I'd rafted the river, then laid down in the middle of the highway. The first spring since Robbie. The first spring since I'd moved to California, on a whim, after seeing El Capitan and Tuolumne Meadows.

I had been living in California for only a few months, subletting my brother's Oakland apartment while he traveled with his girlfriend, when Leila called and said her parents had bought a condo near Palm Springs and she was coming out from New York to visit. Was Palm Springs anywhere near Oakland? Could we meet up?

I checked a maps app. Palm Springs was seven hours and thirty-nine minutes away by car.

"Not really," I said. But then I noticed, on the same part of the map, a green area labeled "Joshua Tree National Park."

Joshua Tree. James kept saying those words, almost as often as he said "Yosemite" or "rad." *Joshua Tree.* The U2 album was named after the place.

Could I even afford the gas, to drive as far as Leila's parents' new condo in Palm Springs? But I had my own Subaru, bought with the spoils of my last New York winter, tutoring teenagers uptown, downtown, from the Lower East Side to the Upper West, from Park Slope to Bed-Stuy to Coney Island, and, in the case of one very dedicated LaGuardia High School theater kid whose single mother owned a famous punk bar, during a weekly session that began after school musical rehearsals concluded at 11:00 p.m. I hadn't bought this Subaru just to drive around Oakland, or Berkeley, or the East Bay, this weird new city that wasn't even one city, just a vague "area," where you couldn't get anything to eat after 8:25 p.m. I had bought it to explore the great new state beyond.

I had a credit card. I could buy gas.

I told Leila I would drive down and we could have an adventure.

I emailed James to ask about Joshua Tree. I hadn't seen him since the road trip, the Valley, the Meadows, the yellow line.

"See you next summer," he'd said pointedly in goodbye, and I hadn't dared get in touch since. But he wrote back, cordially and lengthily, with plenty of advice.

"Go to the Hidden Valley Campground," he wrote. "Ask to see the Space Station."

I printed out his email, stuck it in a folder, packed up the car, and drove south.

LEILA'S PARENTS WERE LIVING in a brand-new condo in a retirement community outside Palm Springs. After drinks and dinner, we went in the "spool," a spa-pool. The spool had a view of the golf course, where I could see two ducks waddling on a carpet of unnaturally green grass.

Leila said she and Simon were going to have kids soon. *Kids*. Weren't *we* kids?

Her life was moving forward, taking form, while mine felt like it was disintegrating into chaos, or hadn't even started.

Leila had always said she never wanted children, that babies were boring. But now that she loved Simon, and Simon loved children, she would do it. "I love him so much that I *want* to have his children," she said.

I had always wanted children. I thought babies were amazing. I wondered whether if I could make myself not want children, then I could make a man who did want me. Watching other people get everything I wanted, I wondered what they knew that I didn't. Was not wanting children the way to actually have them? I was so confused.

I wanted to love someone, and for them to love me back, and not be insane. But I didn't want to want things I couldn't have anymore. I wanted to want what I could have, and for that to be enough.

We sat in the spool, in our bikinis, watching the sunset, the two ducks on the golf course.

"Look," I said. "Monogamous ducks." Even the ducks had each other.

The grass on the golf course was greener than any I'd ever seen.

IT OCCURRED TO ME, the next morning, as we shopped for our road trip to Joshua Tree in a mercifully frigid Target in Palm Springs and wheeled our purchases across the shimmering hundred-degree asphalt, that this could be our last adventure.

We'd had so many. We'd eaten mescaline cactus in the Sacred Valley and magic mushrooms at Machu Picchu. Ridden horses up mountains and banana boats up jungle rivers. Skinny-dipped and scuba dived in bioluminescence. Consumed pure Peruvian blow for a week on a beach at the edge of a vast desert and worked obsessively on a screenplay we never finished while wearing bikinis that exposed most of our asses and eating flaming bananas every night. Danced with old campesinos and coked-up archaeologists in dirt-floored houses in high-altitude towns drinking home-brewed chicha made from corn the local abuelas had chewed up and spit out. Drunk pisco in Peru and rum in Nicaragua and the home-made mezcal in Oaxaca. Tripped naked in a thunderstorm on a deserted beach. Acquired parasitic infections and been mildly electrocuted by live wires left near puddles. We'd bought over-the-counter Valium with which to knock ourselves unconscious for an overnight bus ride on which, while asleep, we were robbed of the chargers for all our electronics, and stumbled out of speeding vans to puke on the sides of winding mountain roads after capping off a twenty-four-hour bender with spaghetti Bolognese.

But then even Leila got married, and soon she—and the whole rest of our New York crew—would all have babies. Then they would have everything, and I would have nothing but freedom. And maybe California.

THE SIGN ON THE Hidden Valley Campground read FULL.

"Welp," said Leila. "Too bad. Guess we'll do our own thing."

But I was still driving. I drove on. I knew what to do when the sign read FULL. James had shown me, in Camp 4.

"We'll see about that," I said. "Let's do a loop." Sure enough, a man immediately offered us the other parking spot in his campsite. I was a little disappointed. I had been prepared to take one by force.

We were unpacking the car when a tall, skinny, long-haired man in a tie-dyed headband strode past. He was older than we were, but maybe not by too much. Upon closer inspection, his tie-dyed headband appeared to be the cutoff sleeve of a T-shirt. The T-shirt he was wearing wasn't tie-dyed, but also had no sleeves. He wore granny glasses, like a hippie, and seemed friendly and nonthreatening and maybe like he had something to offer, like the parking spot we had just scored. He stopped and looked at me.

"Want to go on an adventure?" he asked.

"Let me just go get my friend," I replied.

He said his name was Glenn.

Glenn led Leila and me to a different campsite.

"What are you girls going to do today?" he asked.

"We're going hiking," we said.

"We can show you a place to hike."

At his campsite were other guys. A Derek, a Ryan, and a Fred. Derek and Ryan were young, early twenties, and Fred was older, probably older than Glenn, but he seemed young, too. In his eyes, in the way he held his body. There was a hint of gray in his Samurai man bun, but his body was like the rock itself. He was wearing the kind of glasses that change from clear to shaded. He reminded me of Yoda, if Yoda were from Southern California.

Glenn opened a plastic tub like the one James had kept in his parents' garage and took out some stuff. He handed me a pair of pointy leather shoes.

"Try these on," he said.

"They don't fit," I complained. "They hurt."

"If you can get them on, then they fit."

Next, he held out a climbing harness. "Step in here," he said, making space between the loops. He pulled on the straps at my waist and thighs, gently but firmly, like a practiced dad.

"That fits, too," he said, giving the strap one last, hard yank.

He gave Leila some shoes. She grabbed the harness from him and stepped into it herself. Then he threw the stuff in the back of a copper-colored pickup truck, and the rest of them all jumped in after it.

"Let's go," he said. "Let's go hiking."

We rode a short distance from the campground to a parking lot across the big main road. Then they led us down a trail into a maze of rocks, and then up and over and on top of some boulders, until we arrived at a shady area, where they unpacked all the stuff.

"This is Tumbling Rainbow," Fred said solemnly. "And that's Run for Your Life."

Fred placed a portable speaker on a boulder. Glenn situated himself on some rocks shaped like a chair, uncinched a velvet pouch clipped to his belt loop, took out a glass jar and some brown rolling papers, and started rolling the biggest joint I'd ever seen. The younger guys moved the metal stuff around in a way that was both casual and serious at the same time.

We sat on the rocks as if they were patio furniture, passing the joint. Golden piles and towers and spaceships of rock were strewn around the desert like giant, hardened sandcastles. There was little else here besides the shaggy, Y-shaped Joshua trees, and, in some spots, pinyon pine, sagebrush, spiky yucca, and mean paddles of cholla cacti, the kind with needles.

Someone asked where we were from, and I explained that Leila was from Brooklyn and I had just moved here from there, and we were old friends from college.

"What did you girls get up to in Brooklyn?" Glenn asked, taking a hit.

"Leila's a lawyer," I said proudly. "I tutor kids for money, write for free, and hang out with anarchist punks for fun," I added.

"So, you're an anarchist?" he asked.

"Definitely," I said.

NOW, THE JOINT WAS DONE and I faced the wall. Fred pressed some buttons and the speed metal on the portable speaker changed to the 10,000 Maniacs song "These Are the Days."

I had played that song obsessively in middle school. On summer nights I would lie down on the warm asphalt of my dead-end suburban street with the CD in my Discman and dream of a world beyond.

> *These are days you'll remember*
> *Never before and never since, I promise*
> *Will the whole world be warm as this . . .*

I hadn't heard the song in almost twenty years, but as I touched my fingertips to the warm granite, I felt it pulling me outside of time. Fred couldn't have known that, but he was smiling kindly at me like he knew something.

Glenn pointed at a distant wall. "You see that, over there?" I detected the faintest Midwestern flat "a" in his accent.

"What?" I chalked my hands for the third time. They'd given me a little bag of it.

"The 'A' on that rock, with the circle around it."

I squinted for a moment, before I realized he was speaking metaphorically.

"This is where the real anarchy is," he grinned.

With that, I took my first step into the vertical.

I LIKED IT IMMEDIATELY, this wall in my face. The way it smelled.

The route called Run for Your Life was not, traditionally, for beginners. A beginner route would be chunkier, with plenty to grab. This just looked like a vertical rock. There were maybe some little nubs, here and there. I reached out and up and tried to grab them with my fingers. Then I tried to put my foot on one.

"Spread your legs and trust the rubber!" voices half exalted, half guffawed.

I grabbed some nubs and stepped on some other ones. Without looking down, I made it about four feet up. There was a metal ring bolted to the rock, almost within reach, if I stretched.

"I can almost grab that thing there," I said. "But I can't quite reach it."

"Don't grab the bolt!"

"*Never* grab the bolt!"

"Will I break it?"

"No, you won't break it. But that's not free climbing. You're a free climber."

"Doesn't that mean you have no rope?"

"No, free *solo* means you have no rope. Free climber means you don't pull on the man-made things. You only use the rock."

"Okay, I won't grab the bolt."

Then Leila tried, but she didn't really get anywhere, either.

For a few moments, we each just hung on and hovered, but those guys hooted and hollered like we were really doing something. Leila untied, and then the rest of them took turns doing it while we smoked another joint.

"That was for us," said Glenn. "Now, let's go do something for you."

We walked back down, scrambling over rocks, the climbers offering us their hands and taking our backpacks when we hesitated at heights they leapt from. I jumped awkwardly from a chest-high rock.

Glenn landed gracefully just ahead, then spun around to face me. "You *said* you wanted to go on an adventure."

We arrived at a place they called the Thin Wall, where, they said, there were easier routes. Fred clipped the rope to the belt loop of his jeans and, unattached to anything else, sauntered up to the top of the wall and attached the rope to something up there.

"Having that guy solo up and rig your rope for you is like walking on the field at the Super Bowl and playing catch with the quarterback," said Glenn.

I asked if that meant Fred was an important guy.

"He's a Stonemaster," Glenn said.

I didn't know what that meant, but I liked the word.

I went first again. I trusted the rope immediately. I could hang on it and even sit on it, but quickly learned that I wasn't supposed to. I hung on it for a second, and Glenn, who was belaying, lowered me all the way to the ground and made me start again.

"No hangdogging," he said. "We're old-school."

The next time, I made sure not to hang, or even let go. I kept climbing, which was really just touching. There were all different shapes. You could stick your fingertips inside the dents and holes and curl your knuckles around the edges. You could push on the flat spots like you were beached-whaling yourself out of a swimming pool. There were resting places where you could stand on two feet.

Each thing I held gave my body a little thrill. It wasn't just the grabbing part, it was the way that when I pulled with my hands and pushed with my feet, I could feel the vectors of my limbs converge and rise.

The movement was surprisingly pleasurable. When I reached up high, the counterweight of my body made space between my ribs, like in yoga. The rock felt nice, too. The granite was rough, and the little crystals in it were sharp—later, more than once, a tiny, perfect pyramid would draw a bubble of blood with the precision of a nurse's needle—but it had some kind of energy. Was that because it was big, or because it was old? Or maybe I was just high.

I had never been so acutely aware of my own fear—its taste in my mouth, its tingle in my veins—nor had I ever felt so coolly detached from it. For the first time in my life, it felt like my fear could exist without taking me over completely. I could easily imagine the rope snapping, just as I could imagine my car crashing, but I had to vanquish that intrusive thought with silence. It had never, ever been this quiet inside of me before.

I told myself, *Well, it could happen—the rope* could *snap—but it hasn't happened* yet, and the world would get brighter and sharper, like I was seeing it all for the first time—or the last. It was exhilarating and relaxing all at once.

Pulling up the full weight of my own body, I felt surprisingly light. I didn't need love. I didn't need radical honesty or emotional safety or nonviolent communication or healthy boundaries. Up here, I was free from all that. All I saw were thousands of Joshua trees merrily waving their silly branches at me, while a rock millions of years old held me.

At the top, I looked down. I'd never been afraid of heights, only of my own urge to jump from them. Glenn, Fred, and Leila were tiny on the ground, and the whole Hidden Valley spread out before me in Fraggle rocks and Seuss trees. I lowered down like a spider on silk, and when I landed back on the ground, just as the sky was really pinking up, Fred said, "The only way to end your first day is to see the sunset from the Space Station."

We hadn't even had to ask.

NO ROPES WERE INVOLVED in this adventure, they said, just beers. "You can do it with a beer in your hand," Glenn promised.

We walked up some innocuous rocks, sipping PBR tallboys, until Fred and Glenn coaxed each of us in turn into straddling a ring of rock shaped like a saddle. They instructed us to wrap our limbs around it, slide over to the other side, and step across a narrow chasm that went all the way down to the ground, now by at least a couple of building stories. Next, we sidestepped along a ledge that was the approximate size and shape of the ledges from which suicidal people were talked down by SWAT teams in movies.

That was when Leila whispered, "I don't think this is a very good idea."

You had to not think *too* much about what you were doing, except, at the same time, you also had to pay perfect attention to every move you made. To make a mistake, to fall, to die—those would all be choices, choices just as conscious, or as reckless, as the choice to come up here at all. Finally, I understood everything in the books by dead French philosophers I'd underlined in college. You *could* fall off this ledge. But why *would* you? You *could* choose to die. But why *would* you? You were really choosing to live all the time, just like the dead French philosophers said.

Now they were telling us that we had to climb down and around this dome-shaped rock, which was the outside of the Space Station. It was shaped like an egg, or modernist architecture. But we had climbed up high enough that this dome-egg of rock seemed far above the ground.

"You trusted us with your lives *all day*," said Fred.

"But there were ropes," I said.

"You don't *need* a rope to do this," said Glenn.

"I really think I do."

"All you need to do is turn around—"

"And reach down with your right foot—"

"And there's a hold right there—"

"And then you move your left hand—"

"And there's a big hold right there—"

"And then there's another big hold—"

"It's just like climbing down a ladder—"

"It's like stairs!"

It was not like stairs. It was more like a round rock egg from which you could slip into oblivion, with a few dents in it.

I contemplated the desert. The sun was setting over the rocks we had been darting in and out of all day like Sand People, or desert Hobbits. Down below in the campground, tiny figures prepared dinner. The sky was every color. All myths applied.

I turned around, placed my hands on the rough granite, and with my right foot, stepped down and out, into what felt like nothing.

But it wasn't nothing. There was a little thing to stand on, just like they had promised there would be.

We wriggled through a hole, and then we were inside a round rock cave shaped like a room but missing its front wall, with no guardrail. The round frame of the rock was indeed like the window on a spaceship. It was very civilized. There was even a guestbook you could sign.

We stayed up there for the duration of a joint. As we came down, I took bigger and bigger gulps of my beer every step of the way. When my feet touched flat ground, I felt a rush of sweet relief I would come to know intimately. I would form a chemical addiction to it that would change my brain and life.

Bank balance? Car trouble? Family dysfunction? All that had happened with the pathological liar boyfriend, and everyone else before him? Unfinished essays, the whole book I had tried and failed to write in my twenties, all the bad sex and lost love? Things people had said to me, done to me, how I felt about them, things I had done to people, things I did to myself, rejection letters, callous remarks, climate change, cancer, being a good person, loving a good person, the hypocrisy of government, the hegemony of the system, the quagmire of my own emotions, the weight of love, the lightness of being—none of that was here at all.

There was something bigger, emptier and quieter than all of that, and it was *this*.

Everything was finally okay. It was like finding out you didn't get a parking ticket, or going to bed with the object of your utmost desire, but times a thousand, and all from just stepping on the mercifully flat earth.

"WE ARE CONQUISTADORES OF THE USELESS," Fred said later that night, staring into the fire. "Some people waste their whole lives climbing rocks."

"We have to leave here immediately," Leila said the next morning, "or I will lose touch with everything in my life that matters to me."

I lost touch. I let go. Holding on to the rocks became everything in life that mattered to me.

PART II

RITES

And so—as though unwanting every want,
so altering all at every altering thought,
now drawing back from everything begun—
I stood there on the darkened slope, fretting
away from thought to thought the bold intent
that seemed so very urgent at the outset.

—Dante Alighieri,
INFERNO, CANTO 2, LINES 37–42

4

Crack

There had always been safety in being better, never safety in being equal.

—Eva Hagberg Fisher, *How to Be Loved*

IT TOOK A YEAR TO CREATE a California version of my former New York life. I found some kids to help with their math homework and college essays. I scored a subsidized writing studio at an arts center in the Marin Headlands, renting the corner of an attic in a former military barracks for $140 a month. My garret's skylight framed a sliver of Pacific Ocean and a decommissioned Cold War–era Nike SF-88 antiaircraft missile just down the hill. On certain days of the week, the site was open to tourists, and in preparation for their visiting hours, the missile would rise from bay doors in the ground like an absurd boner. On my night walks, I would startle at the mannequin permanently installed in the security booth.

I lived semi illegally in the studio, until I found on Craigslist a nine-by-thirteen-foot mother-in-law unit next to a redwood tree in an Oakland Hills backyard for $750 a month. It had an old boat kitchen with a mini-fridge, tiny sink, and two electric burners, a loft bed, a very California bathroom with a stone shower and a bronze bowl sink, and French doors that opened onto a tiny balcony, shaded by a grapevine, with a view of the entire glimmering bay. When people asked how I scored these and other plumb deals (my former Brooklyn apartment had been nice, supremely well-located, and rent-stabilized), I always told them ruefully, "Lucky in rental real estate, unlucky in love."

And—I had SubyRuby.

SubyRuby was my first car. I was thirty years old when I bought her, and that was when I knew for sure that everyone who said that love at first sight was a myth was wrong. To buy her, I had tutored almost double through my last New York winter, taking taxis across dark Central Park to protect the cash, wadded in the pockets of my grandmother's old sheepskin coat, for my new life in the West.

The seller was a forty-year-old accountant in San Francisco with two children whose company was transferring him to New York. Movers were loading the truck the day I went to look at it.

"We're changing places," I told him. "You won't need a car in Manhattan."

As we approached the white Outback wagon, the accountant said, "Wait, before you drive it. I haven't done this in a while, but I think—" He fiddled around behind the back seat headrest, pulled on something, and released the seat back.

"There we go," he said. "I thought so. The seats go totally flat."

He went around the other side and flattened that seat, too. Then he popped the rear hatch and gestured inside.

"You're pretty petite," he said. "I think you could fit in there."

I crawled inside and lay down on my back. Out the windows, I could see big patches of sky. I felt like I was in my own spaceship.

"Sorry about the ceiling," said the accountant. "We left a can of Coke in there on a hot day and it exploded."

My eyes roamed the faint stains. Maybe I'd stick some glow-in-the-dark stars on there, make constellations. I reached my hands out wide. This would make a good bed, bigger than a twin.

The back of this station wagon felt, oddly, like home.

"You drive a hard bargain," the accountant said when we shook.

I had gotten him to knock a grand off the asking price. I couldn't tell whether this was a triumph, or if I should have gotten an even better deal. Terrified, as a woman, to be overmatched in my first used-car deal, I had bargained aggressively. Because of what had happened with Robbie, I had to be tough all the time. I could never, ever, let a man take advantage of me again, especially in any way to do with money. We could do dangerous things that risked my life instead of my credit rating, but I would never again be on the wrong end of a bad deal. We could have sex and then he could either never speak to me again or act like it had never happened, just as long as he didn't try to make me pay for his lifestyle, or threaten to kill me.

"So, you're just kind of, like, a free spirit?" asked the accountant, as he signed over the title and I produced the bank check. "Just gonna . . . see where the wind takes you?"

"Something like that," I said, wondering what I'd have to do to make it true.

I drove away, up to the top of a steep hill. The whole city of San Francisco and its blue bay spread before me. I already knew I wouldn't spend much time there. The city was just a golden gateway to a green and wild world. I had already developed a mild dislike for most of the locals; there was something morally vacuous in their facile TED Talk platitudes, something nauseating in their oblivious proclamations of unfettered capitalist greed. I could see all the way to the famous, rust-colored bridge, and I knew where it led—to the Headlands, the Highway 101, and points north, with mist and fog and redwood trees and rocky beaches. To Alaska, even. And inland, toward those mountains, so very sharp, white, and gray.

Just as I crested the hill, the odometer clicked over from 99,999 to 100,000. Even the row of zeroes seemed to be telling me I deserved a fresh start.

SUBYRUBY HADN'T GIVEN ME any trouble in the whole first year I'd owned her. She'd taken me to Joshua Tree, that first time, and on an increasing number of more local California adventures, of which there seemed to be an endless supply.

After I'd met the climbers in Joshua Tree the previous spring, I started going to a local bouldering gym, just north of Berkeley, where a friend of James's let me in for free. (Bouldering is the discipline of climbing without ropes on shorter rock formations, usually up to twenty feet or so. Instead, if the climber falls, they land on their feet, back, or butt, on mattress-like crash pads.) At the bouldering gym, I'd met Noel and Alden, who also vaguely knew James. The climbing community was very small, everyone kept telling me. Big as the whole world and all the rocks in it, but small enough for everyone to know everyone.

Alden lived in his van full-time and bounced from the Bay before Christmas to spend the winter and spring in Joshua Tree. He was there now, Noel said, and if I drove us down, Alden would teach us both to climb crack—meaning climb up rocks via the vertical fissures in them.

"You'll have to buy a harness," Noel added. "Alden only has one extra, and it's my size."

So far, I only had shoes and a chalk bag. I had climbed outdoors a couple more times, once with James, in Tuolumne Meadows, and once with Glenn, on a rock in a Berkeley park, but they had brought their own extra gear for me. I never went to the other climbing gym where I could climb on ropes, because both James and Glenn had told me very strictly never to "pay to climb on *plastic*," and I didn't know anyone who worked at the gym with the ropes who could wave me in for free.

To get my own harness, I went to REI, where I had bought my one pair of climbing shoes, mint-green La Sportiva Mythos I loved like I'd loved my pale pink ballet slippers as a kid. Cutting the tags off the new harness, I detached a small booklet.

"WARNING!" its cover read, in red. "Activities involving the use of this equipment are inherently dangerous. You are responsible for your own actions and decisions."

I had never seen such an admonition in an instruction manual, but I already knew that. It was literally Existentialism 101.

"Before using this equipment," the pamphlet continued, "you must understand and accept the risks involved. FAILURE TO HEED ANY OF THESE WARNINGS MAY RESULT IN SEVERE INJURY OR DEATH," it concluded, next to a skull-and-crossbones graphic.

As if that weren't fucking obvious, I thought, *if you just looked down.*

NOEL AND I DROVE DOWN to Joshua Tree and found Alden's van on some BLM land outside the park boundary. (BLM land was managed by the Bureau of Land Management and was generally free to camp on.) The late March night howled with wind, but the next morning was hot and sunny as we drove into the Hidden Valley Campground to find a spot. I hadn't been back since the year before, when Leila and I had gone to the Space Station with Glenn and Fred. At the campground entrance, Alden stopped his van by the cluster of dumpsters.

"He's pointing at something," said Noel, from my passenger seat.

I left the motor running and got out of the car. There was a futon mattress lying in the dirt next to the dumpster.

"It's brand-new!" said Alden, from his van.

"I don't know," I said. "What if it has bedbugs?"

"Desert sun kills everything," Alden shrugged.

"Where do I put it?"

"Shove it in the back of your Suby," he advised. "Just keep shoving. It'll fit."

I did as directed. The mattress was pristine as promised and fit perfectly in the back of SubyRuby, like they were made for each other.

NOEL WAS SWEET AND GENTLE and spoke slowly and softly, moving like a fair, bearded bear over rock and ground alike. Alden was smaller and slighter and vaguer, with a wispier voice, a wispier, scragglier beard, and faraway eyes often screwed up behind his glasses, as if all the lights were just too bright. He seemed fragile until he was climbing, which he did with an ease that evaded him on flat ground.

Noel told me Alden had social anxiety, which was why he cowered in his van until noon, smoking prolific bowls, until he emerged ready to crush in the presence of others. Alden told me Noel was detoxing from heroin, and that was why he couldn't temperature-regulate at night. I had never heard guys speak with such honesty or kindness about each other, nor seen two people with such supposedly big problems living and functioning under such extreme conditions, though Alden said his social anxiety got worse in cities, and the wilderness was curative.

We developed a little routine. We rose late. The boys smoked bowls in the van all morning. We cooked breakfast in the van, out of the wind, on a battered, grease-caked Coleman stove. Then Alden led us to the base of a mega-classic crack, and the lessons began, at high noon.

From the little outdoor climbing I'd done since my first trip to Joshua Tree, I'd learned a bit more about the system of climbing difficulty ratings, the Yosemite Decimal System, or YDS. The YDS was specific to North America (there were other, different systems in France, Germany, Australia, and New Zealand), and used numbers from 5.5 to 5.15 to rate the difficulty of individual rock climbs. The first part of the number, the five before the decimal, indicated that the terrain was "fifth-class," meaning vertical, and demanded "technical" climbing, requiring a rope and protective gear, anchored, temporarily or permanently, into the rock, to ascend safely. Fourth-class terrain was also pretty vertical and therefore required climbing, probably using both feet and both hands, but wasn't as steep, and could be climbed just with a rope, if that. Third-class terrain was somewhere between a steep hike and real, upward climbing, second-class described a true, steep hike, and first-class terrain was flat ground, or according to Kevin McLane in *The Rockclimbers' Guide to Squamish*, "means you're still in bed."

McLane's description of the YDS is also the best I've read:

5.0–5.7 Easy for competent climbers. Most novices begin in these grades.

5.8-5.9 Levels where the vast majority of climbers become comfortable.

5.10 The happy level that most regular climbers achieve.

5.11 Some talent, training, or lots of climbing. Unemployment helps.

5.12 Even more of the above, especially unemployment.

5.13 Vast amounts of dedication. Permanent unemployment.

From what I'd seen so far, this was highly accurate. Alden climbed 5.12. Alden was unemployed.

The lower grades were often called "five-easy," though no one ever took me on anything below 5.6, even to teach me. James and Glenn and the other climbers I'd met so far spoke reverently of the 5.10s they'd climbed. The muscular, feral folks who seemed to live full-time in the climber campgrounds—or in their vans, behind the bouldering gym— talked incessantly about things that were 5.11 or 5.12, and it seemed like 5.13 mostly got climbed by people who were just boldfaced names in the old climbing magazines I'd found piled up in a corner of the gym and started reading in the sauna. The grade of 5.14 appeared only in the newer magazines in the pile, from about 2000 or so. At the time, there were only a couple of people in the whole world who climbed 5.15, including a Californian referred to simply as "Sharma."

In Tuolumne, the previous fall, James had taken me on one 5.7 that was long, hard, slippery, and scary, and another that was easy and inviting, but I could see how they were roughly the same, and how the 5.6 in the city park on which Glenn had belayed me one sixty-degree Berkeley winter afternoon was just a little easier.

What made climbs easy was one of two things: either they were "low angle," meaning they were closer to being a diagonal line instead of a vertical one, or they were a "sea of holds," meaning there was a plethora of handholds to grab, and all the handholds were "jugs," meaning shaped like jug handles. What made the climbs harder, I quickly figured out, was that they were either steeper, or harder to hold on to. Instead of an edge or even a ledge as wide as the first joint of your fingers to grab on to or stand up on, there would be one as skinny as a dime. Instead of a crack in the rock you could stick your whole hand into until the flesh locked in place and held you there, a harder climb might only have a thin seam wide or deep enough for a few fingertips, with which to pull up the entirety of your body weight. On a hard climb, there might just be a tiny dish or dimple, on an otherwise slick slab, into which you could press only the points of your toes, harder and harder, applying more and more force, until you could stand up and reach up to find something else to pull on, for dear life.

HAVING BEEN A GRADEMONGER ALL MY LIFE, I took to the climbing grading system almost instinctively. Nerdiness was my first extreme sport. From the moment I stepped into a classroom, I was hypercompetitive at school and academics. I saw every spelling test and volcano project as an opportunity to destroy. Not just to crush, but to destroy—or be destroyed, since imperfection, I reasoned, was as good as death. I believed that success, conversely, could somehow ward off pain, and maybe even danger.

Maybe it was because watching the do-or-die 1986 New York Mets repeatedly phoenix themselves from the brink to achieve ecstatic glory was a deeply formative childhood experience. My academic aggression was at the level of a ballplayer charging the mound, but a good grade or a blue ribbon only made me hungrier. I was seeking an unapologetic dominance I'd seen only on television, and only in men. I liked competing academically because, academics, unlike sports, were a venue in which I could compete with boys, and beat them. That was very important to me, both being around the guys and being their equal. I was livid when I had to give up co-ed hardball for *girls* softball. I didn't want to play with only other *girls*. I wanted to fight and beat *everyone*, and we would *all* play together and against one another, and boys would be there, and boys would *see*.

Only the most benign pressure came from my family, like if I got a ninety-eight on a spelling test, my dad would say, "What happened to the other two points?," or my grandmother would purse her lips and ask, "Did anyone else get ninety-eight? How about ninety-nine?" My mother and grandfather, who'd been good students themselves, didn't seem to care as much about my grades, but I got the message. Ninety-eight was okay, but perfect was better.

In high school, I took two English classes both semesters of my sophomore year, doing extra credit projects in both of them in order to buy extra GPA points to offset driver's ed, the following year, from pulling down my GPA, because it wasn't an honors course. (I was hell-bent on taking driver's ed as soon as possible and getting my license on my seventeenth birthday, the youngest you could legally drive alone in New York State. I had this idea that there were places I could go, in a car, that I desperately needed to see. When I finally did get my license, the first thing I did was put my slumber-party sleeping bag and a fresh toothbrush in the back of the family station wagon, to which I would soon affix a decal proclaiming my early admission to a fancy college. I had never heard of people sleeping in cars for fun, but I wanted to be prepared to both sleep and brush my teeth anywhere I might be able to drive to, which hopefully included places far away from Long Island.)

I took AP honors everything, did history competitions and Science Olympiads and the school newspaper and the student council and tried to start a pro-choice club, an effort stymied by the inexplicable assignment of a vehemently anti-choice practicing-Catholic guidance counselor as our adviser. I took an application-only course called Science Research, where we were coached to do science projects in university research labs, to enter into what was then called the Westinghouse Science Talent Search, in which I was a 1997 semifinalist. (The kid who was a finalist went to MIT and became a Columbia neuroscience professor.) Everyone else had to wrangle pigeons in Iowa or petri dishes in Texas for the summer in order to get the necessary data, but I brokered a deal to do my research on my own high school student population, during the school year, so I could still be a junior counselor at my sleepaway camp for art nerds. Under the guidance of a local university sociology professor, I conducted a study about self-esteem and found out that boys had more of it.

I won medals and plaques and trophies and certificates and small amounts of money. I won gold, silver, and bronze shiny objects on varicolored ribbons, but I kept the gold ones, and the blue ones, separate from the others.

I stayed up until two most nights and woke up before dawn to catch a 7:08 bus that delivered me to 7:30 a.m. meetings for the various extracurriculars that I thought would look good on my applications to Ivy League colleges, or that might yield yet more medals, ribbons, certificates, plaques, trophies, or mentions in the school or local newspaper.

It was the best public education privilege could buy a Jewish American princess of Queens, and later Long Island, but it wasn't really about learning or growing so much as joylessly striving toward more numeric, ephemeral proof of my momentary but measurable superiority on some arbitrary metric.

If I wasn't instantly good at something—calculus, basketball—I simply didn't do it at all, because there were so many things at which to be the best. I loved writing the most, and I loved writing for the school paper, but the force that drove me to do almost everything else I did for most of my childhood and adolescence wasn't love or learning or growth—it was fear. Fear of failure. Fear of being anything less than perfect, or the best. And a ferocious hunger for something I could not name.

Growing up, I always felt that somehow, were I to fuck up, or fail, or even just be second-best, that some unnamable fate awaited me, one I could only ward off with relentless achievement. It made my parents happy, and they sometimes seemed unbearably sad. It felt good, inside, in ways that nothing else did.

I turned out tenacious, but developed no tolerance for failure. I'd had so little practice. I knew how to try hard, but I didn't know how to survive my own failure—or the inexplicable shame that even the thought of it made me feel. But here, in the desert, no one cared that I'd gone to an expensive college. No one cared that I'd graduated with honors (in a major I made up myself) after writing a two hundred page thesis that was an existentialist Marxist treatise against homework, but not magna cum laude, because I'd gotten three B's, one in a class called Feminism and Poststructuralism. No one cared that my college classmates were now Barack Obama's White House counsel, Rachel Maddow's lead-in, and one of the stars of *The Office*, or that all my other same-aged girlfriends except for me were neatly married by the time we all turned thirty—the age past which Leila's debutante mom might sniff you'd "married late."

People here didn't have jobs, or even homes. There were climbers here who didn't even live in cars, only tents. Their backpacks were currently inside their tents, but when it was time to move on, their tents would go into their backpacks, and they would hitchhike to the next climbing place. That's why they called the hardcore hobo climbers "dirtbags"—because they slept in the dirt.

THERE WAS NO HONOR ROLL or homework or deadline or rubric at Alden's School of Rock, student body population: two, me and Noel. There was just a granite wall and a rope.

When he finally came out of his van with his rope, Alden said that he would take us on one mega-classic per day. We'd start with Double Cross, then try White Lightning, and then do Sail Away.

"If you don't know how to climb crack after that," he said, "then you never will."

On each of the three Joshua Tree mega-classics, Noel lead-belayed Alden while he hung the rope and made a toprope anchor. Then Alden stayed on top, and we climbed up toward him, or rather, toward his feet, dangling over the edge of a stone block a good seven to ten stories above. No matter what, we little learners, as I had begun to call us (à la *The Big Lebowski*), were on a secure, tight toprope, held safely from above. The only thing there was to fear was the height itself. And the fear itself. And failing. And sucking.

When he could see us, Alden offered occasional helpful advice, shouting, "Find the con-STRIC-tion!"

I'd received one other piece of crack-climbing advice, from James, in Tuolumne, the previous Labor Day. He'd taken me somewhere called Puppy Crack, a perfect "splitter," he called it, that indeed split a big gray rock somewhere near the cold river where we'd swum on our prior trip. He hung a rope, tied me in.

"Don't do this," he'd said, pulling on the sides of the crack like he was prying open elevator doors. "Useless. Do *this*." He karate chopped his hand into the crack, then wriggled it in deeper until it was stuck.

"Make it *stay*," James had said.

"Make it stay," I muttered to myself, six months later, at the base of Double Cross (5.7), a single line splitting the face of the wall.

I repeated the directions. "Find the constriction. Make it stay."

I reached up and into the darkness of the crack itself. It was cool inside. I wriggled my hand into the space, until the rock almost grabbed me back.

Sometimes I could make it stay, first a hand, then the other hand, then maybe even a toe, or most of my foot. The more body parts I could jam into the crack in the rock, the easier it was to pull myself up on them. But then, other times, I couldn't make it stay, I couldn't solve the puzzle, and I couldn't find the good jam, and I slipped and slid and fell out of the crack, flying away from the wall, tearing the skin on the backs of my hands, spinning around on my toprope, kicking the rock. Sometimes the rope was tight, other times, not so much. I wondered if Alden knew about the "girlfriend belay."

"Up rooooooope!" I howled, miserably, into the wind.

But somehow, suddenly, after what seemed like countless tries, slips, and falls, Alden wasn't far away anymore. I was really high up and could see a field of endless Joshua trees previously hidden behind the wall, a few distant mountains. I'd made it to the top. It felt mostly the same as it had that first time, when Fred had soloed up and hung the rope, but also different. More real. I'd fought much harder on my way to the top, and the short journey had been more physically painful. As a result, I now felt more elated, and more exhausted, than I'd ever felt before. I'd been so absorbed in the struggle, in getting past just the one hard part, and then the next hard part, that I hadn't allowed myself to think about the top until I was there, even though I'd only been a few dozen feet away the whole time. At the top was Alden's old, thick rope, slung through two steel rings attached to short lengths of steel chain that looked safe enough. The chains were affixed to steel bolts that were drilled right into the granite, staining it faintly with rust that looked like dried blood.

"Good job," said Alden, and then we went back down again.

THE NEXT DAY, at White Lightning, also 5.7, our campsite neighbors joined us, a couple, Greg and Claire. They lived in a Toyota Sienna minivan and were from Homer, Alaska. They had put wood flooring down inside their minivan, making a tiny kitchen table where the bench seats had been. They made their living working seasonally, rescuing tortoises.

Greg and Claire had cooked us all nachos in a Dutch oven over their campfire the previous night. The next morning, they had the nacho leftovers packed for lunch at the crag in the stacked tins of a stainless steel Indian tiffin. Greg led the hard 5.12 next to our crack. Claire belayed him, and then followed, flawlessly.

"I'm glad he doesn't free solo 5.12 anymore," she said. "But it had to be his decision, y'know?"

Then she sat daintily on a rock, eating her lunch from the little silver bowl, as I thrutched and flailed and bled on White Lightning, stuck at the hardest part, also known as the crux.

"That crack's going to eat you," said Claire's sweet voice from below.

Claire looked so neat and put together. She was chewing her leftover tiffin nachos so carefully. My pants were torn, my unwashed hair a tangled mass. The skin on the backs of my hands was raw and scabbed and bleeding. The pudge of my belly extruded, cold and white, in between my pants and harness. There had to be a reason I was dangling from this rope, sleeping in my station wagon and spending my days with these kind but odd and rumpled men. It felt like the crack *was* going to eat me, and this vague, wholly absurd threat sparked in me like flint. An insane and clarifying rage came through my body, and I let it make me strong.

I jammed my hand back into the crack, into the place where it had been slipping out, determined to *make it stay*. My hand was too small to fill the space, so I folded it into a fistlike shape that would fit more securely in the rock. I flexed all the muscles of the arm and hand until the flesh pushed against the rock. I made it stay.

Now that my hand was basically stuck in the rock, gripped by it, I could pull on it. I pulled up on the arm, feeling my muscles strain and the bones nearly pop, and then I was able to step my foot onto another, higher little nubbin sticking out of the rock.

The previous night, when I'd complained to Alden that jamming my feet in the crack was painful, he'd chuckled and said, "It won't hurt after the nerves all die." Now, I didn't feel any pain, or maybe I did, but it didn't really hurt. I felt light, or made of light, or like I glowed, clean and empty. My senses were heightened, and I could smell the rock, almost taste the difference between a warm patch of granite baking in the sun and a pocket of cooler, moister, mustier air in the shade. I could smell the salt in my sweat, the iron in my blood, the funk of all my rotting biology. Standing on my next little nubbin, I reached up, wedged my hand into a fresh empty space, and roared.

"Yeah!" laughed Alden and Noel. "Get angry with it!"

I was hanging on a rope far enough from the ground that if I fell, I could easily die, but I wasn't remotely scared. Why would I die? Why would I fall? Why would I let go? Why wouldn't I *just hold on* and *make it stay*?

I was thrilled, not only by where I was but also by each individual move and motion. It hurt so good, the tight torque of my feet in the crack. Even the sting on the backs of my hands felt like a trophy, from boxing a rock. I could yoga my feet right up to my groin, and even though I had to try so hard it made me quiver, if I found something to stand on, and another place, high up, to make my hand stay, and if I just pushed and pulled hard enough, I could straighten my legs and stand up, like an evolving monkey—or a baby, learning to walk.

The crack did not eat me. I did not let it. I did not let the chick with the perfect nachos and the perfect minivan and the perfect 5.12 boyfriend see me fail, or give up.

I made it through the crux of White Lightning (5.7). And then I made it to the top.

It had the same view as Double Cross, lots of Joshua trees, repeating and repeating, all the way to the mountains on the horizon.

Why was I doing this? I already knew I would never be that good.

It was because I didn't win anything. Because it wasn't about winning. The whole deal was that I just tried hard—and didn't die.

If I failed, I could keep trying. I had failed in lots of ways, on my way to the top, by hanging on the rope at all, by slipping and falling out of the crack. I hadn't done it perfectly, but I had learned from my mistakes. That felt good, too, to have succeeded at something at which, at first, I had not succeeded.

I was mentally spent by the effort and already sore from the previous day, slack ropes of muscle that burned when I moved. I wasn't yet sore in new places where I would be the next day. It felt like my sinews were emitting icy-hot, from the inside, but even that felt good, when I used the muscles more.

Underneath the body-wide bruise a new and deeper layer was forming, maybe somewhere in the marrow, a living part of me of which I'd never before been aware. I thought of superheroes busting out of their cutoffs, writhing in transformation from spider bites, caterpillars liquefying in their chrysalises before they sprouted wings. My hands looked like someone else's hands. I was becoming something else, something new.

Climbing was the first thing that didn't come easily to me that I did anyway. It was the first thing that actually quieted the demon of my own desire to destroy or self-destruct. And being bad—or not that great—at rock climbing was exponentially more fun than being good at school. Nerds cared too much about school, but climbers didn't even care about death.

THE NEXT DAY, I climbed Sail Away (5.8) to Alden's belay without weighting the rope, and by week's end, I had learned to climb crack in Joshua Tree, a skill that would open up a world of Sierra granite.

And, perhaps equally important—I had a free bed in the back of my Subaru.

5

Bomber

ON THE FOURTH MORNING of our impromptu crack-climbing clinic, Alden and Noel were still hiding in the van when a buff, blond, twentysomething woman from the next campsite put her coffee cup down on her picnic table and began doing pull-ups off the side of her own truck.

"Wow," said Alden wistfully. "I bet she climbs 5.12."

"Her truck has Alaska plates," I said. "Like Greg and Claire. *They* climb 5.12."

I hopped out of the van and began doing yoga stretches, since I couldn't do pull-ups. When I rolled up to stand from my forward bend, she was coming toward me.

"Hey," she said, in a voice at once tough, tender, and awkward. "I'm Kye. Do you have a portaledge? I need a new partner for big walls."

"What's a portaledge?" I asked. "I climbed a 5.8 yesterday. Sail Away. My first one."

"Okay," she sighed. "Ever climbed Toe Jam?"

"Don't think so," I said. "I've climbed Double Cross, though. And White Lightning. And Sail Away."

"Not bad," she said. "Then you'll like Toe Jam." She nodded at Alden's van. "I have to go to work now, but tell those guys that tomorrow is Girl Climbing Day."

Back in the van, I told the boys tomorrow was Girl Climbing Day.

"She's gonna kick your ass!" teased Alden.

"Is Toe Jam a 5.12?" I fretted.

"Toe Jam is 5.7," Alden reassured. "It's easier than Sail Away. But," he yawned, curling up for a nap, "we should definitely take a rest day today, to save your strength."

I wanted to be eternally, maximally psyched, but I was secretly relieved. It would be nice to take an afternoon off from boxing a rock until my hands were bloody while dangling five to ten stories off the ground.

THE NEXT MORNING, Kye was standing politely at the edge of our campsite with a backpack and a rope. She was wearing sporty sunglasses, and the exact same climbing pants I had on.

She came over and sat down at our picnic table. "I made you this coffee in case you didn't get enough," she said, pushing a mug toward me. She shook an American Spirit out of a pack and lit it, then handed me a prepacked bowl and a lighter.

"From Alaska," she said. "Crazy weed grows there in the midnight sun."

"So," she continued, "if it's all right with you, after we climb Toe Jam, I'm going to do a few burns on Bearded Cabbage, which is right next to it. I ran into my friend Reid in town after work last night, and he agreed to give me a catch. If I manage to hang the rope on it, you can try it, too. No offense, but I'd rather he belay me, if I'm on lead. You can belay me on Toe Jam, but I solo that. Bearded Cabbage is my proj right now, so I want to be super-bomber, y'know?"

I didn't know what most of that meant, but I said, "Totally."

"What's your job?" I asked. "In town?"

"I'm a guide," she said. "I take people climbing. That means my gear is always new. Pro deal."

I didn't know what that meant, either, but I said "Totally" again.

"TOE JAM IS ON THE OLD WOMAN," Kye said, as we crossed the campground. "Same as Double Cross."

Having a poor sense of direction and a weak memory for anything that wasn't a story or a vocabulary word, I couldn't really remember which of the five big formations were which, though now, I can list them from memory: Intersection Rock, the Old Woman, the Blob, the Cyclops, and Chimney Rock, named like constellations, for some vague resemblance.

Each of these five major formations contained dozens of routes, as well as plenty of less-technical terrain for tourists from Los Angeles to scramble and take selfies on. Each was a lump of several giant rocks between one and two hundred feet tall, varying in circumference from maybe the outside of a small apartment building to a whole city block. There was a north, south, east, and west face to each rock, and the climbing guidebook even had charts in it, about what times of day different routes were in the sun or shade.

Toe Jam was in the sun when Kye threw the rope down at the base. "Nobody on it," she said. "Good."

"Ever lead-belayed?" she asked.

"Once," I said. "In Tuolumne. With this guy. But not in the gym yet or anything."

Kye was about to climb in a different way from the way I had been climbing up until then. I had been climbing on a toprope that went all the way up to the top of the rock, and was threaded through bolts up there that were permanently drilled in and maintained by the local community, or through no less than three—definitely no less than *two*— pieces of removeable gear stuck into the rock so securely that it was, I was constantly reassured, "trucker," meaning it could hold the weight of a truck.

"Not just a truck hanging there," Glenn had said. "A *falling* truck."

But right now, the rope was all piled up on the ground. How was it going to get on top of the rock, so I could hang, safely from it, while I climbed Toe Jam?

It was going to get up there by Kye climbing up, with the rope dangling below her, not taut above her, and then sticking metal pieces of removeable gear, known as "camming devices," or "cams," into the rock. As she went up, she would attach the rope to each piece of gear, so if she fell, it would catch her, and she would hang from it, below—*if* the metal piece of gear in the rock stayed put, which it would—*if* she had placed it exactly right.

"Ever cleaned gear?" Kye asked. She meant taking out the pieces of gear she had stuck in, which would be my job, as I followed, on the toprope she was putting up.

"Just a little bit," I said. Alden had put a few pieces in as he hung our topropes on Double Cross and White Lightning and Sail Away, but not many, because he routinely free soloed most of those climbs.

"Okay, well," she shrugged. "Should be fine. You got me?"

She showed me her knot. I showed her the position of my hands, the rope, the carabiner on my belay device. Then Kye cast off on lead, and I fed out the rope, like I was fishing in reverse.

When the climber was on lead, putting up the rope and putting in the gear, it was the belayer's job to feed *out* rope, but the rope stayed slack and useless, unless the climber fell, or asked to hang on it. I had caught on that hanging on the rope—sitting in your harness like a kid on a swing and letting the rope hold your weight, instead of holding yourself on the wall with your own strength—was a shameful thing. Or it ruined things. If you were climbing on lead, it blew your send, and your onsight. "Sending" actually meant *ascending*, from bottom to top, without falling. "Onsighting" meant sending the first time you tried. If you fell on the rope or hung on the rope, you could try to send again, by starting over from the bottom, but it blew your onsight forever to weight the rope for a single second. Hanging on the rope before you fell, which was called "taking," was even more shameful—much more shameful—than falling. Falling while in the act of climbing and trying was proud. Taking because you were afraid you were going to fall was weak. Or so I had figured out so far, about the unwritten rules of this unwinnable game.

"Let's close the system," Kye had said. "Tie into the other end of the rope. Then, even if you can't hear me from the top, you'll know it's time to climb when the rope goes tight. But you'll hear me."

I tied the bottom end of the rope to the other side of my belay loop, and we rechecked the knots and the belay. Then she took off her shirt, stuck her phone in her sports bra, and started up the rock.

Like Alden, Kye was a natural teacher. She stopped, partway up, to show me the part of the route that gave it its name. "These are the toe jams," she yelled. "Jam your toes under here!"

"Got it!" I yelled back, feeding out rope from the ground.

She stopped again to tell me that when I pulled out a piece of gear she called "the yellow Alien," I should "think like Tetris," since she had "Tetris'ed it in from the right."

"Okay!" I yelled, hoping that would all make sense when I got there.

Eventually, she went around a turn, or over a lump, and I couldn't see her anymore, and when I looked up, the sun was in my eyes anyway. I could still feel her, though, through the rope. I could tell when she was climbing, and what she was doing, by its movements.

Sometimes, she pulled on it, as she moved, and I helped it along, feeding it out, each long pull a dash of Morse code. But then, when she was still, I noticed quicker, smaller motions coming through, like the dots in the code. We were far away, but also connected. Bound, in fact.

I definitely heard Kye yelling, "Emily! On belay!" and by then, the rope was so tight that it was lifting me off the ground. Whatever "the girlfriend belay" was, the guide belay was even better. As I climbed, I took out the pieces of gear she'd put in and clipped them to my own harness. Up at the top, Kye seemed pleased with both of us when I showed her I had all of it, now clipped to my own harness.

"Great job," she said. "Let's rap down and find Reid. I told him to meet me in the campsite next to where we'll rap."

There are two ways to get down from a mountain or a big rock one has climbed. One way is to walk off a less-vertical part of the mountain. The other way is to "rappel" or "rap" (or, for the Brits, the adorable "abseil"), which means using a device that alternately slides and grips on the rope to travel down the vertical face you have just climbed to the ground.

Kye set up the rappel with a practiced and professional speed I never achieved as an amateur. She was gone in a flash, yelling, "I'll fireman ya!" as she went over the lip. That meant she would hold both ends of the rope from the ground, as I rappelled, to help make sure that they didn't become uneven, which could lead to one end of the rope flying through my belay device and then all the way up through the anchor, until the rope slithered through, and dropped me to the ground. That probably wouldn't happen, but it could happen, and this would make me extra safe. These people were always making me extra safe in dangerous situations, which was the opposite of how unsafe I felt in situations that were supposed to be safe, like relationships, or families.

We lowered down from the sunny top of the climb, all the way down into a cool cave below. As I disengaged myself from the rope, Kye was already pulling on it. It was squiggling, like a snake, moving with faint hissing noises toward a pile she was expertly, speedily creating, some distance away at the feet of yet another rangy and unshaven male.

"Sorry about the rush," she said. "Reid saw another party on their way in, so we need to get on it first so they bail."

She grabbed the gear off my harness that I had removed from Toe Jam and clipped it to her own. When I was free of the rope and the gear, I realized I had to pee. When I came back, Kye was about twenty feet off the ground, and she was yelling. "Watch me here, Reid!"

She was in what looked to be a miserable and desperate position. Both of her hands and one of her heels were all hanging on the same lip of rock, part of a flake that stood out from the wall and therefore had an edge. It was kind of like she was hanging from an open window, from the bottom of the frame, by two hands and one foot, and was next going to hurl herself in, like a cat burglar. She kept turning her head from one side, where the rope was attached to the rock, toward a place up above and to the left, where there was a vertical crack, and back again. She wasn't simply trying to wriggle up on top of the little edge she was gripping with her two hands and one heel. Instead, she seemed to be trying to fling herself far up and to the left.

"Watch me here, Reid!" Kye yelled again.

"Gotcha!" he yelled back cheerfully.

And then she yelled, just as loud as I had, for the past several days, as I was trying to *make it stay,* and tried to fly.

But she fell. Her body described a perfect semicircle as the rope caught her and she came to rest. There were squeaky metal noises, like a swing set on a windy day. Reid was dangling in the air a few feet off the ground, holding the brake end of the rope tight to his thigh. The force of her falling body had yanked him up.

Reid wiggled his eyebrows. "That's why she didn't want you to catch her," he said. "She'd have pulled you even farther off the ground. You're about the same size, but there's more force when she's falling."

"Force equals mass *times* acceleration," I said, quoting from physics class.

"Right," said Reid. "Exactly."

She'd fallen, but with the piece of gear she'd placed in the rock (and the belayer who'd held the rope), she'd caught herself. Watching her fall—hearing her grunt with effort, shriek with velocity, and then curse in frustration, reminded me of the tennis players I grew up watching on the fuzzy screen of my grandparents' television. It was always on, all summer, first during Wimbledon in July and then for the US Open on Labor Day weekend. Some of my earliest memories are the alternating sounds of their groundstrokes and screams, the grunting and groaning that gave way, after sweat-soaked hours, to dazed silence as the winner fell to the ground or collapsed in a heap, often crying, when the battle was won. I was fascinated by the monument of their effort, the way they bent their bodies and minds to their own dogged will.

"There goes my onsight," said Kye, from above.

"Lower me!" she shouted, and Reid lowered himself back to the ground first, then her.

From the ground, Kye squinted up at the place she'd fallen from. "I think I can get the yellow Alien in the crack," she said, "higher up, and then that fall will be more protected."

She went over to her backpack and took out a cigarette. "I should probably have water," she said, smoking.

"Want a bar?" asked Reid.

"Later," she said, handing me her half-smoked cigarette, still lit.

She marched back to the base of the climb and started up again. This time, when she got to the concave edge of the window-frame part, she hung there even longer, reaching over to the crack and managing to put the yellow Alien I'd removed from Toe Jam into it. She stopped, spread-eagled, and said, "Now, Emily, if I fall next time, I'll fall to this one, instead of that one, see?"

I didn't have to imagine it.

"Watch me here, Reid!" she yelled again, and flung herself up the wall. She fell again, this time more straight down.

"Bomber," she muttered, eye level with the yellow Alien.

"Bomber," affirmed Reid, lowering himself back down to the ground.

Then she did it again. And again. And again. And again. She hurled herself at the wall, threw herself up, and tried to grab on to something, I couldn't really see or tell what. Each time she fell, the system made the same swing set creaking noises, but she started yelling louder, not just tennis-player sounds but "Fuuuuuuuuuuck!"

"Yeah, Kye," said Reid, softly, each time.

I was transfixed. Was she going to make it? Was she going to do it? Could she? Would she?

"I'm sorry, Emily," she said, shaking her head, hanging on the rope above, looking dejected. "I wanted to put this up for you so you could practice, but I don't know if it's gonna go today."

"It's okay!" I said. "This is fun! I'm learning a lot just watching!"

"One more," said Kye.

"Yeah, Kye," said Reid.

"Yeah, Kye," I repeated.

She wormed her way along the window-frame-shaped part, wriggling her hands and then her heel.

"Nice, Kye," said Reid.

"Nice, Kye," I repeated.

She got into flinging position and looked up at whatever it was she was flinging herself toward.

"C'mon, Kye," said Reid.

"C'mon, Kye," I repeated.

Her eyes got wide, then narrowed. Her whole body tensed, and then she flung herself, again.

But there were no swing set creaking noises. She stuck it. Reid stayed on the ground. She was up there, yelling "slaaaaaaack" as she marched over a bump and out of sight.

"It's five-seven hands to glory!" she shouted gleefully from somewhere up above.

"Told ya," said Reid. "*Nice*, Kye."

"Do you want to climb this, Emily? Should I build a toprope anchor?"

I wasn't sure I did. It looked ungodly. I had smoked the rest of Kye's cigarette and was dizzy. But I understood that she had done this, in some way, for me. So I could practice. So I could learn. So I could try. So I could fail, and flail, and fall, and not die.

"Sure!" I said, gamely. "I'd love to!"

Kye came down and released Reid from the belay. We all smoked a bowl, and then Kye and I shared another cigarette while Reid had a bar, and then Kye proceeded to belay me while I took toprope whippers on the crux of my first 5.10c, talking me through it in a way that was almost hypnotic.

"*Good*, Emily, *good*, that's right, keep going. Nice heel hook, nice high foot. Keep going, keep traversing, left, *left*, now reach up, and try to get that jam, no, don't clean that Alien, just unclip it, nope, don't pull on the Alien, don't pull on the gear, you're not French-freeing, good Emily, *good*, yeah, GET IT!"

I flung myself and flung myself, but I never grabbed what she had reached. I never made it past the crux, but I didn't stop trying until she lowered me down. That was the day I learned that I could be the weaker one—even the weakest one—and the pack would take me in, and keep me safe, while I tried—and even failed—but didn't die.

6

Valley

GLENN HANDED ME A FRAGRANT PINT JAR. "For your trip," he winked.

"Good place to cut your teeth," he added.

Then he gave me a hug, got in his truck, and drove off.

I stood there, in the parking lot, outside the Yosemite Lodge, clutching a pint jar full of weed and a brand-new park map, all alone in Yosemite Valley.

I'd been ditched in the Ditch.

"COME TO THE VALLEY!" Glenn had messaged, several weeks prior.

If I ditched my last day of school-year tutoring work, we could overlap in Yosemite for one single day.

It had been a little more than a year since I'd first met Glenn in Joshua Tree. Since my more recent, second trip there, I'd been spending even more of my evenings in the local bouldering gym—or smoking and talking shit on the ripped-out car-seat couches behind it, or reading old climbing magazines in the gym sauna until the glue melted and the pages fell out. I had my own harness, shoes, belay/rappel device, and chalk bag. As with any activity for which there existed helmets, my parents insisted I get one.

Driving to tutor some San Francisco rich kid the day before my departure to Yosemite, I improbably saw Tori Lutz's muscled, bespectacled figure traversing SubyRuby's windshield. I had met her only once before, on a weekend visit to Glenn's then-illegal off-grid organic Mendocino County cash crop farm. Before legalization, he employed climbers looking to fund their expeditions by seasonally working ten- or twelve-hour days in a quasi-communist, somewhat elevated sweatshop environment, preparing the cash crop for sale.

Tori was a Rock Monkey—the Stonemasters' sequel lineage—as well as an internationally known skydiving and wingsuit-flying badass, though at the time, this context was lost on me. All I knew was that, when she'd offered me a sip from her yerba maté gourd on the cash crop farm, she'd said "Don't move the straw" in a way that inspired the same mix of fear and awe I now felt about the Valley itself.

I shouted her name and pulled over. "I'm going to the Valley!" I announced. "Tomorrow!"

"Then you better get your scene dialed," said Tori, leaning, unsurprised, into SubyRuby's passenger-side window. *Get scene dialed*, I noted, nodding, as Tori elaborated:

"When you go around in the morning looking for partners, have your stuff all packed. Don't walk around in flip-flops—go around in your approach shoes, so if you find someone who wants to climb, you'll be ready. If you can't get a site in Camp 4 and need to sleep in boulders, keep your climbing gear in one backpack and your bivy gear in a different one. Make the bivy backpack small, and don't put the sleeping pad on the outside where the tools can see it. Find a bivy spot before it gets dark, and don't use your headlamp there. Whatever you do, *don't smoke weed in Camp 4*. I hear the conditions are good. Have fun!"

From Glenn, I had gleaned that some climbers referred to everywhere they slept, even someone's guest bedroom, as a "bivy," short for "bivouac," which means a "temporary camp" for "soldiers or mountaineers." In Joshua Tree, the climbers in the Hidden Valley Campground referred to the National Park Service law enforcement rangers exclusively as "tools." This could also be a verb, as in "getting tooled," which could mean anything from getting dinged for "forgetting" to pay your campsite fee to being written a ticket for a hefty fine to being tased or even chased into the river to your own death by drowning, if you saw fit to BASE jump off El Cap, which was illegal.

The Joshua Tree tools were comparatively benign, and easier to evade than the ones in Yosemite, who sounded like the SEAL Team Six of tools. In Joshua Tree, it was at least legal to sleep in your own car, in your own campsite, and the tools were mainly concerned with making sure there weren't more than the allotted two cars in each site. But the Yosemite tools sounded legendary in the extremity of their federally funded efforts to prevent illicit smoking or sleeping. So far, I had heard more about them than the climbing routes.

Tori's advice would enable me to camp, illegally, beyond the boundaries of Camp 4, beyond the sign I'd seen with James that other summer, the one that read NO CAMPING BEYOND THIS POINT. Tori was essentially explaining to me how to dirtbag, also both a noun and a verb. A dirtbag dirtbagged by avoiding paying for things at all costs, like camping, so that that the dirtbag could spend more time dirtbagging— climbing and living as freely as possible, in all senses of the word. Dirtbags, as I'd already learned, were called dirtbags because they slept in the dirt. Sleeping in the dirt was usually free, especially if you slept on dirt you weren't, technically, supposed to sleep on.

I liked how, in her instructions, Tori said "conditions" instead of "weather." It made it all sound more official, like a mission.

Thus blessed, I drove east. But when I arrived in Yosemite, Glenn announced that his girlfriend had a splinter, the wound was now infected, and they would have to leave a day early to go see a doctor.

Instead of going climbing, Glenn took me to the Yosemite Lodge, bought me a burger and a beer, opened up the park map I'd received at the entrance station, and marked it with an X.

Park & sleep, he wrote.

"Employee parking," he said. "Don't sleep in your car anywhere else. They check. They use heat-sensing technology."

He drew a circle around another place, which he labeled, *LeConte Memorial*.

"This is a library," he said. "You might like it if you're a writer."

"You may be able to get a spot in Camp 4," he added, "but you know, you can't smoke weed there."

Glenn and his girlfriend showed me a bivy near their bivy. The next morning at dawn, he stood over me with a fresh cup of coffee and a burning roach. Over breakfast in the lodge, he told me about a guy who'd lived for years, in a cave, on pilfered ketchup, mustard, and mayonnaise packets, then pointed out all the food the tourists left behind on their cafeteria trays.

"You can eat that," he said.

"So, am I gonna climb with strangers?" I asked.

"Randos," he corrected.

"But how do I know if they're . . . okay?"

"Suss 'em out," he shrugged. Then, jabbing a finger, he said, "Don't climb with a guy named Spewer."

Some years later, I would find out *why* not, but for now, I filed the information away. *Get my scene dialed*, I thought. *Don't climb with a guy named Spewer. Don't smoke weed in Camp 4.*

Then Glenn gave me the pint jar and the hug, and left.

STANDING IN THE PARKING LOT, wrapping the map around the jar to obscure its contents, I began to fret. Where would I park? Where would I sleep? Where would I *park & sleep*?

I looked at the map, saw that I was near Camp 4. Might as well try for a real campsite. I drove SubyRuby to the Camp 4 parking lot. It was just as I remembered it, from when James had brought me here, shaded by tall pines and carpeted with their needles. There were picnic tables and bear-proof boxes for food and metal fire rings and one small bathroom for everyone to share, all neatly arranged—and heavily policed—in one of the most famously beautiful places in the world.

At the kiosk, the person in the little booth told me there was exactly one spot left in the whole campground, at the very edge, right by the parking lot. I pitched my tent, hung the tag from my rearview, stashed the pint jar in a bear box with my food, and looked around at the remaining randos, who appeared to be ripped, punk Neanderthals. I strode purposefully to the library Glenn had circled on my park map, where I spent the afternoon, cowering.

In the round, stone building, I curled up in a window seat with a book about tall tales and legends in Yosemite history. I read about how, around the turn of the last century, a newlywed couple had left on their honeymoon to go boating down the Merced, the river that ran through Yosemite Valley, but they disappeared, and their boat was found empty. The man's body was later recovered with a blunt trauma to the head, while the wife was never heard from again. Years later, at a campfire, an old woman revealed herself to be the erstwhile bride. Her husband had turned abusive, she said, so she killed him, hiked out, and started a new life.

I slammed the book shut and left the library. If a woman had survived *that*, I reasoned, then surely I could brave the randos.

I walked the length of Camp 4 to the slacklines at the rear. I stood up unsteadily, holding a tree, took a few steps, and hopped off. There were two other people there, a tall, blond-haired guy and a short, dark-haired one.

"Hey," I said. "Either of you guys named Spewer?"

I ASKED EVERYONE IN CAMP 4 if they were named Spewer. No one was, but a polite, twentysomething fellow with a British accent was named Ian. He had just arrived and wasn't busy the next day. He mostly climbed ice, he said, because his mother was from Norway, where, in fact, he himself was a member of the Norwegian ice-rescue team.

I hadn't known that ice was something one could climb, much less be rescued from, but these sounded like good credentials, in addition to not being named Spewer. Hopefully, that was what Glenn had meant by "Suss 'em out."

That night, by headlamp, using a bear box as a table, Ian and I consulted a guidebook and chose a five-star route called Munginella that we could walk to from the campground.

"It's 5.6," shrugged Ian. "Should be all right."

We hatched a plan to climb the route in the afternoon, after the overly keen morning crowds dispersed. At exactly high noon the next day, he appeared at my bear box, wearing an orange helmet and carrying a green rope.

We walked on a touristed path through some trees and past the base of the ginormous waterfall that the tourists were all dutifully photographing, then up a faint trail through some more trees to the base of a big stone wall, where we tied ourselves to opposite ends of Ian's green rope. I put Ian on belay and he cast off on lead.

I was once again tied, with a rope, to a near stranger, holding their life in my hands, hoping they didn't accidentally get me killed. But this had happened several times before already and was beginning to feel less like being bound and more like a bond.

I fed out the slack in the rope that let Ian continue upward unencumbered, and looked around at the living Yosemite Valley postcard come alive, a landscape in which I was now a tiny and animated figure.

It really *was* a ditch. A ditch full of giant granite rocks, which anyone who could climb at all could climb, and people who *really* liked walking uphill could hike up, on the backside.

Ian stopped at a tree and tied the rope around it. He pulled up all the remaining rope on the ground until it went tight on my own harness, and when he yelled down, "On belay!," I started up.

The climb was as easy as the views were spectacular. As soon as I was above the trees, I could see farther into the Valley's heights and depths. The landscape's major features seemed to change position as you moved around, forming tricksterish vistas in which I could never quite orient myself.

While actually climbing, I felt zero fear, only a disbelieving delight. I could smell the rock, and myself, both clean and summery.

I was so much less afraid of everything up here. I wasn't afraid of anything up here.

After my week in Joshua Tree with Alden and Noel and Kye and Reid, I moved upward with greater ease. If you did this right, it was easier—and far more fun—than walking uphill. I'd never liked hiking. Trudge, trudge, trudge. Schlep, schlep, schlep. You had to keep going, while thinking of something other than the trudging and the schlepping, and every step was the same. But with climbing, instead of taking steps, you made moves, and each move was different. And you *had* to think, but not about anything else—about this and only this. That was the best part—using your brain, but also *not* really thinking at all. Thinking with your body *and* your mind, about only one thing, in a state of effortless focus and total flow.

After another rope length, I arrived at another, higher tree where Ian sat, barefoot, on top of the rock next to a pile of rope.

"Well done, Emily," he nodded.

"Thanks, Ian," I said, sitting down next to him and the tree and the pile of rope. "You, too."

From the top of the route, we could see the Valley's massive rock walls sloping down to its floor, while Half Dome loomed ogrishly above. The Valley was densely forested in ponderosa pines, themselves sometimes over a hundred feet tall, though from the top of the rock, the trees looked like miniatures in a model-train tableau. It had been a wet winter, the last one before California's unprecedented drought, and the grass in the Meadow was green in what was still, in early June, Sierra springtime. Trees that would later be consumed by beetles and fungus were still green and alive, but the giant rocks dwarfed them, even as they climbed some of the slopes in patches I soon realized were steep, deep gullies—ditches within the Ditch. The rocks themselves were mostly bare, glimmering silver-white in sun, or shadowed almost black in shade. They were bare of trees because they were vertical, or nearly so. And I had climbed straight up one of these walls, high enough that the tall trees were tiny. I felt primal and alive, at peace and unstoppable.

I want this, I thought, with my body, feeling whatever it was already draining away. It was the kind of desire I had only ever felt for another person. Now I felt it for a feeling.

"Yosemite," Fred had said, in Joshua Tree. "You can have an adventure there."

JAMES HAD TOLD ME. Glenn had told me. Tori Lutz had told me.

But in my joy, and in my freedom, I forgot.

I smoked weed in Camp 4.

They came from everywhere and nowhere, all at once, stepping out of the darkness into the light of our fire. Their clear leader had the most recent buzz cut and the greatest number of deadly weapons in little black pouches Velcro-ed onto his tactical belt.

"Hey, guys," was his opener.

He paused as his cronies circled our site, looming above us sitting, unarmed, on tree stumps, rocks, and camping chairs. A Camp 4 campsite held eight people and got split between as many as four parties, all sharing one bear box, one picnic table, and one fire ring. I was sharing my campsite with three Brazilians and a family of four Danes, three of whom were asleep. Now we were joined by at least a half-dozen tools, all armed to the teeth like any red-blooded American out hunting for terrorists and illegals and joy and life to annihilate.

The alpha tool went over to one of the Brazilians and kicked over his beer, then picked up the empty.

"What's this?" he asked, squinting at the can as if it were evidence. "Drinking some Budweiser? Drinking some *American* beer?"

"How about some weed?" the tool said suddenly. "You guys smoking some weed?"

Neither I nor the three Brazilians nor the Danish dad said anything.

"We saw you," said the tool. "We *know* you were smoking weed."

"It was a cigarette," said Rafa, holding up his tobacco pouch.

"We *saw* you," the tool repeated triumphantly. "We saw *her*"—he pointed to me—"take out the *weed* and give it to *you*"—he pointed at Rafa—"and then we saw *you*"—Rafa again—"mix the weed *with* the tobacco and roll it up before you *all* smoked it."

I hadn't entirely believed James when he'd said that federal law enforcement agents were using military-grade night-vision goggles for campground doobie surveillance. Because of this, I hadn't truly understood the gravity of the threat until it stepped out of the shadows and into my campsite. These were militarized federal agents with the same guns and goggles our blessed Special Forces used to maim and murder. They had been watching, from the bushes, *waiting* for me to do what I'd done—which was to give Rafa some weed to roll us a spliff to share by the fire over beers after a day of climbing.

I had always suspected I was naturally lawless, but once I stood on top of the rock and saw the tiny trees, I knew. Now that I had seen the majestic Valley from on high, I didn't think there was any authority in the world that still applied to me. By the time I came down to the campground and the bear box where I'd stashed the pint jar from Glenn, given Ian a warm beer for his trouble, and devoured most of a bag of chips, I'd fully released myself from even the idea of anything as binding as law or society. I had tasted the freedom of the vertical through the defiance of gravity, which was no man's law, but nature's alone. Yes, we were all going to die. But so what? We were living now.

Nothing went better with these mountain-sized sentiments than a spliff. I had charged into the campsite at sunset, gear clanking, thrilled by our successful ascent. The Brazilians were already drinking beers, and Rafa was rolling a cigarette. I offered to trade him some weed for some tobacco, and he suggested that we instead create, and together smoke, a shared spliff—the very one the tools had watched us roll through their night-vision goggles and chosen to interrupt while heavily armed with deadly weapons provided to them via the expenditure of our tax dollars, while children went hungry and human beings slept in their own filth on the street.

As night fell, the spliff was constructed, then passed around the campfire. The tools let us smoke most of it before they barged into our campsite and kicked over the Brazilian's Budweiser. Or maybe there was an arcane federal law that the spliff had to go around the campfire a certain number of times to prove it was a spliff, and then and only then could you mount an armed invasion of the campsite to seize the evident weapon of smokable destruction.

"Empty your pockets," said the tool. "Give us the weed."

"And what if I do not consent to be searched?" I asked experimentally.

"Then we can take you in right now," the tool said smoothly.

He was speaking of the federal courthouse not far down the road, complete with its own in-park jail cell. I'd heard tell of it from the seasoned climbers employed at Glenn's off-the-grid organic cash crop farm, and behind the bouldering gym on the car-seat couches. The climber slang for the place the tools took you if they caught you smoking weed in Camp 4 was the "John Muir Hotel." I couldn't go to the John Muir Hotel after my very first climb in Yosemite Valley.

I cursed myself for my rookie mistake. I knew better—or should have known. I had been told, but I hadn't listened.

So I reached into the pocket of my Patagonia R3 fleece hoody, purchased at steep discount from an outlet store in Utah after a multi-day whitewater-river trip, and handed over the mint tin containing my stash, lighter, and rolling papers to the tool.

"Now," he said, "I will need to get your name."

And that was when I made my second mistake.

"My name," I told the tool, "is Meg Pfefferson."

I don't know what I was thinking, except that they had no power over me, or if they thought they did, then they were wrong, or if they really did, then they shouldn't.

I had climbed a giant vertical rock wall. I could have fallen off and died, but I didn't. Their law was a joke and a lie.

Stealing other people's weed was the least of what these strapped-up tools did with the power vested in them by their many deadly weapons. Even then, in 2012, before Ferguson and George Floyd, I knew about the police's predilections. I'd grown up watching crewcut cops from the white-flight suburbs terrorizing Black boys my own age on the streets of our own city, in broad daylight. The NYPD did not hide in the bushes, nor wear night-vision goggles, and that made me loathe these federal forest tools even more.

"The person," Fred had said, "who fails the test to become a regular cop, and *then* fails the test to become a *mall* cop—*that's* who becomes a tool in Yosemite."

I'd always loathed the tools, but I no longer feared them.

The alias didn't go over particularly well, but somehow, I managed to talk my way out of a several-hundred-dollar ticket by doing a combination of improvisational theater and amateur jurisprudence. (My dad always said, wistfully, that I would probably breeze right through law school.) I did, at one point, place my hand gently on the alpha tool's forearm. I did apologize profusely for the inconvenience, tacking tactfully to the crowd-pleasing observation that of *course* these fellows were *just doing their jobs.*

In short, I white-womaned my way out of it, like I was unlocking a particularly technical boulder problem at the gym, with special magic chalk made of my own white privilege.

At the end, the beta male tool turned to me and said, "You seem like a nice lady. You should try harder not to get yourself arrested."

The tools melted off into the night, to go steal someone else's weed, or smoke ours. I went to the bear box, to grab another nug from my plentiful stash, for a new spliff I would be sure to smoke well hidden in the boulders. And smoking it, all alone on a rock in the dark, staring up at the stars and the summits between me and them, one of which I had stood upon, on this very day, I realized that there were four things I now knew about the Valley:

1. Get your scene dialed.
2. Suss out the randos.
3. Don't climb with a guy named Spewer.
4. *Don't smoke weed in Camp 4.*

AFTER THAT, Valley life picked up speed. If you weren't afraid to talk to the randos, it was pretty easy to suss them out and make sure they weren't named Spewer. With ten males to every female, it wasn't hard to find someone with a rack and a rope but no partner for the day.

Within a week, I had climbed with Scott, a bespectacled, self-assured

VALLEY

young fellow Easterner whose dad had dropped him off at the start of the Appalachian Trail during a turbulent period in his quite recent high school years with a handwritten list telling him where to pick up the resupply boxes. We sent (climbed without falling) the Nutcracker (5.8), with Scott ropegunning (leading every pitch, or rope length), and me "tronsighting," meaning "onsighting"—climbing on my first try, without falling, but on toprope, which meant it didn't really count, hence the term "tronsight" rather than "onsight." I climbed with lanky British big-wallers Harold and Will, who begrudgingly took me over to hard cragging areas in the afternoons, after they had completed their list of Things to Do to Get Ready to Climb El Cap, and gave reserved British encouragement while I struggled up the first pitch of Outer Limits, 5.10c, and then, another afternoon, Lunatic Fringe, also 5.10c. I climbed with Calvin Wade Thompson, a heavily tattooed, painfully sensitive, active-duty US Marine marksmanship instructor with a raspy Southern drawl, who was on some kind of extended leave that enabled him to finally smoke weed, which he said greatly reduced the many symptoms of his complex trauma from two tours of duty in service to our supposed freedom, one in Afghanistan, and another in Iraq.

One afternoon, in the campground, the three Brits decided it was time to teach me to lead climb. Lead climbing was what I had seen Kye doing in Joshua Tree, what Ian and the rest of my new buddies had been doing this whole time in Yosemite.

We went over to the Swan Slabs, where paid guides took their paying customers on routes just right to learn on. The rock slabs there were low-angle, meaning not fully vertical, and they had good cracks and easy features (things that stuck out that you could hold onto), making them ideal for teaching new techniques.

Ian took the initiative. Harold and Will dragged over camping chairs and cracked beers while Ian walked up the back of the rock and hung a toprope for himself from a tree. Then he instructed Will to lead-belay me on a different rope while he hung next to me, on his own rope, hands-free, and I tried to do the new and scary thing, all by myself, but supervised.

What made climbing on lead different and new and scary and real was that I wasn't already technically hanging from the rope before I even left the ground, the way I would have been on a toprope, and in fact had been all this time. A toprope was attached to the top of the rock before you started climbing it, and it sometimes almost tugged you off the ground. On a toprope, if you got tired or scared, you could just let go and hang there.

There was nothing to be afraid of—ever—on a toprope. Toproping, according to serious climbers, wasn't even *real climbing*. On a toprope, you could never really fall, only hang. It was the risk of falling—really falling—that made it all real, and taking that risk was the only way to truly be brave.

Now, I could begin to fall for real. But first, I had to hang the rope.

For the first time, I tied into the end of the rope that would go up the rock first, often called, ominously, "the sharp end." Higher up, I would keep myself from "decking" (falling all the way to the ground), by sticking the same brightly-colored metal pieces of gear I'd seen Kye using in Joshua Tree into cracks in the rock, but until I climbed high enough to place one, I would actually be free soloing. That was how lead climbing started—free soloing up just a little bit, maybe ten or fifteen feet, until you could place your first piece. Then climbing without falling while making sure you placed the gear correctly that would catch you if you did.

A new thing to do right, every time, under pressure. Not just the pressure of possible failure. The pressure of possible death—or just maiming.

I suddenly realized that I wasn't wearing my helmet, but Will said, "Well, you'd rather be dead than paralyzed, wouldn't you, Emily?"

"*Course you would,*" he answered for me, in his Queen's English.

Ian was dangling on his toprope about fifteen feet above me. "Climb on up to me, Emily," he said, patting the rock like it was an empty seat on the bus, "and place your first piece of gear here."

Americans would spot you at the base, standing like a basketball player in a defensive crouch, ready to catch you if you fell before you could stitch the rope to the rock. But the Brits did not.

"Go on, Emily," Will nodded Britishly.

My heart was pounding. They were all watching, plus a few other ripped, punk Neanderthals who had wandered by and stopped for the sports action.

"When you get up to where I am," said Ian, "there's a perfect spot for a number one. That's the red one."

"I know," I said.

Harold's and Will's well-used gear dangled from my harness. Not too much of it, because Ian had sussed out what he'd thought I would need, so for my first time on lead, I wouldn't have too much weight pulling me back down.

Before I even left the ground, I understood, bodily, why climbing on lead was called climbing on "the sharp end" of the rope. It was because the risk of falling, and therefore the fear of it, was so much sharper on "the sharp end." As I felt the fear first tickle, then poke, then stab me in the belly, the words "the sharp end" reverberated in my mind, reminding me of the way the talking heads on television had used the words "the tip of the spear" to describe the first invasion in my generation's war. I wondered whether Wade—as Calvin Wade Thompson had instructed us to call him—had been part of "the tip of the spear" when he was in the war. I wondered if being in a war was even scarier than this was.

Wade was here, too, now. Everyone had beers. I wanted one, but I had to earn it. I looked at Wade, the only fellow American in the peanut gallery.

"You got this, darlin'," he drawled, toasting cheerfully.

Look sharp, I thought, brushing off the soles of my shoes.

There were so many *boys* watching, and I hadn't even done anything yet. I could feel their kind and curious attention. I wanted to impress them, and also not die or get paralyzed.

"How about a little encouragement?" I joked, so the Brits did an impression of American climbers, shouting "Yeah, dude!" and "Yeah, bro!" and "Come on, man!" with fake American accents and enthusiasm.

I threw a grin over my shoulder at all of them at once.

"Here goes!" I said gamely, and put my foot into the crack, with no rope above.

I needn't have worried. The crack was so secure that I didn't really need a rope at all. I had heard various posturing twentysomethings scoff at topropes. The climbing writer John Long had famously said that toproping was "great practice for climbing." James had said that lead climbing was better than toproping, because there was "no rope in your face," so it was "just you and the rock," and free soloing was even better, because there was no rope at all. But it was really true. For lack of a better simile, it was like having sex without a condom for the first time, and realizing that there was indeed a difference between human skin and powdered latex. It was as if some kind of barrier had just been peeled off of all of it, and it was more bare, more raw, more free, more dangerous.

Back in New York, Leila was eight months pregnant. We were both thirty-two years old.

I wouldn't be doing this, I thought to myself, *if* I *had a kid*. But I didn't.

Don't think about that, said a voice from within. *Don't think about that right now.* I realized, when I stopped thinking about it, that I thought about it a lot.

I climbed up to just below Ian. His flip-flopped foot was dangling above my head.

"Just a little higher," said Ian. "And you can put the red number one right here."

But I didn't want to go any higher. "I think I'll just put the green 0.75 right *here*," I said, slotting it into place. I had discovered, climbing with Ian, that he was solid but bossy, and we were prone to epic political arguments if the conversation veered away from rock and ice. I think he might have been a banker.

Ian sighed. "If you place a piece down there, I'll have to lower myself down to check it for you."

"Yes, please do," I said to Ian, realizing that my hands were shaking as I clipped the rope to the green cam.

Stop, I told my hands, now stuck in the crack, holding me, hovering, onto the wall. I let out a long exhale and willed myself still. Surprisingly, it worked.

Ian was using a device that enabled him to shimmy up and down on his own toprope. He lowered down to me and yanked on my green 0.75 cam, hard.

"Yeah, well done," he said.

Then he belayed himself another fifteen feet up.

I don't think any of the Brits reminded me to breathe. No one was rolling a doob, since we were in Camp 4, right by the road. We weren't, technically, in California, even—we were on federal national park tool-patrolled land on the other side of some weird mini-Midwest in the middle of California full of giant windowless megachurches with names like The Father's House. *Why not just give up on the idea of God as big-box retail and turn the place into a proper BDSM dungeon?* I wondered, looking for the next place to tether myself and longing for the boredom of a long, seated drive through a region where the white people seemed like they could easily be incited, by the right far-right radio broadcast, to commit genocide with yard tools. *Don't think about that.*

I stopped again under Ian's dangling foot. "I think I like to place my pieces just a little closer," I said.

"It's supposed to be every *ten* feet," said Wade, in agreement. "Body lengths."

"That uses too much gear!" exclaimed Ian. "You'll have to climb everything with a double rack! That's not good style! That's not alpine style!"

"It is her first lead, though," said Wade.

"Fair point," said Ian, lowering himself down again to check my next gear placement.

"It *would* be perfect," he concluded, "if it were a little bit higher up, but it is good."

This process repeated itself until I had climbed on lead and placed approved gear up to the height of my old apartment building in Brooklyn. It was decided that since it was dark, I should learn to build the anchor that went at the top of the rock another time, so I lowered off my last piece of gear after Ian checked it, and we pulled the rope, and Ian "cleaned" (removed) the gear I had put in on his way down, and the lesson was over.

I felt kind of proud that I was learning from the British guys. Californians were very tough and unafraid of death, but they still had American feelings. I'd always wanted to see what it felt like to have a truly stiff upper lip. Learning to climb from British hardmen seemed like as good a way as any to become so stoic that my emotions could never endanger me again.

HAROLD AND WILL HAD picked out that weekend to climb El Cap, but there was weather in the forecast, and clearly visible on the horizon, so they bailed.

"Shall we go to a rodeo?" asked Will, as we sat around the campground. Will had gone on the internet intermittently available in a certain spot by the lodge and found out about a rodeo on the other side of the park, up and over the Sierras on the eastside, near the border with Nevada.

"A rodeo!" said Harold, in a slightly different accent, because he was from a different part of England. "Emily, have you ever been to a rodeo?"

"Not too many rodeos on Long Island," I said. "Lacrosse is really big, though. There're hot springs on the eastside, too," I added. "We could go there, and camp, before the rodeo."

We quickly packed for a rodeo road trip in what seemed to me to be record time. Harold and Will were traveling in an ancient, tiny purple car Harold had bought while ice-climbing in Canada, which he insisted was his true passion. Harold's car was missing both its fourth gear and entire back seat, so we took SubyRuby instead. Scott couldn't come, but Ian, Wade, Harold, Will, and I filled SubyRuby's five seats.

"Do you think we'll see any guns, Emily?" Will asked as we drove out of the Valley.

"Yeah, are we going to see any guns?" added Harold, before I could answer. In his Northern accent, it sounded more like a cross between "gowns" and "goons."

"I don't know, guys," I said. "Maybe at the rodeo. That'll be your best bet."

"Do *you* have a gun, Emily?" asked Harold.

"Yeah, sure," I said. "I got one for my bat mitzvah."

"Really?" exclaimed Will. "For your bat mitzvah!"

"No, not really!" I laughed. "Though maybe that happens in, like, Texas or something. And besides, I never had a bat mitzvah."

"Why not?" asked Will.

"Because my family hates God and thinks all religion is total bull-shit," I replied.

"My family's actually quite religious!" said Will.

"Oh, sorry," I said.

"You're all right," Will said cheerfully. "Takes all kinds, innit?"

I HAD NEVER BEEN to the Green Church Hot Springs before, but I had a hot springs guidebook. I had noticed that true dirtbags never bought guidebooks, only took pictures of them with their phones, often surrep-titiously, in bookstores, like spies.

We arrived after dark and spread out our sleeping pads in the sage, then stripped naked and got into the hot tub with cold beers. Harold, Will, and I outlasted the others, until it was just us—and Flying Frank.

Flying Frank talked a lot, but Harold and Will were enthralled by his sheer American reality. A middle-aged-to-older fellow, he had a twang I couldn't place, beyond the sense that it might portend "These Colors Don't Run" T-shirt ownership.

Flying Frank flew planes. Flying Frank had yarns. Flying Frank was pretty lit. Flying Frank was not naked, but tubbing in his tighty-whiteys. Suddenly, Flying Frank moved toward me.

"Now, Emily," he said, "I won't come any closer because you have these two protectors. But if you didn't—"

Harold and Will closed ranks around me like naked male elevator doors.

"I'll just leave my card right here," said Flying Frank, exiting the tub, now that he had made a credible, if hypothetical, threat of sexual assault. After he toddled off toward his RV in his transparent tighty-whiteys, I picked up the card and checked it with my headlamp. It really did say "Flying Frank."

"Wow," said Will, beginning to roll a spliff on the edge of the tub now that we were alone. "I wonder who we'll meet at the rodeo!"

I WAS JUST STIRRING IN THE SAGE the next morning when I heard Wade's voice saying, "Get in the vehicle."

"Give me your keys," he said to me. "Get in the vehicle."

"Get in the vehicle," he said to Harold and Will and Ian, who were muttering, "Oh my God!" as they hurried from the hot tub.

"Get in the vehicle," Wade commanded, again, as I tried to deflate my Therm-a-Rest from inside my sleeping bag. He took it from beneath me and shoved it into SubyRuby's back hatch. Once we were all in the vehicle and Harold and Will stopped saying, "Oh my God," I found out what happened.

Everyone else had risen with the sun and gone for an early-morning soak. Harold and Will and Ian and Wade had found themselves all in the tub with our old friend Flying Frank, who was now toting a breakfast beer.

Flying Frank said he wanted to show them all something. He climbed out of the tub and, beer in hand and naked this time, walked the short distance to his RV, from which he soon reemerged with a firearm.

I don't know if he was waving the gun or brandishing the gun or just holding the gun, because I was still sleeping in the sage, but Flying Frank definitely *had* a gun. And he was doing something with the gun that led Calvin Wade Thompson, United States Marine, to feel that it and he should be immediately disarmed.

Everyone agreed that Wade was very calm as he took the gun away from the drunk, wet, naked American pilot before our terrified English hardman friends, almost the way you might gently take a forbidden toy from a small child. They said Wade took out the clip and emptied the bullets into his hand so quickly and smoothly that they almost didn't see it happen. He put the bullets in the pocket of his board shorts and gave Flying Frank back his gun. Then he gathered us all up, collected us in the vehicle, and drove us to safety.

Wade didn't say anything until they had finished, and then, all he said was, "He could have hurt somebody."

I don't remember if the rodeo was rained out or if we just didn't go. Instead, we drove all the way to the other hot springs, on the other side of the Highway 395, north of the Mobil station, instead of south, the ones you had to hike down a steep hill to get to, so RVs couldn't get there, the ones by a cold river, where we soaked for so long, going from hot stone pool to cold river and back again, over and over, so late into the night, that we all fell asleep, in the shallows, in a row, sitting up, looking up at the stars with beers in our hands.

BY NOW, we had all been living, for the better part of a month, in one Camp 4 campsite, under one or two people's names, keeping all of our bivy gear in the one tent to which we were entitled, only taking it out to sleep once it was dark (it rarely rained without warning), and using up the allotted ten days on each person's ID before substituting another. We shared all of our dishes and never washed them. When we finished eating from the pots we had cooked in, we just shoved the dishes back in the bear box, and when we wanted to cook again, we cooked on top of the crud. I sort of remember sharing a toothbrush with someone, or maybe even two other people, or maybe that is just how close we all felt. Closer than family, closer than blood. Like soldiers, or tribe.

I was eventually sleeping with one of them, though I won't say which (a lady never tells), but what I liked best that summer was being one of the guys. Even though it was largely my tragically straight sexual interests that drove me toward men, I'd always enjoyed their company and comradeship and valued them as human beings. I was genuinely happier when men were nearby, and more bored when they were excluded. I'd never understood the point of purposefully avoiding the male species through participation in anything deliberately gender-segregated, like "girl time" or "women's circles" or—God forbid—"women's only workshops" billed in serious whispers as "safe spaces," as if the mere presence of a dick in the vicinity were a danger akin to an active shooter. I had zero interest in saying or doing anything that couldn't be said or done in the presence of any person of any gender. What was the point of being homosocial if you were heterosexual? Why voluntarily segregate yourself from men, as if you could only speak or climb freely without them? And, most important, how would a woman ever get laid in this pink and dickless Barbie world?

ENJOYING A LAZY REST DAY AFTERNOON in El Cap Meadow, swimming in the river and reading in camping chairs, Harold, Will, and I were approached by Big Wall Bob, this guy who had asked to borrow my hot springs guidebook, copied my phone number off the title page, where I'd scrawled it under the words "If found, please return to Emily Weinstein," and then texted me several times, asking if I wanted to drink malt liquor with him in the Meadow, or perhaps go to the hot springs together, which was a frequent line in the great state of California, land of the Not Necessarily Sexual (But Probably So) Co-Ed Naked Hot Tub.

Big Wall Bob was something of an El Cap fixture, known, in addition to the type of creepy behavior I had personally experienced, also for aid-climbing El Cap, which meant using a blacksmith shop's worth of metal tools to "nail" your way up the wall. Big Wall Bob was rumored to free climb no harder than I did at the time.

I hadn't seen Big Wall Bob since I had repossessed my hot springs guidebook from him in the Meadow and continued to ignore his intermittent texts, but he now approached us with some urgency.

"Conrad Anker is giving a talk in town! At the high school! It starts in fifteen minutes!" announced Big Wall Bob.

It was like he had said magic words to Harold and Will.

"Conrad Anker!" they exclaimed, nearly flipping their camping chairs. "Let's go let's go let's go!"

I left Big Wall Bob to sort out his own transport and let one of the boys drive SubyRuby, but it was an hour's winding road from El Cap Meadow to the high school in the nearest town, and the whole caravan arrived there just as Conrad Anker, whoever he was, was wrapping up his slideshow. Harold and Will were crestfallen, but at least somewhat thrilled to be in a real American high school gym.

When Conrad Anker found out that Harold and Will had missed his slideshow after driving at top speed from the Valley on their first rest day after sending El Cap *and* the Regular Northwest Face of Half Dome, he immediately invited us all back to the restaurant his family owned, at the top of the steep road that led up out of the foothills and into the true Sierra. He said that if we ordered some burgers and stayed until after the restaurant closed, then he would show us the slideshow again, over free beers.

Harold and Will were completely beside themselves at the mere invitation, making me curious about what could possibly be in this slideshow. We went outside, where the sun was slowly setting over a freshly mowed high school athletic field, which is one of the most wonderful things that can happen in America.

"Conrad Anker!" the boys were exclaiming, nearly skipping with delight, saying these pleasing words like a spell. Big Wall Bob was still with us, having hopped on to the private slideshow by standing unnervingly close to me during the actual Conrad Anker encounter.

"Hey, Emily," said Big Wall Bob, "want to hear a joke?"

"Not really," I replied. "But we have time to kill."

"There are these two bulls standing on a hill watching this herd of cows grazing below. And the young bull says, 'Hey, let's run down that hill and fuck one of those cows.' And then the old bull says, 'No, let's *walk* down that hill and fuck *all* of those cows.'"

"That was deep, Bob," I said, meaning it.

Big Wall Bob then proceeded to challenge Harold and Will to a race, which he badly lost.

WE RALLIED OVER TO THE CAFÉ at the end of town, at the top of the steep hill that led out of the foothills and into the proper mountains. Inside the café were several framed magazine covers featuring Conrad Anker, many of them either *National Geographic* or *Outside*. He was movie-star handsome, but like all climbers, looked more like nature than television. Like Fred, and Glenn, and Tori, and Kye, and Harold, and Will, and all the true hardwomen and men I had met in the past year, Conrad Anker looked like a rock, like he was made out of the stuff he climbed.

After the restaurant closed, Conrad Anker turned out all the lights, filled up two pitchers of beer, and led us to a table on the patio, where he opened his MacBook and began the slideshow, which was about a very big, white, snowy mountain he had climbed. It wasn't Everest (though he had climbed Everest), but it was also in the Himalayas. It was called Meru. He had both climbed it and failed to climb it. At first, he failed, but then he succeeded. He had done it with two friends, also professionals—both climbers and filmmakers—and they had taken most of the footage of the three friends climbing the mountain no one else had ever climbed, using axes and crampons and wearing bright shirts and snowsuits that popped against the pure gray, white, and blue of the death-zone peaks.

We crowded around Conrad Anker's glowing laptop for what seemed like hours, but the two pitchers of beer stayed eternally full. I was conscious of being neither as large nor as British nor as high-profile nor as high-altitude as the others at the table, and taking care not to get too drunk around these giant mountain men whose veins probably ran with iron and beer. Harold and Will had endless questions about how they had finally succeeded in climbing the giant white Himalayan mountain, and Conrad Anker seemed more than happy to be speaking to two actual alpinists who had climbed some real snowy, icy, deadly mountains themselves, like Denali in Alaska, and the Alps in Chamonix. It was fun just to be a fly on the wall, but eventually, I had my own question.

"Hey," I asked Conrad Anker. "How come all your stuff in all the pictures says North Face on it?"

"Because they sponsored the expedition," answered Conrad Anker.

"Oh, nice!" I said. "So they bought all that stuff?"

"Well, actually," said Conrad Anker, "I'm the head of the North Face climbing team, so they sponsor any expedition that I want to lead, and give us what we need to make it happen."

From a Himalayan height, the penny dropped.

"You're the guy," I said, drunkenly, to Conrad Anker, slapping his arm as if I were Elaine on *Seinfeld*. "*You're* the guy. *You're* the *guy* who actually uses the *stuff*, on the north faces of *stuff*, so they can *call* it *The North Face*. You're the guy who makes it *true*."

"Yes," said Conrad Anker, kindly. "I am the guy."

Conrad Anker squinted into his laptop, flicking his fingers through the rooftops of the world. Images of a peak that, as of this writing, some years later, the three men in his pictures are still the only human beings to have ever seen in person floated by in blue-white stillness.

"Oh, hey," he said. "This one is cool."

It was a video, of him and the guy named Jimmy, on or near the summit of the giant mountain, sharing a cigarette as casually as if they were sitting around the campfire.

"Let's never, ever do this again," said Jimmy to Conrad, in the video, laughing.

I thought of something Fred had said, in Joshua Tree, after he had said that some people wasted their whole lives climbing rocks.

"The whole point," Fred had said, "is to get to somewhere cool and burn one with your friends."

The real Conrad Anker closed his laptop and told us we could all sleep in the parking lot if we were too drunk to drive back to the Valley. The next morning, we ate breakfast with the great alpinist, and his mom.

WHEN WILL AND HAROLD went back to England and the Valley finally spat me out, I had enough voicemails from Leila to know I should call her right away.

"You had the baby, didn't you?" I said, when she picked up.

"I'm nursing her right now," she said, sounding like a mom. "She's perfect."

And she was. Her face appeared in my phone, just then, by magic and by miracle. It was a face I'd known forever, pulled from the ether and delivered through the portal of a mortal body. It was Leila's face, and Simon's, mixed together. Even though she was just born, she was already her own self, lying on the bare breast of her mother, which I recognized from all our skimpily-clad college parties, for which we would prepare, for hours, trying on and trading sparkly and metallic and animal-print bikini tops to be worn, with miniskirts and thigh-high boots, under half shirts made of fishnets.

I wanted to do that—make love that made a baby with someone I loved who loved me. But now I also wanted something else, which was to get back on top of all of the rocks again and again and again and again, where no one could tell me what I did or did not deserve or could or could not have or should or should not do or say or smoke or feel. I wanted to be free and wild, maybe forever, and definitely for now.

What I could see of Leila's body looked strong and soft and ripe and new. My own body felt similarly alien. I had noticed, over the past few weeks in the Valley, that the muscles that had quickly carved themselves into my flesh had a life and an agenda of their own. They felt like they were humming or even twitching with energy, maybe even desire. They needed to be used for the purpose for which they had created themselves, which was to climb mountains and rage like a monkey.

I felt less like a woman and more like a boy, in the way I'd always felt like a boy, in the part of me that always was one. Like a man, even. Or a woman who was truly equal to one.

Leila and I both crossed over some kind of threshold that summer, both got forged by Mother Nature herself into people we had never been before, but on divergent paths. I knew I was on the road less traveled, and I didn't know—or care—how to get back on the main one.

There was nothing for me there. No one wanted me, not for anything good.

But here on this road less traveled, they thought I was pretty. Here in this ditch, they treated me like I was brave.

7

Stonemasters

Wuzu Fayan guided people with more humility than that
of a hungry and thirsty man. He once said, "I have no
teaching—how can I encourage disciples? I am a true
criminal in this school."

—Zen Lessons

FRED NEVER REFERRED to his contemporaries as Stonemasters. In his stories, he described each of his friends affectionately as "another knucklehead." It took me a while to realize that the other knuckleheads to whom he was referring were other legendary climbers, some of whom were no longer alive.

Fred's stories were often about the first time he'd climbed whatever route we were climbing, or sometimes the first time the route had ever been climbed. Or they weren't about climbing, exactly, they were about the shenanigans and capers and adventures and minor crimes and misdemeanors and encounters with the law or the edge or the face of death that wouldn't have happened if not for climbing.

The climbing stories were ancient and epic. They sounded like myths, or an undiscovered manuscript about an outlaw stoner warrior poet mountaineer subculture that was somehow hippie and punk and anarchist and apolitical all at once.

I had been home from the Valley for less than a week when Glenn told me he was rallying up to Tuolumne Meadows, Yosemite's high country, even getting a proper campsite, and Fred and his partner, Flora, would be coming up from Joshua Tree to climb with us. I repacked SubyRuby and rallied myself.

I HAD MET FRED on my first trip to Joshua Tree, but had not yet met his partner, Flora, who was also a Stonemaster. One of the first things I noticed about her was the pure genius of the simple machine she built to hold the garbage bag while we cooked on the picnic table. She had taken a twig from the ground and put it through the two handles of a grocery store plastic shopping bag. Then she placed the twig over the space between the planks of the picnic table, perpendicular to it, so the bag hung securely from the twig under the table while you cooked. What I didn't know, looking at this plastic bag on a stick hanging from a picnic table, was that Flora had done pretty much exactly the same thing, but with her body, and used these combined ingenuities to climb El Cap and become one of the few female Stonemasters.

In 1980, my first full year of life, Flora and Lynn Hill, the most legendary female Stonemaster, made the first all-female ascent of the Shield, one of the most difficult aid routes on El Cap. El Cap itself wouldn't be climbed "free"—without using aid gear like fishhooks and knife blades and forged metal piton spikes, until 1988, and in 1993, Lynn Hill herself became the first person—not woman, just *person*—to free the famous Nose route.

Fred and Flora weren't legally married, but their love story was better than marriage. They had grown up in Glendale, a part of Los Angeles, fifties-born Boomers, just like my parents. Fred had already graduated high school when one of his buddies asked for a favor. The friend was supposed to take Flora to the prom, but at the last minute, he decided he wanted to ask some other girl and asked Fred if he'd help him out by being Flora's date.

"So I took Flora to the prom," Fred would say, "and we've been hanging out ever since."

Around the same time my parents had met at Queens College, Fred and Flora and a bunch of other SoCal adventurers had started driving out to Tahquitz and Suicide Rocks, then to Joshua Tree, and then finally to Yosemite, where they lived in the Camp 4 parking lot unmolested and changed rock climbing forever by making it rock and roll—or that was what I understood from the stories I had started to hear, about smoking weed with impunity and climbing without fear while showing no respect for the law and living on almost no money.

Nowadays, there are articles about the Stonemasters in glossy magazines. There is a coffee table book about the era, featuring photographs by the official Stonemaster photographer (my friend Dean Fidelman) and writing by the official Stonemaster scribe, John Long. There is a feature-length documentary film and an oral history, officially called the Joshua Tree National Park Historic Resource Study of Recreational Rock Climbing, conducted by an anthropologist out of UC Riverside under the auspices of the National Park Service. But back when they lived the legends they told me, almost nobody knew about it.

"Those guys acted like they were too cool for school," one of their contemporaries scoffed, when I met him in a distant mountain parking lot and told him who had taught me to climb. "Like they ruled the Valley!"

It took all of the humility they had taught me by example not to tell the guy in the parking lot *They were! They did!*

By the time I met Fred and Flora, in the early 2010s, they had been walking the line between dropout dirtbagging and sustainable adulting with masterful precision for decades. They had real jobs in Los Angeles, as a dockworker and a scientist, before they retired to their Joshua Tree spot. It was a house they had built on once-barren land now covered in native plants they'd nurtured into adult Joshua trees and flowering cacti, which was also a sculpture garden of Fred's welded pieces of metal and granite. They built an off-grid little house out of a shipping container that ran on solar power that I got to stay in when I visited. Their property backed up onto a roadless wilderness of BLM land where they went mountain biking.

The first time I went there, Fred pointed out a metal peace sign strung like a necklace across the space between two rock formations behind the house, maybe a hundred feet high.

"That's a memorial," he said, "for our friend, John Bachar."

Bachar was a famous Stonemaster and free soloist who'd died, free soloing, a couple of years before I met Fred and Flora.

"He didn't know himself," Fred said. "He didn't know himself anymore."

I think he meant that Bachar hadn't admitted to himself that his capabilities, in his fifties, and after a car accident, were not the same as they had been in his youth. That was the same time Fred had told me, "Climb all you can now, in your twenties and your thirties, while you're at your youngest and strongest, because one day, you won't be able to do the same things"—though Fred and Flora were both emphatic that you could climb for a long time, if you were careful and lucky and didn't make mistakes.

"Pilot error, every time," they told me, when I fretted about accidents other people had.

WHEN FRED AND FLORA ASKED if I wanted to climb On the Lamb with them, I didn't know that there was a famous photo of Bachar soloing the route, in the seventies, naked of any rope or gear, and most clothing, save for some red short shorts and matching red climbing shoes, accessorized with the kind of pulled-up sweat socks with the stripe that my dad still wore, and a chalk bag that covered more than his shorts did. I didn't know that On the Lamb was unique in the vertical world, for it was almost entirely horizontal.

"It's a geological oddity!" Flora said gleefully, on the approach. The climb, which was rated 5.9, was a five-hundred-foot traverse—a sideways climb. It was made of a nearly continuous horizontal crack in the rock that ran across the upper face of Lamb Dome. The handholds were jugs, said the guidebook, but the feet sometimes "disappeared."

The thing about a traverse or sideways climb is that the follower faces the same fall as the leader. On a vertical climb, the leader belays the follower safely on a toprope from above, but a toprope isn't a toprope if it's coming from the side. Fred would lead the climb—or more like solo it, and then build a belay. Except, Flora reminded him, he'd need to put some gear in, or if we fell off, following him, the rope would swing all the way down from the anchor, leaving the climber dangling by as much rope as there was between themselves and the belay—which, on a five-hundred-foot sideways climb, could be a lot—well below and out of reach of all the jugs on the climb. To prevent me from taking a big, sideways swing if I fell as I followed, we would use a "backrope belay," which meant that as I climbed, there would be a second rope attached to me, that went the *other* way, back to a *second* belayer who was behind me, and I'd be suspended between the two ropes, and not fall too far, even if I let go. We'd bring a fourth climber, Ben Bloomberg, to hold the rope on the backrope belay for me. Compared to some of my most recent shenanigans, it sounded extremely safe.

Ben Bloomberg described himself as "the Jew from New York!" He was from upstate, near the Gunks, the East Coast climbing area. The Gunks had Stonemasters, too, but they were called Vulgarians. They rode around on the roofs of their vans naked, on acid.

So we set out to climb On the Lamb, a "geological oddity," on a bluebird midsummer day in the subalpine, two Stonemasters, and two Jews from New York.

But we couldn't find the start of the climb. It's hard to find, they say, because unlike the starts of most climbs, the start of On the Lamb is not at the bottom of a rockpile, but several hundred feet up, in the middle of it. So we "scrambled"—really free soloed—up and over the entire Lamb Dome, looking for the beginning of the climb and finding, instead, the end. It was normally climbed from left to right, but we would climb it from right to left.

"Like Hebrew!" I joked to Ben. "Backward!"

While we looked for the beginning of the five-hundred-foot-long horizontal crack several hundred feet up Lamb Dome, Fred and Flora bickered just like my parents trying to decide whether to stay in the dead-stopped traffic on the Cross Bronx Expressway or Cross Island Parkway, or get off and take the streets—except there was no 1010 WINS or Newsradio 88 to provide traffic reports. There was, in a guide-book called *Tuolumne Free Climbs*, a verbal description of how to find the spot where the geological oddity began, but no real map. The location of the beginning of the five-hundred-foot-long crack in the dome rising from the subalpine meadow at over 8,500 feet of elevation was only in the Stonemasters' reptile brains and muscle memory.

When we finally found one end of the climb, Fred was soloing east-ward before Flora even had him on belay. "Don't forget to put in some gear!" she reminded him, one last time, and Fred stepped into the sky, yelling, "I will, Flo!" Soon he disappeared around the dome's curve, out of sight.

Before she followed Fred's rope, Flora checked that I was all set up with my backrope belay. The two ropes on my harness, both tied to my belay loop, reminded me of the Jolly Jumper, a contraption my parents had hung from the ceiling of our Flushing, Queens, apart-ment when I was a baby, before I could walk. It suspended me in a little baby-bucket harness seat, taking the weight off my legs so I could bounce and jump. Later, when my mom studied neuroscience on her way to a clinical psychology PhD she earned in her fifties, she lamented that the Jolly Jumper was a developmentally unsound toy for infants, and had probably overstimulated me. I didn't just bounce in it, but took big rides, as my dad pulled me backward, by the diapered butt, into the living room, and then released me to swing-fly into the kitchen, cheering "Woooooooooo!" I can't scientifically prove that raging in the Jolly Jumper in Queens in 1980—probably while Flora and Lynn Hill were high up on the Shield, on El Cap, dangling from similar nylon straps in their portaledge, a special cot-platform designed to be hung from the side of a cliff—led directly to my own desire, thirty-two years later, to tiptoe along a rock ledge in the sky, but it was a curious parallel.

Once Flora checked that I was tied into my backrope belay as securely as I'd once been strapped into the Jolly Jumper, she stepped out onto On the Lamb.

It was the first time I saw Flora climb. She moved like a ballerina, but a casual one. She was petite, and her moves were precise, deliberate. Careful. Purposeful. Intuitive and scientific at the same time. Masterful, worthy of the moniker "Stonemaster." Then the rope went tight, and three tugs came, and I followed in her footsteps.

As we left on foot for Lamb Dome that morning, Glenn had yelled after us, "Make sure when you get to Fred's belay that he's not belaying you off of just one nut!" Technically, climbing anchors are supposed to have *at least* two pieces, and preferably three, and there should never be one piece, especially just one nut.

But after I did my best to imitate Flora's skywalk on the geological oddity, and came to Fred's belay halfway between the end of On the Lamb and the beginning of it, which was our ultimate destination, I came to the belay to find Fred not only belaying me off just one nut, but also smoking a joint that Flora leaned out to pass me before I even attached myself to the intermediate anchor.

"Don't worry." Fred grinned. "It's a *good* nut."

Ben Bloomberg the Jew from New York followed, and we repeated the process a second time, for the geological oddity was two rope lengths wide.

Except that this time, after Fred had led and Flora had followed and the rope went tight and the three tugs came, Ben Bloomberg was curled up in a ball, hanging from the anchor he'd have to take apart, while hanging on, when it was his turn to climb.

"Migraine," he barely croaked.

"But you're supposed to belay me," I squeaked. "The backrope."

"You'll be fine," he rasped, clearly in pain.

"But what about you?" I asked. "How will you make it?"

"I'll make it," he said, looking like death in the bright sun. And then he buried his poor head in his hands.

This is interesting, I thought, as I took my first step on the second and last sideways pitch (rope length) of the geological oddity. I didn't totally entirely understand what would happen if I fell off the climb and dangled from the rope without the second rope firmly held behind me to catch me, but I could well imagine it. *Don't think about that.* But I had ended up in the vertical with useless ropes before—with the Brits, on an impromptu accidental semi–free solo of the Great White Book. And there was that first time in the Space Station with Glenn and Fred, with no ropes at all. This wasn't what I had expected, or planned, but here we were. Or rather, here I was. On the Lamb. Somewhere up ahead, to the east, back toward New York, a Stonemaster I trusted completely was holding my life on this wall, on at least *one* good nut.

As I tiptoed toward New York, technically going backward, technically facing a lead fall, I didn't think about anything but moving along. I placed my hands in the perfect horizontal crack, and held on to jug after jug, stepping my feet along, usually on little nubbins and dents and edges and footholds. The guidebook was right. Sometimes the feet disappeared, and I had to just smear them on the wall like a lizard and, Fred and Flora had said, "trust."

It was too beautiful to be scared. To my right, back toward Ben and the Pacific Ocean, was a perfect view of Tuolumne's domes and peaks, rising proud and free above the green pines below, and, at the end of that landscape, a flash of Tenaya Lake, mirroring the sky. Up ahead, to my left, was endless blue, then harmless, happy little clouds below, then more domes and peaks, and way, way down below the tree line, were the forest and the meadow and the road where I'd once lain down and done it and not died. Walking through that particular patch of sky, I thought to myself that it was worth even death, just to see it.

I waited until I was anchored into the next belay, which, this time, was more than just one nut, to tell Flora that my backrope belayer had been felled by a migraine, and no one was really holding the rope. All Flora said was, "Then it's good that you didn't fall."

"I figured," I said.

When he appeared, Ben was in some kind of pain cave where the high-altitude sun couldn't reach him but to torture his eyeballs and brain.

"I left the red Alien," Ben confessed miserably to Fred, when he arrived at the end of the climb, which was really the beginning, a comfortable ledge on which Flora and I were chilling.

Fred yelled with the same tone I'd heard in my dad's voice when I spilled milk, or the Mets lost.

"Aw, man!" he exclaimed. "Flora, put me back on belay!"

Before she could even do it, Fred was headed back west, toward the red Alien. He came back in minutes with it clipped to his harness. Before we coiled the ropes and started down, Fred held up the red Alien, squeezed its triggers and made its lobes wiggle. The part that lodged in the rock was maybe about the diameter of the big marble, the one that hit the little marbles. Aliens were so named because the loop that connected the cam to the nylon that linked it to the carabiner, which held the rope that held your life, was shaped like the head of an alien.

"This is a really good piece," he said, almost conspiratorially. "It's bigger than a 0.5, and smaller than a 0.75, so it fits in the places that neither of those do."

The way he said it reminded me of the way my dad would hold up his hands and say, "With these two hands, I can make anything!"

Fred reminded me of my dad, if my dad had been put in a California stoner Catholic-childhood-dockworker filter, instead of a Brooklyn-Queens Jewish accountant baseball-fan filter. They were both about my height, and the same size as their mates, and they both had strong hands and hearts that radiated love through irreverence and *Twilight Zone* references.

"Well," said Flora, as we began our descent, "at least we know the way down."

The red Alien was the first piece of gear I bought, at full price, from Spain. If Fred said it was a really good piece, then I wanted the best and most expensive one. No reason to try to save money on saving my life.

BEING IN THE MOUNTAINS was a new way to love, and be loved. It wasn't about needs or wants or feelings. Sometimes it was about fear, or death, but you didn't have to talk about any of it, because it was all beyond words. You didn't talk about your feelings in the mountains because your feelings had no place there. You didn't have to tell too many stories because you were living a story, every time. And the stories my climbing elders and teachers did tell weren't scary. Sometimes the person in the story suffered with mental illness or died climbing—or both—but that was part of the story, part of the history.

Since I was little, the grown-ups in my life had told me scary stories, every chance they got. My grandmother told me, over and over, about how her father beat her with a belt, when I was so little I didn't know things like that even happened. My mother told me, over and over, about things relatives and other males did that left her feeling traumatized. Along with physical beauty and back trouble, the lineage harbored secrets and violence, fathers and brothers doing things to their daughters and sisters that no one should ever do to anyone.

Growing up, I was scared of rooms without windows and didn't know why. I was scared of the dark, scared of the night, scared of my nightmares, scared of a man coming into my room, scared of the stories I'd already heard, scared of what I could sense, without being told, beneath the words.

But up in the Meadows, up on the wall, with these Jedi Stonemasters, there was so much room and light and air, and I didn't have to mutely listen to any scary stories about what happened long ago in dark rooms in tiny apartments on flat earth for these grown-ups to keep me alive. I felt safe, utterly safe, even hanging from one nut—one *good* nut—hundreds and hundreds of feet above the ground, safer on the wall than I felt on the ground. In a way, I was re-parented, in the vertical, by two Stonemasters from Southern California who have adopted many misfits like myself, loved them well, taught them all they knew—and set them free.

In California, Fred told me once, "There's room for all of us to be ourselves."

I had to leave before we could climb anything else. My family was going on another family river-rafting trip with my brother's then-girlfriend's entire family. I had to wake up at dawn to drive to Oregon. I already planned to take the inflatable kayak through every rapid on the whole river, hoping I could find someone to regale with my tales about how climbing was better than rafting, because you could smoke weed whenever you wanted, and you didn't have to deal with paying customers.

"We'll get up with you," Fred and Flora said, "and make you coffee." They made me a mocha latte in the subalpine dawn, and after one of Glenn's doobs went around, gave me the roach for the road.

"That drive," said Fred, "is gonna fly right by."

THE RIVER TRIP WAS ALL PAYING CUSTOMERS, mostly families. It was only four days, plus a night on either side to put in and take out, but I felt caged, even though we were in wilderness. I said to my parents, for the first time, that it felt weird to me, being the lone solo traveler in a party of five, or maybe seven, with everyone else in couples. My parents were a couple, and my brother always had a girlfriend. Except for the one summer that the one college boyfriend I'd met on a semester of study abroad visited America, I rarely dined with my family in a restaurant without hearing the maître d' call out, "Weinstein, party of five?"

I was always the fifth wheel. I always sat at the end of the table while the couples faced each other on either side. I prayed, for years, to have a boyfriend—even a temporary one—to make a party of six, to eat, even just once, in an even number, at a table with my family and my own person, too, but I never managed to have a boyfriend at the same time that my brother had one of his nearly unbroken parade of very serious girlfriends. Starting in college, he would move in with them, sometimes after only a few weeks, and then enter a carousel of breaking up and getting back together that went on for months or even years, drama swirling at the center of our family that left me feeling, after any holiday, like maybe relationships and families were all a big mistake. But the river girlfriend was my favorite of all the girlfriends, and her family was kind and welcoming, too.

There were no other single people on the trip, besides my brother's girlfriend's younger brother, a college student. Sitting around the fire one night, one of the paying customers asked me what I did, what I was good at, what my thing was. I wanted to say I was good at charming strangers into liking me but bad at getting people to love me. I was about to say something about my adventures in Yosemite Valley and the "geological oddity" in Tuolumne I had just climbed, sideways, with Stonemasters, without falling; about the book I'd been writing in New York about my punk rock friends that I hadn't touched since I'd first touched rock; about the tutoring business that supported the ramshackle ecosystem of my broke single artist life that I'd left behind in New York and built back up from scratch in California, in little more than a year, before adding a new, all-consuming, and life-threatening hobby to the mix.

But my brother's then-girlfriend's brother spoke first, and spoke for me.

"Living," said the college kid, emphatically. "The thing Emily is good at is *living*. Living *life*."

8

Rope

"C'MON," SAID GLENN. "Let's go watch Rosie take whippers on Spider Line."

"Who's Rosie?" I asked. "What's Spider Line?

"You'll see," he said.

It was almost New Year's Eve, almost 2013. I'd been back in Joshua Tree, the winter spot, since before Christmas—since right after Hanukkah and before the solstice. It was one of the years in the early 2010s when an end-of-the-world prophecy gained traction on billboards.

The Solstipocalypse party was raging in the desert as I reeled away, hit all at once by the tequila and the beer and the weed and the whiskey and the tobacco and the mushrooms, all organic and of the highest quality, and most homegrown or homemade. This was advanced partying, I realized, as I hollowed my stomach, heaving over a cactus. Luckily, my earlier, twentysomething punk rock–adjacent adventures had prepared me for this moment by involving even more—and worse—drugs, even less sleep, retching in alleyways, not wilderness, and neither kale nor kombucha.

My vision steadied and the vague shapes silvered in moonlight took form. In the center of the dark desert was a glow of living color. It was the bonfire, hidden from the road behind a carefully selected boulder, burning and sparking and popping and smoking higher and higher into the night sky with each log someone hurled in.

I gathered the strength to stand upright. To my surprise, it felt wonderful. Maybe the world wasn't ending. Maybe the mushrooms were kicking in. Maybe the party was just beginning.

I made my way back toward the fire boulder, stopping to find my water bottle, stashed between rocks, half frozen into a needly slush that stung the roots of my teeth as I rinsed out my mouth. Tipping my head back to drink, I saw the stars, so densely visible that they formed those milky clouds people point at and name as the galaxy itself—that other, streaky part of it, spiraling, somewhere long ago and far, far away.

CHRISTMAS CAME AND WENT. Glenn ran a Secret Santa in the campground and dressed up as Satan-a-Claus. I received a plastic shopping bag with two wine coolers, two condoms, and two cigarettes, which I thought was very romantic and was even able to put to use. After Secret Santa, everyone just went climbing. No families, no bullshit, no stupid carols, no baby Jesus, no gift receipts. I never wanted to do anything else, ever again, on any other national holiday.

After Christmas, people started pouring into the campground for New Year's. James showed up, with Jacob and Clark, two friends he'd grown up with and was teaching to climb. They filled a campsite Glenn had reserved for them with tents and trucks and the dirtbag riches of beer and firewood.

It was in this festive holiday environment that Glenn asked me if I wanted to go watch Rosie take whippers on Spider Line, in nearly the same spot where, not very long ago, he had asked if I wanted to go on an adventure.

What Spider Line turned out to be was a 5.11 climb—5.11d, to be exact, a grade hard enough that I, a born moderate climber (if no other kind of moderate) would never really attempt it in my whole climbing life.

Rosie turned out to be a rad chick who would try to send the hard, 5.11d climb. I had never met or even seen her before I watched her walk up to the base of Spider Line and tie herself in to the sharp end with a golden helmet on her head.

Rosie, unarmed but for her fists, proceeded to do battle with the steep, hard crack, roaring like a lion and screaming like a tennis player. Each time she placed a piece of gear was its own precarious struggle, as she hung on with one hand while finding a place to hang her life with the other. Then she got to a spot that was especially hard, and took a fairly big fall, while screaming with what was clearly rage and not fear. Falling didn't seem to stop her so much as inspire her. She charged so hard from the end of the rope back to the last piece of gear that she almost seemed to levitate, and then she charged harder back toward the part where she'd fallen, managing to get some more gear in to catch her before she fell again. Like Kye had done, on Bearded Cabbage, which at 5.10c was "moderate" compared to this 5.11d route, Rosie took a number of huge, growling whippers. The way she whaled on the rock, it was hard to say whether she was battling it, or herself. It looked like she was trying to give the rock the beating it was giving her.

Climbers were always saying that it was "all mental." It was all in your *mind* that you couldn't climb the 5.11d, or the 5.10c, or get on the sharp end (lead the climb, instead of follow it on toprope), or whatever it was that you just couldn't bring yourself to do. You really could do it, if you really wanted to. It was "mental." The flesh was never too weak if the mind were truly willing.

Climbers were also always talking about "the ego." If it were "mental," it was just "the ego" that was stopping you. It was always either "all mental" or "just your ego."

The day I watched Rosie take whippers on Spider Line, I saw how mental it really was. Maybe it was because she didn't hide her emotions as she went ten rounds with her nonexistent opponent, so even the by-standers in the peanut gallery could see what was going on in her head and heart. I had never minded telling people what I *thought*—in fact, I shared that freely, at every opportunity, through every medium, any time I had an internet connection, or even a passing thought, but I was petrified to show people what I felt, and even more so, what I wanted. I'd never been ashamed of my opinions, but I was ashamed of my feelings, and my desire, and terrified of other people's feelings, and what they might do to me because of them.

I had always wanted to win things and make it to the top and be the best and prove I could do it, but I couldn't stand it if the game went on after I had failed to win it. When, as a junior in high school, I found out I was ranked second in my class instead of first, I wrote an editorial in the school newspaper and then gave a speech at a school board meeting, following which the school board voted to end class rank for all classes after ours. I was applauded by parents and students alike for my good-will in eliminating this system in which I appeared to be dominating, but no one but me realized that I had flipped the table of the game simply because I hadn't won.

Watching Rosie battle on Spider Line was the first time I saw for real that there was no one to dominate or beat but your own self, fear, or ego. And you could be honest about what you wanted, and you could let people see if you failed.

I was afraid of Rosie for years after I watched her throw herself at Spider Line, which, she later pointed out, she never even sent. It wasn't because of anything she said or did, besides be a beast. It was because I couldn't fathom how someone that ferociously powerful could also be kind.

Eventually, I got what it was all about. Being powerful with this kind of power made you kind, and being kind—maybe even to yourself—made you powerful.

———————————

THE ROPE WAS A BRIGHT, vernal green, sixty meters long. My brother had bought it for me with his REI dividend.

The night he gave it to me, I took it home and slept with it in my bed, under the covers, still in its factory coil. I've repeated this process with all new ropes since. My intention for the ritual is for the rope and I to cleave to each other, in some way more tightly bound than its nylon fibers, closer to the blood that binds siblings, even as we fight.

My brother had sometimes unconsciously grabbed the back of my life vest as he rowed and I paddled in the same boat, through the rapids on the rivers he guided. I had felt the tug as we went through the biggest water, his hands momentarily free because his oars were shipped— placed along the sides of the boat, out of the water, to prevent their breakage on rocks. I told myself that the rope my brother had bought me would be like his sure, silent grip on my life vest, a human touch, tethering me, keeping me from falling into churning water—or thin air.

The next morning, I packed the green rope into SubyRuby and together we three drove south to Joshua Tree, for, once again, it was spring.

GLENN DIDN'T JUST LEAD CLIMB, but frequently free soloed, often before breakfast. Glenn and Fred and everyone I'd met since didn't believe that any other kind of climbing was really real, only "practice" for what *was* really real, which, if it couldn't be free soloing, was leading. Not tying in to the end of a rope someone else had hung, but taking the rope and hanging it yourself.

Though I'd practiced a few times, on short, easy climbs, this would be the first time I would lead climb for real in Joshua Tree. It would be like what I had done in Yosemite, with the peanut gallery of beer drinkers in camping chairs, but without Ian hanging above on a separate rope and making sure the gear was good.

Because I was mentored in climbing by feral, van-dwelling free soloists, Stonemasters, and hardman Yosemite big-wall climbers, my risk-benefit calculus was always a little bit skewed. "I climb like the Jewish grandma I hope to one day become," I quipped—though I wasn't sure how a Jewish grandma would climb trad on lead, when I brought the new green rope my brother had bought me to Joshua Tree to do exactly that.

Climbing trad, or traditional climbing, was one more danger-ous thing I was doing. Climbing trad meant that you had to carry all the metal gear that would catch you if you fell with you as you climbed and place it in the rock yourself. Sport climbing, which Glenn and Fred frequently derided "was neither," meant that the metal that caught you if you fell was permanently drilled into the rock. Placing the gear yourself was one more layer of danger, and therefore one more layer of responsibility, but I was growing to like it. I liked the parts that were like a puzzle you had to solve with your body and your mind at the same time.

I TIMED MY TRIP with another rare visit from Leila. She had a work thing in LA, so she visited her parents in Palm Springs and drove down to meet me for a single night and day in the Hidden Valley, while Simon was with the baby, who was almost one, back in New York. I prepared for her arrival by making the bed in the back of SubyRuby as cushy as pos-sible, and also making myself a separate sleeping place under a pinyon pine at the back of the campsite Glenn had reserved for us, next to his. She arrived just after dark, after dinner with her parents in Palm Springs.

Excited, I showed her the bed in the back of my car.

"Check it out," I encouraged her. "It's all yours."

Dubiously, Leila folded herself into the back of the car. She was tall, but I'd hosted many taller overnight guests there before, albeit all of them males, wild-caught. But they had been climbers, and were accustomed to sleeping in uncomfortable places. Leila was not.

"I don't fit," complained Leila. "I'm too tall."

"Go diagonal," I instructed. "The hypotenuse."

"I don't want to go diagonal," Leila said, in a tone that portended no further discussion.

"And I have something to tell you," she continued.

I knew what it was before she said, "I'm pregnant again."

"Wow, that's amazing!"

"Really? I feel like I'm letting you down."

"What? Don't be crazy! That's amazing! The baby you already have is amazing! This is gonna be amazing!"

"It happened really fast. We thought it would take longer, because it did the first time, and I *just* stopped nursing, right before this trip."

"Fertile Myrtle," I ribbed her. "Practically Irish twins!"

Leila rolled her eyes.

"You don't have to climb, obviously," I added.

"Oh, I'm gonna climb," said Leila. "If it's gonna stay in there, it's gonna stay in there. If it's not, then it's not. I'm not gonna *not* climb."

"The first trimester feats of strength." I sighed.

"One more thing," she said. "I don't want to tell anybody else, because it's so early. I didn't even tell my parents yet. So you have to finish all my beers and joints."

"I got you," I promised.

I dragged the mattress out of SubyRuby and put Leila to bed under the pinyon pine. Then I sat on the rear bumper with the hatch open. I had forgotten to tell Leila that I was going to try my first real lead climbs the next day, that we would climb for the first time on my brand-new rope. I wasn't sure she'd understand—or care—what that meant anyway. I realized, with an extra layer of fear, that it would be my anchor Leila would climb on in her delicate condition, while with child (or embryo).

Our gang back in New York was in such a prolific phase of child-bearing that one of them was always pregnant or on maternity leave. When I visited, they took pictures of me holding the babies. Sometimes, sleeping in the back of SubyRuby somewhere without internet, I gazed at them. Cradling the newborns, the muscles in my arms looked impossibly large and defined. After one of my friends gave birth, they'd be just a bit softer and paler than usual for just a little while, but by my next visit to New York, they'd have marathon'ed or yoga'ed their way back to their old bodies, before the babies even stopped being babies.

From the back of SubyRuby, I could see into the Space Station, looming above the campground, really not so high. By now, I had climbed things that were much higher than that. I hadn't been back up to the Space Station since the time Leila and I had gone together, with Glenn and Fred, two years ago. Now she had a husband and a baby and even another on the way, and I had—a rope.

The thought of carrying the bean-size potential baby of someone I loved who loved me felt so precious, and so impossible, that my gut knotted with envy and longing. If I made a mistake and died the next day, I thought, dramatically, I wouldn't have to feel this anymore.

The first time we'd come here, Leila had said that if we stayed, she would *lose touch with everything else in her life that mattered to her.* But I had gone back, and back and back and back. And I *had* lost touch—with everything. Brooklyn and babies and men who got married.

I wasn't here because I didn't want that. I was here because I couldn't have it. This was what I had instead.

It was a still night in the campground. Often, after dark, the wind died down completely. I stabbed out my spliff and sat without moving until I could hear my own pulse from inside my body. I thought about the next day and felt my pulse quicken, then practiced using my breath to slow it down.

I looked up at the sky and saw Orion, his sword fully rendered, every stud on his belt sparkling.

Shoot your shot, he seemed to be saying. *I'm stuck up here forever drawing back my bow, and I never get to let it rip.*

Maybe, I thought, if I could do it—could send the climbs on lead and hang the rope and not fall and not die—then maybe I'd become the kind of person who could do other impossible things, like make someone who wasn't crazy love me in a way that felt okay. Or maybe, on the other side of this pit of fear and gut punch of envy, there was something else. Something I would come to learn, from the sharp end. Maybe I could show everyone, including myself, that underneath the fear in my lonely, empty belly, I had guts, and underneath my guts, I had balls.

"YOU GOT THIS," said Glenn, as he helped me uncoil my new green rope from its factory packaging and recoiled it so it could be backpacked. I reached for it, but instead, Glenn put it on his own back.

"Leader carries the rack," he grinned, handing me a clinking sling full of dangling gear to choose from. "The anchor takes big stuff, so take doubles up to number three. I'll climb on your rope and check your anchor before anyone else climbs on it."

Toe Jam was a traditional beginner lead. It wouldn't be an onsight, for me, since I had climbed it before, on a toprope, following Kye, the previous spring, but I could go for the send. It had plenty of places to put in the gear that protected you from falling off the rock, and I hadn't fallen, or even rested on the rope, when I'd climbed it the year before.

I racked up, clipping the big blue threes, then the meaty gold twos, then the bright red ones, then the green 0.75s, on down to the small, also blue, 0.3s, onto my harness, symmetrically on either side. They were all this one kind of cam called a Camalot, that was color-coded in the most pleasingly organized way. Though it was heavy, I liked the way the gear felt my harness, pulling down on my hip bones, the calming sound it made when I moved, like wind chimes. There was even a rhythm to the carabiner wires snapping shut.

And then there was the sound of the rope zipping through Glenn's sure hands, softly piling onto the tarp that unfolded from the rope bag my brother had thoughtfully included in his gift. It had taken only a moment to walk across the campground to the base of Toe Jam, a journey of which I had absolutely no recollection.

A small crowd had gathered. There was Leila, not looking pregnant at all, standing there with her harness on already, in an old T-shirt with widespread angel wings across the chest that she had worn in the peak of our adventure heyday. There was Lucas, who had rerouted his morning free solo circuit to take in the sports action and was now cheering encouragingly from a nearby ledge, shirtless. He had a tattoo of wings on his real chest that oddly matched the one on Leila's shirt. Glenn's girlfriend at the time, Jessica, had also come over, and Fred was on hand for the big event. And there was a crusher kid I hadn't met before, who was injured. He was hobbling around the campground with a splint on his ankle, looking bored and stoned and restless. He was here, too, reclining on a boulder with his hands clasped behind his head and a giant smile on his face, like he had nothing better to do than watch me try not to fuck up, or die.

I was too scared to shake. I was so scared that I had come out the other side and was calm.

Glenn had taken the top end of the rope and already tied the first figure-eight in it before laying it over a rock at the base of the climb. I sat down next to it and put on my climbing shoes.

I tasted metal in my mouth, like the electric smell before a rainstorm. Bitter, like the poles of city playgrounds, like the giant chains on squeaking swings I'd stood on, and jumped off of. Sometimes, I used to tear open my palms, swinging on the monkey bars. I could go from end to end. I could do this. I could do this.

There was a toothmark on one of my family's dining room chairs. "When you were a toddler, and first got your front teeth, you climbed up onto the dining room table to get a balloon," my mother would explain. "We didn't know you could do that, so we didn't babyproof it. But you fell off, and hit your open mouth on the chair, and your front teeth pushed back up into your gums. But the doctor said they would come out again, and they did."

I'd always focused on the part of that story where I fell off and got hurt and bit the chair, but lately I'd been thinking about how uncanny it was that when I could barely walk, I'd chosen to climb. I could do this. I could do this.

I strangled the Alien and stabbed it in the eye, and showed Glenn my knot. I dusted off my shoes on my pant legs, while Glenn and I re-stated the plan that I'd build an anchor and then he'd follow my lead and come check the anchor, and then Leila would toprope it, too.

"On belay," he said.

"Climbing," I replied.

"You got this, Em," said voices.

The fear disappeared as soon as I put my hands to the stone. I could do this.

I remembered how casual Kye had looked, leading this, the year before. How easy it was for her. It wasn't that easy for me, but it wasn't that hard. It was doable. Very doable. I could do this.

I was pretty sure my gear placements were textbook. For the past year or so, I'd been practicing placing gear at the bases of crags, then asking more experienced climbers to check it. I'd built a number of practice anchors, and had read a book called *Climbing Anchors* and even another one called *More Climbing Anchors*. I'd looked at anchors other climbers built when I followed their leads, taking in the various options. I could do this. I could do this.

There was one part of Toe Jam that was supposedly kind of hard. "Really only one move where you need the rope on that thing," anyone who routinely free soloed it would tell you. It was at the top, this ostensible crux. Or, not even a crux, just a move. You had to step left, which was totally safe on a toprope, and more scary on lead, or ropeless.

But even that was casual. When the time came, I just did it. I did it without thinking, thinking maybe even less than I might have, if I were on a toprope.

I got to the top and built the anchor like I'd practiced, shouted down to Glenn, for the first time, that he was on belay. He was at the top in no time, with my water bottle clipped to his harness. "Thought you might be thirsty," he said, handing it to me. "Good job."

He checked the anchor, yanking. "Bomber," he said. "Textbook. Nailed it."

Then we rearranged the rope, so Glenn was belaying Leila. As she came into view, climbing up, I was reminded of the irony of all this. She'd been the star of her high school basketball and volleyball *and* field hockey *and* softball teams, was so good that her coach would have to put her in even after he'd benched her for skipping practice to smoke weed with the skater-punk boys. She was absurdly naturally athletic, almost six inches taller than I was, with naturally flat, ripped abs and less cumbersome boobs, and long limbs perfect for dunking and spiking and hitting and climbing. Despite not having spent the past two years sleeping in the back of a car for several months of the year and climbing with the itinerant, the houseless, and the feral, she was charging. Despite being less than a year postpartum and now six weeks pregnant again, she was charging. If she had stayed and I'd escaped, she'd probably be leading at least 5.10 by now.

She paused momentarily at the step left.

"Do you want beta?" I asked. "You step left."

"I don't want beta," she said. "I'm just catching my breath."

And then she stepped left, and continued charging, until she reached the belay. We had sent, both of us. All of us. Even the embryo.

We had done a lot of stuff, she and I, over the years and years of our friendship, but this was a new one. I'd stood right next to her while she'd gotten married, and toasted her after. (And made out with her cousin. And later slept with her brother-in-law.) We'd held each other in bear hugs through all manner of drug-induced freakout and party foul. I knew things about her, and she about me, that we would take to the grave. But she had never climbed, newly pregnant, on my rope or my anchor before, a humbling act of complete trust.

WHEN WE RAPPED BACK DOWN to the base of Toe Jam, Fred announced, "Well, you've got the send, now it's time to go for the onsight."

We headed back to Glenn's favored campsite, Six, for doobs and lunch and afternoon route selection. We passed around the battered guidebook, considering the weather and light. It was a warm day, in late April, the tail end of the climbing season, and in the afternoon the sun was hot, making the rock "greasy." We needed a cool spot, it was decided. There was a 5.8 not far away called the Flue, Fred said, on the aptly named Chimney Rock. Shade all afternoon.

Leila and I ended up alone with the joint, which she passed off to me.

"It's so sad to watch you not inhaling," I said, sucking down the smoke like it might help me float or fly. "Gonna climb this one, too?"

"Hell no," she answered. "I'm gonna lie in the sun and eat snacks."

"Are you nauseous?" I asked.

"Sometimes," she said. "But it's more that I just have to make sure there's food in my belly. That helps."

While I was learning how not to shake while I sewed myself to a granite rock wall with a 9.8-milimeter-wide rope and a rack full of color-coded aluminum Camalots, she was figuring out how not to be nauseated by the biology of the miracle of life, but I was just happy to be together.

"You did a great job, back there," I told her. "I'm really glad you're here."

"You, too." She smiled. "Me, too."

AS THE MOTLEY CREW AMBLED over to the Flue for the afternoon activity, I thought about how funny it was that I wasn't going to pass a test or get a card or be certified at anything. There was a bandana I'd been eyeing at the Coyote Corner in town, when I stopped in to shower, that had a map of the park printed on it. There was a similar bandana in the much vaster Yosemite store. I'd get one for each new level I sent, I decided. Park map bandanas. A reward.

This time, Fred belayed me.

"Make it good," he said softly, before I left the ground.

But the Flue was different from Toe Jam. It was a grade harder, 5.8. It had a hard and awkward start, and the first piece of gear was a few body lengths up. But that was normal for Joshua Tree. A lot of the climbs had hard, unprotected starts. I had to learn.

There was a little ramp you could walk up to get yourself established, and then a little pod that you could kind of shove your butt in and hide. Once I was in the little pod, I had a hard time coaxing myself out of it, but Fred was able to do it, step by step, like he was taming an animal.

"Breathe," he kept saying. "Get some of that *good oxygen*."

I decided that I'd feel much better about climbing if I could get a piece in, so I set about doing that. But this gear placement wasn't like the ones on Toe Jam, or the earlier climbs I'd practiced on. It was up above my head, about as far as I could reach, and I'd have to wriggle out of the little pod and hang on with one hand while I blindly tried to place the piece, with nothing to stop me from decking if I slipped. And the rock bulged out just there, making it even harder to see over, let alone climb over.

But I was barely fifteen feet off the ground, no higher than a boulderer climbing a boulder. If I slipped and fell, I might sprain or break an ankle, but I wouldn't die.

Don't think about falling, said a voice in my head. *Think about climbing*. Someone had said it recently at the gym, but I couldn't remember who.

I made my way out of the pod and scrabbled my hands up into the crack above, trying to judge its width by my fingers. A green one, I decided, but when I managed to place the cam in the rock, it was rattly, and I never got to clip the rope to it. Ever so delicately, hanging on with one hand, I removed it, clipped it back on my harness, and selected the next size up, the red one. But the red one was slightly too big and, even when I squeezed it down to its smallest size, didn't fit far back enough in the crack to be *good*. Someone suggested that I find a nearby, tighter spot for the green cam, which I did, though it wasn't as perfect as the placements had been on Toe Jam that morning, which scared me even more.

"Looks marginal," said Glenn.

This wouldn't have been that big of a problem, if the piece weren't my first piece, and it weren't protecting the hardest part of the climb.

"I want to take on it," I said, meaning ask Fred to pull the rope tight, so the cam took my weight, and I could rest. The other benefit of weighting the cam would be that I would know that it would hold my weight and wouldn't be guessing about that as I tried to climb past it, with it and its marginality now being the only thing between me and the deck.

"No!" shouted the peanut gallery, as they had, two years ago, when I'd tried to grab the bolt. "You'll blow the onsight!"

"Climb till you fall," Fred said softly. That was the game.

"How do I know if it's good?" I asked.

"Pull on it," said Glenn. "In the direction of the fall."

The direction of the fall was not hard to figure out. It was straight down.

I pulled and pulled. One lobe of the cam wiggled slightly—that was what made it marginal—but it stayed put. I reached for a sling to extend the piece as I had been taught, but Fred said, "Extend the next one, this one is so close to the deck."

I clipped the rope directly to the marginal cam, and promptly crawled back into the pod below, to rest before I tried to climb above.

"Breathe," Fred said again. "Get some of that *good oxygen.*"

I peeked out at the peanut gallery. Leila was lying on her back with her head propped at a perfect viewing angle, one hand delicately placed on her belly, the other lazily, rhythmically moving between a bag of—probably dried mango, her favorite—and her mouth. When she saw me looking out, she waved encouragingly. The crusher kid was there, barefoot but for his ankle splint, his foot soles black and his wide grin white.

Part of me wanted desperately to back off, to lower down—not even lower on the rope and trust the marginal cam, but just climb down. And yet as soon as I imagined it, I rejected the idea. I couldn't do it in front of the crusher kid. I just couldn't.

So I stopped thinking about going down. I started thinking about going up. I peered out of the pod, then climbed back up to the holds from which I'd placed the marginal cam.

"Yeah, Em!" cheered the crowd encouragingly.

But I couldn't do it. I couldn't climb past it. Not without knowing that I would definitely not deck, definitely not die. I would probably not die, but I might deck. Break things. I crawled back into the pod, the cave of fear and shame.

"Breathe," said Fred. "Oxygen."

I made my heart slow down like I'd done the night before. No part of me was shaking, but I wanted to be completely still before I tried to move. *Oxygen really is good*, I thought to myself. *Oxygen is great.*

I thought about another route I'd climbed, with Glenn, only on toprope, something harder, maybe 5.10a or b. I'd been trying to do the hard part, but I kept slipping off. Glenn, always an impatient toprope belayer, had said, "You're wasting your one good go."

That came to me now. Every time I crawled out of the pod, only to crawl back in, I wasted energy. It took energy away from a good go. Next time I went, I had to make it a good go.

Fuck it, I thought.

Don't think about falling, think about climbing, I muttered internally. *Show that crusher kid you're not a pussy, or a weenie, or a wuss, or a loser, or a coward.*

Don't fuck this up, Weinstein.

And I didn't. I crawled out of the pod and got back to my high, cam-placing position. I yanked on the marginal 0.75 one more time, knowing that I could not apply one-hundred-plus pounds of falling force with one hand. But that didn't matter, because I wasn't going to fall. I felt the urge to crawl back into the safety-shame-fear cave/pod, and knew it was now or never. I started climbing, for real, climbing up, not thinking about falling, but thinking about climbing.

I fell.

It happened so quickly there was no time to fear it. I had fallen so short a distance that it was over before it began. The cam had held. I was hanging from it.

"Bomber," said Glenn.

"Nice whip," said Fred.

"There goes the onsight," I said.

"See?" said Glenn. "The system works."

I took so many whippers on that marginal green 0.75 that they had to change belayers from Fred to Glenn. I couldn't work it out, this one little bulge, couldn't get past it. It was probably mental. I kept slipping and falling and hanging on my one stupid cam, which caught me and held me and never budged. Out of the corner of my eye, I saw Glenn's girlfriend serving guacamole to the peanut gallery from a tray. I had been too nervous to eat much all day and was suddenly acutely aware of my hunger in addition to my mortality. Leila looked bored. The crusher kid looked to be either totally fascinated or completely zoned out. I wanted a beer. I wanted a joint. I wanted a snack. I wanted a hug. I wanted a bandana with a map of the park printed on it. I wanted out of here, out of this loop of trying and failing and trying again. I wanted to send this thing, or get to the top, or whatever the technical term was for getting to the top after you'd already fallen and blown the onsight.

I remembered Rosie, on Spider Line, just a few months ago, in a similar situation on a much prouder climb. She hadn't given up just because she'd blown the onsight. I remembered how hard she had tried, how hard she had charged. She hadn't given up just because she'd fallen. Kye, neither. Glenn and Fred and James never fell, not on the climbs that I could do with them. The whole summer in the Valley, I hadn't seen Harold or Will or Ian or Scott fall, either. It probably wasn't even allowed, in Britain. But I had two examples of what to do if you did blow the onsight, how to keep trying even after you'd already kind of failed. And I had that *good oxygen*. I took a few slow breaths, then a few fast ones.

Some other day, Glenn had told me some theory about breathing fast, to force more oxygen into your blood. It sounded like one of the many supposed childbirth breathing techniques that my now-childbearing friend group were telling me were all bullshit. Hypnobirthing? Bullshit. Lamaze? Bullshit. I wasn't going to take any stupid birthing classes if I actually got to do it. My intention was to scream my babies forth like I was in the upper deck of a Mets game or the mosh pit of a punk show in a basement club in Germany. That was my whole, secret future birth plan. Screaming at the top of my lungs.

I thought breathing techniques were bullshit, too, but now I did Glenn's thing. It sort of happened naturally. It was kind of like "breath of fire" in yoga, or some other culturally-appropriated method by which San Francisco tech douches tried to force more money into their blood and more blood into their money. This was all *mental*, anyway. This really was mental. Totally mental.

I didn't plan to start yelling, it just came out of me. At first I didn't even realize that it was me. But then I heard the others, down below, yelling with me. We were all yelling.

It worked. I got past the stuck part. I found a new place to stand on and a new thing to hold on to. And then another, and another. It wasn't impossible, not at all. It was possible. It was easy. It had all been mental.

I was charging so hard that I forgot to stop and place a piece and had to be reminded. The next placement was bomber, and the next after that, and I was up on the top in no time.

It was the same time of day as it had been when I'd first topped out the Thin Wall, on toprope, two years before. The golden hour, just before sunset. I wasn't even all the way on top of Chimney Rock, just at the top of this one route, The Flue. But I could still see how tiny we all were, how silly this all was. I clipped myself in to the bolted anchor and felt something orders of magnitude beyond anything I'd ever experienced on a toprope, or even leading the easier climbs. It wasn't just a rush but a flood, an influx of relief, power, freedom, and joy. I had faltered, but I had not failed. I had fallen, but I had not given up, given in, turned back, or backed down.

"I made it to the top," I whispered. That was all I had to say to myself, as I half wept, half laughed, at the top of a two-star 5.8 any Stonemaster, Rock Monkey, or crusher kid would surely free solo.

Glenn lowered me down and gave me a high five and a burning doob. Fred tied in to check and clean my gear and pronounced all my placements "good," even the marginal one.

"Marginal, but *good*," he said, beaming with pride I could feel, washing away all of my doubt like water.

I WAS NEVER BAT MITZVAHED. My vocally irreligious family believed in nothing but natural childbirth, vitamin supplements, and the New York Mets. I was glad for this, because I have always believed that all organized religion is violently and immorally patriarchal, and much of it murderous, or genuinely perverted in the worst ways. But, lacking for faith, my family lacked for rites of passage. There was no clear event to mark the transition to adulthood, and even if there were, my parents would never have truly let me go.

It was Passover, I realized, though no one else in the campground was Jewish. I hated that holiday, always had and still do. The believers said it was all about freedom, but if you actually read the story, it was about praying to God to free you by killing other people's children.

But this—this was a truly tribal rite. What the Jews were meant to do in the desert. Not pray to some fake God for a real brown child to die and then pretend their murder was our freedom and God's love, as the Passover horror story annually celebrated in cheerful song, but to take matters into our own hands, to save our own lives, to set our own damned selves free.

That night around Glenn's fire, the dirtbag mafia raised their ever-present Sierra Nevada Pale Ales to me.

"Hip, hip, hooray!" Glenn led them in cheering, three times. And that was it. There was no diploma, no medal, no trophy, no certificate. All I got was a beer and a cheer, and the chance to do it all again the next day, when Leila finally told her secret.

"I'm pregnant!" she announced breathlessly to Glenn, as she styled her way to the top of another one of my early leads.

"Mazel tov," said Glenn, looking at me for confirmation. "That's what I say, right?"

He handed her his water bottle. "In that case," he said, "you should hydrate."

Then Leila went back to New York, and I dragged the mattress back into SubyRuby. On the nights I led, I slept like the dead, as if the danger and thrill of it finally exhausted my demons, and they rested, too.

The night of my first lead—my climbing bat mitzvah—before I passed out, I had the clear and present thought that I'd never before achieved anything so cool by fucking up so much. This was better than religion, better than Judaism, better than Passover, better than a bat mitzvah. This was real liberation, the kind that didn't hurt anybody— the kind that truly set you free.

9

Rack

OVER INDEPENDENCE DAY WEEKEND a few months after my climbing bat mitzvah in Joshua Tree, I went with James and his two friends, Jacob and Clark, to climb in an area called Patricia Bowl, on the east side of the Sierra, past the important Mobil station and toward the rest of America. Compared to the greener, wetter western slope of the Sierra one first encountered when approaching from the San Francisco Bay, the east side was grayer, drier, and steeper. The line of demarcation between the two was the ridgeline of the Sierra Crest itself.

Since we'd met, via James, in the shirtless drumming fire cave the previous New Year's in Joshua Tree, Jacob, Clark, and I had coalesced into a tight crew. We spoke in a secret sibling language of inside jokes and self-help psych. We climbed together once or twice a week at the gym in the Bay, and one or two weekends a month, outside, in silent agreement to be continually and mutually stoked.

At Patricia Bowl, I led the one 5.8 at the crag where James and Jacob hung the rope on the 5.10s with ease. I got lost on the approach on the way up the steep trail to the cliff, almost circumnavigating the cirque, a ring of rock eroded by ancient glaciers. I was so much weaker and slower than the rest of any group with which I climbed that I frequently got lost on the approach. Clark was a distance runner who woke up every morning before dawn and ran for miles, at altitude, before breakfast, and James and Jacob seemed to hike at the same pace no matter how many fifty-fifties we smoked at every opportunity. The boys seemed genuinely relieved when I finally found them, and claimed to have been worried about my whereabouts—though not so worried that they didn't climb a couple of routes while I found my own way.

When it was time for my lead, James queued up a soothing playlist and Bluetoothed it to his portable speaker, then hung the gear sling around his own neck and came over to me so I could rack from it, selecting the gear I wanted to use for the climb and clipping it to my own harness. We were still hooking up then, or we were on that trip, wrestling some nights according to no discernible pattern on my dumpstered futon. The smell and warmth of his body made me dizzier and thirstier than the altitude already had.

"I feel like I'm shopping," I said, as the carabiners click-clacked between us.

"Shopping for your *life*," laughed James.

I wondered, fleetingly, whether we would still be hooking up if I hadn't gone so all in on his death wish, then selected a blue Alien James grabbed back, shaking his head. "You won't need that," he said. "I've soloed this."

The music from the Bluetooth speaker echoed off the shaded stone as I started up the wall.

"Yeah, Em," one of the boys said, occasionally, as I spaced out the gear a little farther this time, though I never weighted it, and got the onsight.

"Nice, Em," said the boys, when I came down.

I HAD MY OWN ROPE and had already whipped on it, but I still didn't have my own rack, a complete collection of my own protective, life-saving gear to attach myself and the full, nearly two-hundred-foot length of my rope to the wall, at body-length distances. I had a few pieces of "bootied" gear, equipment that other climbers had found, left behind, stuck in the rock, and managed to free. Plus, I had the red Alien I had bought, brand-new, from Spain, after I saw, climbing On the Lamb in Tuolumne, how much Fred valued his.

"Just get doubles," Glenn had suggested, meaning two of each size. Doubles would be a lot of cams, or at least enough. "Get doubles on a pro deal. Sawyer's got one. Use his."

A pro deal was a steep discount from a gear company, offered to guides and ambassadors and other professionals of the sport. Sawyer was the crusher kid who'd been hobbling around that past spring in Joshua Tree, flirting with me or simply grinning at me, I couldn't tell which. I'd thought he was in his early twenties, maybe just out of college, but on the last night of the desert trip, he'd mentioned that he was eighteen, and my jaw had literally dropped. He'd dropped out of *high school* to become a dirtbag, not college. Horrified, I'd gone home and confided to a female friend close to my own age that I felt like a pedophile for even having considered it.

"I'm thirty-three!" I exclaimed. "Eighteen is a *teenager*! I can't have sex with a *teenager*! I didn't even have sex when I *was* a teenager!"

"Emily," she intoned gravely, "these are some of the last years of our *lives* we can sleep with eighteen-year-olds."

The eighteen-year-old had messaged me from Glenn's off-the-grid cash crop farm in Mendocino, saying that if I came through, he'd buy my rack for me online with his pro deal if I paid with my credit card. "Missing ya, sister," he'd signed it, which I found inscrutable but interesting. I hadn't picked a weekend for this mission until, on a girls' trip to hot springs, also in Mendocino, I had improbably met an Israeli at the Mendocino County Fair.

I'd been standing between the prizewinning kale and a trifold billboard warning of the dangers of smoking meth while pregnant, complete with distressed plastic fetuses glued to the cardboard—when I heard the unmistakably guttural sound of spoken Hebrew. The voice was coming from an animated ginger fellow, but when I turned in its direction, I saw only the blue eyes and dark stubble—Robbie's coloring, though the face was open and the eyes were kind. I smiled, almost involuntarily, and he was smiling back before the guy who was actually talking saw me looking and said, "I bet you don't know what language we're speaking."

"It's Hebrew," I said, and the blue eyes crinkled at the edges.

"How do you know that?"

"Because I'm Emily Weinstein from Queens."

The one who was looking at me was named Yoav. We somehow exchanged information amid the loud, aggressive Hebrew. I had to drive my girlfriends back to their real jobs in the Bay, and he was going back to Israel at the end of the month, but we quickly made a plan to meet up the following weekend, again in Mendocino. That was when I'd messaged back the crusher kid with the pro deal and said I'd be up at the farm on Sunday.

YOAV MET ME AT A POST OFFICE that was the entirety of a small town in his American friend's borrowed Burning Man van, an eighties- or nineties-era Dodge that was carpeted inside on every possible surface. His manner was shy, but his movements were swift. With the efficiency of a trained relocator, he wordlessly reached into my car and grabbed one of the wicker baskets I used to organize my things, then marched it over to the borrowed Burning Man van and came back for more. He somehow managed to transfer all the stuff I had in the Suby into the Burning Man van himself, taking even the things I hadn't wanted him to take.

We drove toward the coast on a two-lane highway that snaked through the redwoods from the 101, stopping at a vineyard and a goat farm to buy wine and cheese. Then we went out to the beach to watch the sunset on a blanket.

"I think it might rain," I said.

"Then we'll dance in the rain," he said with a shrug.

Instead, as soon as it was dark, we made love in the sand.

We stayed on the beach until it began to rain in earnest. When we got back to the Burning Man van in the parking lot, we were met by the bright lights of several state park rangers.

"Park's closed," said one of them. "Can't sleep here."

"We're leaving," Yoav said softly. "Right now."

"Can't smoke weed here, either," said another one.

Yoav, standing in the cop light, faced the direction of the voice and slowly opened his arms and both sides of his jacket, turning in a slow circle to show he had nothing on him, a peaceful gesture of supplication before the long tool arm of the idiot law. I wondered if Yoav had learned the move from making other people do it, at gunpoint. It was as if all the war had made him extra peaceful, like Wade the US Marine.

"Park's closed," said the voice again.

We got into the borrowed Burning Man van, and I told him to drive up Highway 1, where I knew an apple orchard in a ghost town I thought we could sleep in.

"Man," I grumbled. "I hate rangers. Fucking tools."

"We trained with some rangers," Yoav said mildly. "Nice guys. Your guys."

I thought for a moment and realized he meant Army Rangers, elite units of the US Army, while I was talking about park rangers. I had climbed with an Army Ranger, once. He'd been trained to climb by the military, on beige ropes that blended into the occupied deserts, so he could stay for days in little sand cave pods, waiting to possibly kill somebody. He told me that when the operation was over, they'd buried the gear in the sand before they hiked out, so as not to give away the position.

"Those rangers just now weren't the same kind of Rangers," I explained. "Those were *tools*."

Yoav chuckled. "You have a lot of fire," he said, "for someone who has never seen war."

I almost asked him if he thought that what he had done was really war, or if it was something worse, but it felt like we were far away from wars, and even words.

WE SPENT THE NIGHT in the apple orchard in decadent Burning Man van warmth, while it rained and rained and rained, sleeping only in brief interludes. When I woke in the damp, gray dawn, he was sitting on the van's doorstep, brewing coffee and smiling and whittling with an actual knife. (He'd started his trip in America by shooting a moose in Alaska.) After breakfast, we took a long walk on the beach, peering into empty houses and discussing which ones we would buy.

We didn't talk much about where he was from, but I was desperate to ask him what he'd done, and why he'd done it, because he was so kind—gentle, even. It didn't come up until he mentioned he was in his late twenties, not his early ones. In my previous travels, I'd encountered many Israelis in nearly every foreign city and beach town, all on long trips after finishing their military service, Jewish Rumspringas on which Palestinians were curiously never invited. When I asked why he was older than the usual Rumspringa Israeli, he told me he'd spent extra time in the military, in the Special Forces.

"Whoa," I said. "You must have seen some things."

"Yes," he replied.

"And done some things."

He nodded.

"Why'd you do it?" I asked. "Whatever you did."

"I thought I had to," he said. "To protect my family."

He thought. So he knew.

But it was the wrong question. I should have asked him if he was busy the next night. But I already had plans, to go up to Glenn's farm and buy my rack on Sawyer the crusher kid's pro deal.

I CROSSED THE HIGHWAY 101 and headed for the county's vast interior, where Glenn's farm was located half an hour up a dirt road, outside a tiny town that was itself an hour's drive up a steep, two-lane road from the 101 dotted with roadside memorials to car crash victims. I'd been to Glenn's farm a couple of times before, once when I'd met Tori Lutz and she'd told me not to move the straw in her yerba maté, and another time, when the now-late Ammon McNeely, the El Cap Pirate, showed me the scar where the Yosemite tools had tased him for illegally BASE jumping in the park.

This time, I recognized the one reflector that marked the turn between thick trees, and for the first time, didn't miss it.

"Muscle memory," the climbers were always saying.

There had been a slight misunderstanding the first time I'd gone to Glenn's farm. He'd invited me there, soon after I'd met him and Fred in Joshua Tree.

"I'm only inviting you, though," Glenn said. "Not anyone else."

"Okay," I said. "I won't bring anyone else."

I'd arrived at the farm and taken a tour. There were huge, healthy pot plants growing in what Glenn called "the garden," where he slept in the center in a real bed in a gazebo, and there was even a lower garden down a hill, with its own cabin, where someone else was growing their own crop. There was a trim room with a big table, where several young hippies and climbers were shaping raw stalks of marijuana into nugs for sale, throwing each completed ganja bonsai into a large plastic bag at their feet that Glenn would weigh at the end of the day, paying them by the pound. After we left the trim room, Glenn whispered the bona fides of the climbers around his trim table, this one just back from a first ascent in Patagonia, that one saving up to make a second attempt on some peak in the Himalayas.

I followed him and Fred up to a loft above the workshop, a big building the size of a small church or school gymnasium where the weed was drying, everywhere, hanging from clotheslines like allergenic Christmas garlands. In such quantity, it stung my eyes and throat, even uncombusted.

We'd been hanging out in the loft for the better part of the afternoon, smoking weed and talking shit, when Glenn said, "You know, it's fine if you want to hang out, but most people don't come here to hang out."

"Why do they come here?" I asked.

"To work," said Glenn. "To trim."

"Ohhhhh," I said, realizing his confusion. "I'm not—I don't—I don't work . . . for other people. I have my own job. I work for myself."

(I considered my self-employment as a tutor of teenagers part of my anarchism. One of my favorite lyrics from my favorite punk band was simply the shouted words: "I DON'T WORK FOR YOU.")

"But," I added, remembering the unwritten code of the anarchist-hippie collectivist spirit, "maybe I can help out. Like, alphabetize the library."

"Sure," said Glenn. "You can alphabetize the library."

I tried to trim the weed but didn't have much flair for it. But, eventually, I discovered a way I could help out around the farm. It was the early days of podcasts, which ran all day in the trim room. One afternoon on an earlier visit, I'd wandered in there, taken a few bong hits, and started talking to the trimmers. Someone had turned off the podcasts and reported that night at communal dinner that my stoned rambling was "better than a podcast," a compliment I treasure to this day.

THE CREW WAS THIN THIS YEAR, Glenn reported when I arrived Sunday night, after my one-night stand in the Burning Man van, so they would each work longer hours, trim more weed, and make more money. It was almost dark when I arrived, and still raining, but the trimmers were doing an after-dinner shift.

A thunderstorm raged outside while I provided conversational podcast alternatives. Sawyer, the crusher kid, was making heart-hug hands over his actual heart at me across the table, looking at me with guileless man-child eyes.

As the trim room emptied out, Sawyer said something to me about the location of his van. I couldn't tell if he was telling me I should park near it or sleep in it. But finally, he took me by the hand and led me, through the downpour, through some mud and some puddles, into the dark field, where the van was warm and dry.

"YOU THOUGHT I WAS OLDER." Sawyer laughed later, as we passed a joint, wrapped in the whispering fabric of a single high-end extra-long pro-dealed sleeping bag. "I saw you. When you found out I was eighteen, your jaw dropped. I *saw* it."

"I thought you were, like, twenty-four," I said. "I thought the age difference was more reasonable, like, less than ten years."

"Well," said Sawyer, deftly levitating me back atop him, though we had only just collapsed, "I turned *nine*teen, so I'm older now!"

I thought about trying to explain to Sawyer that though he was older now, I, too, was also *the same amount* older, but math and time didn't seem relevant, and it was already too late for more talking, and the rain pounding down on the van's hard metal drowned out all the softer sounds inside.

THE NEXT DAY, in the trim room, at Glenn's breakfast suggestion, everyone brought in their racks and threw them in the center of the table.

"Get to know the gear," said Glenn. "See what you like."

There were piles and piles of it, some old and some new. I was going to get Camalot doubles, this had been decided. But what did I want for "small stuff"? Did I want Aliens? Did I want offsets? Did I want offset *nuts*?

The risking-my-life part, I was down for. The having-sex-in-cars-parked-in-remote-rural-and-wilderness-areas part, I'd taken to with ease. Sleeping in the dirt soothed my soul, and I was pleased to see that petty theft and low-grade rule-breaking was part of dirtbag culture, never having believed in the concept of property nor the rule of law. I loved the people and culture of climbing, the itinerant, traveling lifestyle, the way everyone was an accidental Buddhist because you had to get a little bit enlightened, just to do it, and doing it further enlightened you. But this was something I had not bargained for—the need to understand, purchase, use, and maintain tools.

My father and brother were both epic maker-builder-woodworkers. They could and would build anything—custom furniture, modifications to and improvements on store-bought machines and gadgets, whole speaker systems from scratch. My brother had once put my car on a lift and tried to show me, uselessly, how to do something important to my own brakes. They both had every tool. Every size and type of screwdriver. Little briefcases full of wrenches. Giant, terrifying sharp and motorized objects I was afraid to touch, even under supervision. I'm sure if I'd wanted to learn, my dad would have taught me, but I honestly preferred that he just do it for me, and he did. In all of my dorm rooms and Brooklyn apartments, he'd helped me build and install bookshelves and bed frames and desks made out of doors I'd found on the street, made clothes-hanging poles out of metal pipes, painted and repainted and bolted things to walls. All of it felt like love made tangible, surrounding me with comfortable, helpful, useful, beautiful things. But I had never thought of myself as a buyer or owner or user of tools before.

"I don't do DIY," I joked. "I'm into YDI—*you* do it."

But now I had found something I wanted to do, with tools. Simple machines, really. I understood these tools. I understood how they worked. I understood how they fit together and how they came apart. I had memorized angles and learned to gauge by eye or feel which one fit where.

There was a guy in the trim room I'd never met before, named Kyle. He was quiet at first, but when we started talking about the gear, he lit up. He showed me the offset cams and the offset nuts, explained the difference between them and the regular kind, and then recited from memory all the places on all the different climbs I had already done that each individual piece of gear would fit. He seemed to have an encyclopedic mind for the mountains themselves, like they were all contained inside his brain. He had his own inventions, ways he had come up with to use the tools and cords and slings and ropes that made new things possible. Kyle and Sawyer had a long conversation about some certain kind of device they both used, to climb "light and fast," "alpine style," in the mountains.

It took most of the day, but with the help of the group, I fine-tuned my shopping list. I got out my laptop and got on the Wi-Fi and put all the Camalots in the cart. Sawyer held my hand and kissed my knuckles each time I clicked on a new piece, shopping for my life. I bought two of each, like Noah's ark, but Sawyer had one edit. Still holding my knuckles to his lips, he reached out his other hand and removed one of my number 3s, the biggest, blue cam, from the cart.

"Those are really big," he said, sweetly. "Really heavy. You don't need two of those. Only one."

I did need two of those, it turned out later. Sawyer only needed one number 3 cam because he free soloed so much that he barely placed any gear even on the rare occasions he used a rope. As a scandalously older woman who climbed like the Jewish grandmother she hoped to one day become, I definitely need two number 3s. I had to buy the second one later, at full price.

I'D PLANNED TO HEAD BACK to the Bay on Monday, before I had come to know the specifics of Sawyer's van. Now that I knew about the van, I decided, on impulse, to stay another night, not remembering that I had told my brother I'd be back from my trip on Monday and maybe we'd get dinner.

The rain stopped, overnight, and the morning dawned sunny, but we did not exit Sawyer's van until nearly noon. It had no windows in the back, and curtains in the front for stealthiness, and until Sawyer kicked the back hatch open with his enormous, bare, black-soled foot, it was too dark inside for me to make out the words on the book that was tucked behind some of the interior bedside metal. As the sunlight blasted in, I saw the words, "PATIENT, HEAL THYSELF!"

I read the words aloud and looked quizzically at Sawyer.

"Yeah!" he said, stretching affably and chuckling. "So you don't need *doctors.*"

I made some coffee and wandered into the garden.

"Oh, good," said Glenn, passing by with a load of lumber on his shoulder, "you're up. Now can you call your parents and tell them I haven't kidnapped you before they call the state police and send them to my house?"

"What?"

"I think your parents think I am keeping you in a hole, like in *Silence of the Lambs.*"

I quickly pieced together what had happened. My brother, expecting me back Monday, had texted about dinner. Glenn's farm was off the grid, so I had not yet received the text. My brother had mentioned to my parents back in New York that he'd thought I'd said I'd be back Monday, but added that I hadn't answered his text, and therefore was not back, which caused them to feel the need to confirm my location immediately. When I did not answer their text, they made further moves. It was known that I was going to Mendocino, possibly even known that I was going to Glenn's farm. So my brother, or my parents, had somehow figured out how to message Glenn on social media, of which he was an avid user, to ask if I was there.

But this was the crazy part: when Glenn messaged back that yes, I was there, had stayed the night but just hadn't yet appeared that morning, they hadn't accepted this as proof of life. In their panic, they had asked—possibly demanded—that Glenn have me call them immediately. And they didn't even know about the Special Forces Israeli in the Burning Man van!

Glenn had not explained to them that I was currently within the confines of a blacked-out white van, tucked among the trees on the far end of his field, now muddy after several days of rain. Glenn had not, to his credit, come a-knockin' on the door of said van, a-rockin' or not. Though it was the height of trim season and Glenn's daughter was also nine months pregnant—and planning to birth right there on the farm, where she herself had been birthed in a school bus, before the big house got built—Glenn had respected my privacy until I emerged, even as the threat of some law enforcement agency storming the not-entirely-legal cash crop farm loomed over the day's project, which was to complete the birthing room for his daughter before her labor began.

"Use the landline," he instructed. "Call your parents."

I figured out how to text or email or message them using the Wi-Fi, explaining that I was fine, had stayed an extra day, and would be back later that same day, to tutor the next day. I went back to the garden with my coffee, where the thin staff of this year's grow was clipping stalks from the big plants with a different model of the same brand of orange-handled scissors they used to trim the nugs.

"Did you not see your parents for a really long time?" an accomplished alpinist asked politely, not breaking the steady rhythm of his shears. "Is that why they're trying to track you down? Because once, I hitchhiked down to Patagonia and I didn't have a phone and I didn't want to waste money on a phone card, so I just didn't talk to my parents for like a year, and after a while, they started looking for me."

"No," I sighed. "I talked to my parents a few days ago."

More than one head swiveled, more than one pair of orange-handled weed-trimming shears paused in midair.

"Then why are they looking for you?" asked the same curious climber.

"Because we are Jewish," I answered. "And very anxious, and afraid of death."

"That's actually also why Israel is doing apartheid genocide in Palestine," I added.

"I try not to get too political," the alpinist shrugged. "It's really negative. Lots of fear."

WHAT I DID NOT EXPLAIN to the curious climbers and accomplished alpinists in the Mendocino marijuana garden was that my parents had done this before—several times. Once, when I didn't respond quickly enough to an email they sent while I was traveling with Leila and her then-boyfriend in Peru while also, coincidentally, ensconced on an off-the-grid farm with a man of at least passing interest (the expatriate ex-Marine), they had called Leila's parents, two calm WASPs who drank cold martinis every night at six o'clock sharp. My parents even managed to panic the WASPs.

So much of what they said and did felt like infinite love to me, except for this part. This part felt like fear.

As the seasonally employed alpinists turned back to their labors, I pondered the irony of my parents' obsession with my safety, when I had just bought a whole box full of bright, colorful aluminum devices that I would soon use to stitch myself to vertical walls with my very own sixty-meter length of bright green rope. Somehow, I did not think my parents would take much comfort in the fact that I was getting this equipment at a steep discount.

At Patricia Bowl, on July Fourth weekend, I had debated, with Jacob and Clark, whether to get my own rack, since James let us borrow his.

"If you can get it on pro deal, then you should definitely do it," advised Jacob.

"Why's that?" I asked. "What for?"

"Independence," said Jacob. "It's independence."

10

Whip

THE BOX WAS WAITING FOR ME on the steps of the tiny cabin one night when I got home from the gym. Each Camalot was wrapped in its own plastic bag. Each came with its own thick booklet of warnings and instructions. There were illustrations showing "good" placements, marked with green check marks, and "bad" ones, with red X's, and skulls and crossbones.

I had already learned everything it said in the booklet, in the real world. The green check mark was what Fred meant by "Make it good."

The gear arrived just in time for a weekend trip to Sugarloaf, a sunny crag, even in winter, on the south side of Lake Tahoe, with Clark and Jacob and Jacob's new climbing buddy and not-quite-girlfriend, Summer. James couldn't come, but he called the night before to wish me luck.

"I'll need it," I said. "I just got my own cams."

"Now you can take *huge falls* on them," he chuckled.

"They say learning to lead is the most dangerous time in your climbing career," I fretted.

"Well, you're well past *that*," James replied charitably, though I had only ever led one 5.8 without falling before, and partly because he'd been watching, and I'd wanted him to think I was invincible, or immortal, or some other thing that no human being could be. I thought that if

I did something impressive or suicidal enough, he might like me more, or treat me better, or fuck me more often, and I still did not understand that being liked or treated well or even considered fuckable were not, actually, things you had to earn.

IT WAS A LONG, steep hike up to Sugarloaf, but I didn't get lost this time. It had been decided at the gym earlier in the week that a three-star 5.8 called Pony Express should be my next quarry. Clark and Jacob disappeared around the formation toward a 5.10, leaving Summer and me alone with our business.

Summer, I'd learned on the drive up, *lived* in Yosemite—she was a naturalist who went out on long wilderness backpacking trips for her actual job. She was a strong climber—she climbed Valley granite most days, after work—but she never led. She could have, without ever falling, as she followed 5.11, a much harder grade than I could climb, without weighting the rope. But, Jacob had already confided, she didn't have the "head" for it. She would theoretically never fall, because she was so strong and athletic that even legitimately hard climbs were easy for her, at least physically. But she cried and shook when she tried to climb above her gear. It was the mental game. The lead head.

That was what I supposedly had, in addition to the green rope my brother had bought with his REI dividend and the primary-colored gear I had bought on Sawyer's pro deal—some semblance of a "lead head." The ability to put the gear in the rock, and *make it good*, and then trust that it was—trust yourself, to place the gear correctly, and trust the rock not to break. Trust in your own ability to climb, and to think clearly enough to solve a series of puzzles, to keep yourself from splattering on the ground if you fell and becoming what Fred called "strawberry jam."

It was easy to make myself do it—I wanted to, even. I thought maybe, on the other side of the fear, the fall, the void, there might be something that felt like love, or better yet, an escape from my constant longing for it.

I did not have Summer's rude youth or mountain fitness or nearly Olympian athleticism. All I had was a greater willingness to step just a little bit closer to becoming "strawberry jam," and then try to put my proximity to that possibility completely out of my mind.

WHAT THE GUIDEBOOK DESCRIBED as "an obvious flake" beckoned in the afternoon sun. It was a continuous, zigzagging, not-quite-vertical crack. I was only going to climb one rope length, or really half of one, as I would need the other half to get back down.

The rope was all in a pile on the ground. I would be the one to take it up there, and this time, no one who knew any better than I did would be watching.

I tied my shoes with shaking hands and checked my knot and Summer's belay device three times each before chalking my hands three times more.

"You got this," said Summer.

"I hope so," I said.

Once I started up, I couldn't believe that what I was doing was allowed. I wished even one guy were watching, not to provide safety but to open the door to danger, so I could forget my fear and lean into my own boy-crazy desire to impress with my death wish. But then I forgot about who was or wasn't watching, and began to enjoy the simple solitude. Summer's voice was so kind, so encouraging, even as it grew more distant. As I climbed higher, I felt less lonely, though I was getting farther away from the one other person on God's green earth who knew where I was at this exact moment. I was tied to her, for lifesaving reasons, but I felt less worried about life the higher I went. It was like a weight incrementally lifted with each piece I placed in the rock, as if each body length or building story of upward progress I made lightened the burden of atmospheric pressure on my shoulders. I could do this forever.

Then I came to the business, which was what we called the hard part, or crux.

It was more serious business than I'd seen before. The hard part ahead looked longer and more demanding than the easier hard parts of routes I'd climbed before. It had fewer resting places, and more uncertain-looking hands.

I was standing on the last little ledge. There was certainly gear to be had. I reached up as high as I could, placed the blue Camalot that was wider than my fist, and pulled on it to see if I thought it could hold my life.

"Bomber," I murmured, comforted by the sound of my own voice whispering this word to the granite. I clipped the shiny silver carabiner to the cam's brand-new bright blue webbing. I extended the still-white sling with its absurd red stripe as far as it went. I pulled up my green rope from between my legs and clipped it to the shiny silver carabiner. I was protected. Even if the weight of my plummeting body went literally screaming past this blue thing, and then pulled on it with all the falling force of its earthbound mass, multiplied by the acceleration of gravity's only desire, to bring and hold matter to earth, the Camalot would definitely "hold." I checked several times that it was placed exactly like the picture in the folded instruction booklet. It was textbook. Trucker. Bomber. Trustworthy. *Good.*

"Watch me here!" I yelled down to Summer, more gaily and nonchalantly than I felt on the inside.

"Got you," she said. "You got this."

Looking down at Summer turned my gaze from the rock wall to which I was clinging to the beauty all around—the snowcapped pine forests of Tahoe and the church-white Sierras ramping skyward like stairways to heaven. It was almost distracting, being in a place so beautiful, doing a thing so dangerous.

IN MY SENIOR YEAR OF HIGH SCHOOL, not six months after I got my driver's license, I totaled the family station wagon on my way to a calculus test for which I had not studied. I was making a left turn against oncoming traffic when a UPS truck ran a red light and slammed into the Ford Taurus, sending it spinning through the intersection, only coming to rest after taking out three parking meters.

My life really did flash before my eyes. I had two clear, simultaneous thoughts: *It was all so beautiful* and *I can't believe I'm going to die a virgin.*

I would have been at peace with it, except for the part where I'd only kissed five people and never had sex, but I didn't die a virgin. I walked away with little more than the airbag's brand name stamped, backward, into the flesh of my hand, and a sprained ankle that was not, technically, a casualty of the accident itself. (Mistaking the smell of the air bags' gunpowder for a sign that the car was on fire, I'd kicked frantically at the mangled door, injuring my foot in the process of freeing myself before the paramedics got there.) An ambulance came and took me to a nearby Catholic hospital, where everyone kept asking if I could possibly be pregnant before they would x-ray my swelling ankle to see if it was broken. I was tempted to tell them I'd conceived immaculately, from making out with Christopher Christensen, the fifth person I had kissed, on his bed, underneath a crucifix, one weekday afternoon when his parents weren't home.

I walked away from the smashed up station wagon with a piece of important knowledge I hadn't had before. Death wasn't necessarily scary, or even sad, if you were the person busy dying.

While the car had been spinning and the glass had been breaking and the metal had been crunching and the sounds were all around, I had been at the calm center of it. It was an oddly religious experience, though it had nothing to do with God, unless God was the force that was making me feel so completely unafraid, so wholly at peace. I was grateful for all seventeen years and five months of my short life, almost relieved that I would never have to grow old, or even finish growing up. For the first time in years, I forgot all about college, where, after all that, I'd never go. I was thinking, as usual, about sex and love, but now I was finally thinking about life instead of death.

It was a long trip through the intersection in slow time. It felt like a joke, how life only made sense if you were staring death in the face. *I can't believe I wasted all that time*, I grinned. *How silly of me. I get it now.*

When I came to rest and wasn't dead, I was scared again, scared the car was on fire, scared I was injured in some way I hadn't noticed yet, scared the accident was my fault. Years later, when I met hippies who waxed poetic about how various hallucinogenic drugs were actually the same stuff that got released in your body at the moment of death, I wondered if my overeager adolescent brain had started the process. The memory of the second or two it took to smash up the station wagon lodged in my reptile mind like a secret, or a siren song.

Death wasn't scary. It was the fear of it that was.

And besides, as adventurous people were always quick to point out, you could totally die, just driving a car.

The next day, my dad marched me, on my crutches, out to the remaining car I hadn't totaled, and handed me the keys.

"Can't be afraid," he said. "Can't give up."

Sometimes, my parents gave me their fear, but other times, they gave me their courage.

NOW, JUST BELOW THE CRUX AT SUGARLOAF, twice as old as the seventeen-year-old who hadn't died a virgin, I mustered the courage to climb beyond the shiny object, to another place where I could free a hand and insert another shiny object. There was a place, up above, where this appeared possible.

I coaxed myself above the gear, into the hard part, charging past the piece without fear or trembling. But the next rest did not present itself as easily. It was not as close as I had hoped, nor was I moving as fast as I would have liked to be. The crack I was climbing had changed size and shape and no longer held my hands and feet so perfectly in its comforting grip. What had been working just moments ago was no longer working as well.

My hands were slipping. My feet scrabbled for purchase.

I wanted to hold on. I willed myself to hold on. But I couldn't.

It felt good to even start to stop trying, for once. Free.

Screaming wordlessly, I hurtled, once again thinking two clear and simultaneous thoughts: *I hope I did everything right* and *That was a good run.*

The pines and peaks went by in a beautiful blur. I had no regrets, no wish to be anywhere else. It was happening so fast, but my mind and soul were in the slow and okay place. It was okay right now and always had been and always would be. Even if this was the end, that was actually also okay.

It was okay I was falling, okay that I might die. It was okay that I'd failed to *just hold on*; it was good that I had tried to *make it good*; it was a relief to be plummeting, a thrill to have finally let go.

IT WAS CALLED "TAKING A WHIPPER," or "taking the whip," or "going for a ride" or "getting some air," and now I understood why. I understood why people jumped out of things, or off things, why they tried to fly, even though they were always really doing what I was doing—falling. It felt like the air itself had been cracked by a whip, into an invisible before and after balanced on the tipping point of my failure of grip.

In the summer of 1970, my mother's boyfriend's VW bus stalled out on the train tracks, as the bells rang and the whistle blew and the lights of the oncoming train grew closer—but the engine sprang to life just in time. In the winter of 1944–45, my grandfather's unit got surrounded by Nazis, in the same dark European woods from which he and his parents had already fled the Ukrainians' and Poles' pogroms when he was an infant, but the next morning, the Nazis were gone.

These and all my other ancestors had come all this way through all this threat and terror and given me life and eight years of orthodontia and four years of debt-free Ivy League college education so I could hang my life on a green rope from a piece of blue metal I jammed into a granite crack. A thousand generations of Jews and fifteen thousand dollars of orthodontia and a hundred twenty thousand dollars in higher education, I was frequently reminded—and now all of that capital investment was suspended, at my leanest and meanest hundred twenty-seven pounds, hanging from a point in the Sierra Nevada so high I could see for miles and miles and miles and miles.

I dangled, dazed, from the number 3, more exhilarated than frightened.

"That's the coolest thing I've ever seen," said Summer, holding the rope that had broken my fall.

"In some ways," I said, "that's the coolest thing I've ever done."

Fear always tasted like metal in my mouth, but this freedom was sweet. Taking a whipper was suicide you survived. It leased you your life, again and again.

Boys were watching, it turned out. Jacob and Clark could see us from where they were climbing, and were hooting and hollering and cheering for me, for taking the whip. They managed to make it over to us before I went to the top and made the anchor and came down, in time to leave a freshly rolled spliff in the crack for me. Then Jacob climbed on my toprope and cleaned my gear.

"All of it was good," he said, as he lowered off with the colorful pieces of my new rack, "but you knew that. That part where you fell was probably rattly hands for you, huh?"

He squeezed my shoulder affectionately. "Sometimes I forget that you're really just a little guy."

We hiked down from Sugarloaf and made it almost all the way back to the Bay before my ankle blew up and turned purple. I'd whacked it in the fall but hadn't even noticed.

"Adrenaline," said Jacob, when I wondered, at the In-N-Out Burger, why it had taken so long to register. It reminded me of the car accident, half a lifetime ago, to have a smarting ankle and a new lease on life.

This failure hadn't killed me. This error wasn't fatal. It wasn't even, technically, an error. It was just a whipper.

I'd protected myself. *Saved* myself. Done everything right. Not perfectly—I'd blown the onsight, yet again—but *right*.

I'd survived my own death wish, by making it *good*. Good enough, which was all I had to do, to live.

11

Epic

I had really learned that you can't fall off a mountain.
Whether you can fall off a mountain or not, I don't know,
but I had learned that you can't.

—Jack Kerouac, THE DHARMA BUMS

I HAD HEARD THE TERM "EPIC" BEFORE, both in noun and verb form. It was something more serious than a "shenanigan," as in "I had to pull some shenanigans, but we managed not to epic." An epic was what happened when the shenanigans failed. An epic would be a mistake or bad luck that you paid for in hunger, thirst, time, pain, fatigue, and fear, in exchange for escaping with a story to tell.

Epics, as I heard them described around campfires, involved either many hours of unintentional, overnight, overland travel, or a "shiver bivy,"—bivouacking (sleeping) outside in the cold with no tent or sleeping bag, waiting out the darkness. You could get stuck, pretty much anywhere on the climb or the mountain, or wander "off route" on the climb and suddenly be faced with a blank, unclimbable wall, or you could get the rope stuck, or there could be weather, rockfall, accident, injury, or calamity. That was when you would start learning the shenanigans.

AFTER SEVERAL DROUGHT-RIDDEN WINTERS, Yosemite Valley was already hot and crowded when I made my way back there in mid-June, after preparing a half-dozen high school juniors for their SATs and spring semester finals by showing them pictures of my weekend climbing trips in my phone and exhorting them to release their fears. I was plenty keen to escape the crowds and heat by heading up to Tuolumne Meadows with Dave Gold to climb Eichorn's Pinnacle.

My original intention had been to climb Cathedral Peak, which I had not yet climbed. Cathedral Peak was a truly iconic nearly pyramid-shaped hunk of granite that loomed over Tuolumne Meadows, with two needles rising from its very pointed top. It looked like what you might imagine a mountain to look like, the pointy picture a kid might draw, the one that later became the emoji. The true summit of Cathedral Peak could be achieved by easy—entirely 5.6—climbing, and most hardpeople free soloed it exclusively and called it a "romp."

Eichorn's Pinnacle was a subsidiary rock spire on the same mountain that was slightly harder to climb. It was accessed by a different and slightly longer hike, and would therefore theoretically be less crowded. On a summer weekend, there could be lines at the base of any easier and therefore more popular climb, and part of the game was to figure out where you could enjoy a favorable balance of sun and shade without encountering too many tourists, noobs, gumbys (noobs), weekend warriors, or the dreaded gym climbers released into the wild. But realistically, you had to climb at least 5.11 to truly even begin to avoid weekend crowds. An alternative solution was to rearrange your entire life to climb only on weekdays.

At that point, I had only ever led 5.8 and followed 5.10, so I was hesitant to swing leads on the harder climb, Eichorn's Pinnacle. I hadn't yet led anything that hard (5.9) at that altitude (ten thousand feet). But Dave Gold said he'd rather ropegun (lead all the pitches on) all of

Eichorn's Pinnacle than spend a summer Sunday on the easiest route up Cathedral Peak.

I didn't know Dave Gold all that well, but he was not a rando. I'd met him a few times before, in Joshua Tree, and he was loosely connected to the wider world of all the people Glenn seemed to know everywhere. Dave Gold lived in a Volkswagen Eurovan on the streets of the posh Marin suburb where he taught kindergarten, and there was something childlike about him, though he was my age, mid-thirties. His *Sesame Street* demeanor could also have been the effects of another of his subcultures—he mentioned that he was an avid electronic dance music (EDM) festivalgoer and though he refused both weed and beer, he partook frequently of EDM's sister acronym, MDMA (ecstasy, in the parlance of my micro-generation), which seemed to have made him cheerful, if not outright giggly.

We got an early—but not alpine (middle of the night)—start, hiking in from the road and uphill from Tuolumne Meadows. Come mid-morning, at the base of Eichorn's Pinnacle, there was plenty of sports action already underway. There were several other parties on the route, each communicating (or miscommunicating) in their own native spoken and emotional languages.

There was a tense couple of fellow Americans, an impatient boyfriend aggressively encouraging his girlfriend to trust that her recently broken ankle had fully healed while she fought back tears on lead not twenty feet from the ground. Behind them in line was a petite, impatient woman irately naming to her beleaguered buddy all the other, better, harder routes they could and should have climbed instead today. Finally, some Euros appeared, fighting loudly in a Slavic language, until the chick convinced the dude to begin climbing off route, in an attempt to overtake the distressed American girlfriend, which failed when he found himself thirty feet up a blank slab with no place for gear.

We sat at the base in the hot sun, drinking too much of our water.

By the time the first pitch finally cleared of drama and Dave Gold set off on lead, it occurred to me, fleetingly, that it was no longer morning, or possibly even midday.

As the tugs came and the slack went, it was finally quiet. I could see the shadows lengthening as I cleaned the gear on my toprope and fed out the rope from my belay.

By the end of the third pitch, Dave was yelping, "Make haste! Make haste!" whenever I came into view, giggling like a madman. What did this giggle mean? Was it a crazed giggle? A fearful giggle? A gleeful giggle?

By the fourth pitch of five, the sky and the rock were pink. "Make haste!" Dave giggled, tugging. "Make haste!"

Finally, Dave yelped from the summit.

"Make haste!" he shouted.

It was twilight. As I followed the last pitch, the full moon rose over the spire. When I topped out, the sky was navy.

I sat astride the spire, benighted on a peak under the light of the full moon. It would have been the most perfect and complete moment of my life, if not for the looming question of how we were going to get down from the top of the mountain, in the dark.

I scuttled down from the summit to the bolted rap station, where Dave Gold had already efficiently threaded the rest of the rope through the rings. In the course of changing out of my climbing shoes and into the approach shoes (sneakers with climbing rubber soles) that were clipped to my harness, I dropped one of the approach shoes from the summit. It tumbled into an inaccessible gully, into the darkness, falling so far it became too small to see before it came to its inglorious rest. I started our descent in one approach shoe and one climbing shoe.

The first part was straightforward. There were bolts near the summit and we rappelled down to a notch on the steep side of the peak, where we unroped to begin, ostensibly, walking down the mountain.

"There are two descent options," I read aloud by headlamp from the guidebook I had insisted on bringing, which took up most of the space in my small backpack. "'One, scramble down third-class slabs back toward Cathedral Lake and the John Muir Trail; or two, walk up a few hundred yards and pick up the descent trail for Cathedral Peak.'"

"That means nothing to me!" Dave Gold giggled.

"Do you know where the descent trail for Cathedral Peak is?" I asked.

"Never climbed it!" he said cheerfully.

I had no interest in scrambling down third-class slabs, let alone in the dark, or rather the moonlight, which was beautiful, but challenged my depth perception. I had not felt very scared at all on the whole climb up. Now that I had begun leading, I never felt any fear at all on a top-rope, where the only way I could fall or die would be if something catastrophic happened—a falling rock cut the rope (rare); a falling rock hit my buddy on the head, knocked them out of consciousness or existence; and they let go of the rope while for some reason using a belay device with no automatic braking function (unlikely); or we got struck by lightning. But now that I was still on a mountain, but not tied to it by a rope, I was scared.

The slabs of Tuolumne Meadows were famous. These so-called death slabs were the less-vertical parts of the big granite domes, but they were still sloped slabs of granite. They were often polished, by both glacial action and foot traffic, slippery as the granite slide in the fanciest playground in Central Park. Hikers and climbers alike died on the ones on Half Dome, down in the Valley, every year. Most climbs found the proudest, most vertical lines up the steepest faces of the domes, and then their descents involved walking or "scrambling" down the fourth- or third-class slabs on the mountain or dome's backside, which were still plenty steep, and sometimes slick, or wet. On a "sketchy slab descent," you had to tiptoe your own switchbacks back and forth down the rounded, sloping side of the dome, until you got low enough that there were trees to grab and dirt to stand on—or the slick slab slope led right to the asphalt road.

It was terrifying enough making sure you were stepping on the most level, highest-friction places in daylight, so I made an executive decision to pursue option two, which was to avoid the "scramble" down the third-class slabs from the third-class ledges by walking up a few hundred yards and then picking up the descent trail for Cathedral Peak. How hard could that be?

We walked "up" "a few hundred yards" until we saw some sign of a trail. We high-fived.

There were a few cairns here and there. Then there weren't. There was an obvious trail. Then there wasn't. We got cliffed out (got stuck in an area where we could no longer proceed up or down), doubled back, tried higher, got cliffed out again.

We wandered the third-class ledges on the side of this mountain for what felt like hours. It was not unpleasant, being on the side of the mountain in the moonlight, looking for a way down, though the lights in my headlamp were dimming, and we had long since run out of food and water. But for all of our efforts, by midnight, we were still very much on the mountain, quite high up on it, in fact.

No one had ever really told me what to do in this particular situation. Most of our efforts and strategy had been geared toward getting *to* the mountain, or *onto* the mountain, or *up* the mountain. I made a mental note to ask more about how to get down, from all mountains and especially this one, but then realized that by the time I would have the opportunity to pose this question to anyone who might be able to offer any insight, I would have already solved the problem.

I heard a voice, inside myself, as we teetered and tottered hither and thither about the slabs and ledges from which we could have easily fallen. Maybe not fallen off the mountain, but fallen ten or twenty or fifty feet, onto another ledge, below. It was my grandmother's voice, or maybe it was my own, from the future, the voice of the old Jewish lady I would one day become, but only if I didn't anticlimactically tumble a few dozen feet to my maiming or death after surviving a seven-hundred-foot technical climb. The voice said, in the way that only a Jewish grandmother can, *Now, this would be a good way to get hurt.* Down on the ground, the next sentence would be *This is a lawsuit waiting to happen,* but up here, whom would you sue?

But it was ridiculous! To be stuck on a mountain, with no one to ask for directions, and no one to sue! Or not be stuck on the mountain, but moving freely around it, having gone all the way to the top and tagged the summit, only to be unable to find the way down. Everyone who had taught me to climb would have free soloed Cathedral Peak, simply climbing around the many parties tied to the wall with their silly ropes and gear, and then loped down the slabs in time for sunset beers. I felt like an idiot for not knowing how to get off the mountain, but then I realized I'd feel like an even bigger idiot if my body were found on *third-class* ledges. Though I would already be dead, I could not live that down.

The summer solstice was little more than a week away. If there were ever an ideal night to be stuck on the side of a subalpine peak waiting for dawn, it was this full moon summer evening. Sunrise was five hours away, first light maybe four. I patted my pockets, felt the ever-present lighter. We had the means to make a fire. I kind of had to pee. We had the means to put the fire out. Or so went my brilliant—and our only—plan.

"It's not an epic until you're spooning your buddy," said Dave Gold. But spooning, it turned out, was no warmer than curling singly around the fire.

I wanted off this mountain like I'd never wanted anything. Actually, I wanted off this mountain with equal fervor to how much I'd wanted on it about twelve hours before. I'd never been able to scrape together the money to go on an Outward Bound or NOLS trip, where you could have a lightly surveilled "solo experience" and even write about it in a trademarked journal and share it in a branded sharing circle afterwards. You could pay people to take you out in the wilderness and pretend to leave you there all alone, or you could just be a dumbass and do it to yourself, for real—and for free.

I had to stop thinking of my mother, and how very much she would not want me to be where I was. But looking out at all the granite, the moonlit lakes below and the starlight sky above, not another human being in sight, why would I want to be anywhere else?

I had always been afraid of the darkest hours before the dawn. It was when I was most prone to waking up, from nightmares or wracking coughs, delirious and fearful when I would rather have been safely asleep.

An acupuncturist had once told me that each organ system of the body had designated hours when it was replenished by sleep; the hours from 3:00 to 5:00 a.m. were "lung time." Each organ system also had an associated emotion, she said, and the lungs' was "grief or sorrow."

My predawn sorrows never felt like they were really mine. Like a case of mistaken identity, someone else's demons at my door. Awake and scared in the night, the darkness always seemed superlative, eternal, vast, in what Fitzgerald called "the long dark night of the soul, where it is always three o'clock in the morning."

But I was less scared up here at three o'clock in the morning than I was in my own bed. Even at three o'clock in the morning, this night was not dark. The moon was there, whole and full, a maternal and abundant presence. There was a lake down below, and beyond that, slabs and walls of undulating granite. There was really nothing to be afraid of at this altitude, or this hour, only more things to see.

In the thin air, my lung time harbored neither grief nor sorrow. As I watched the night world from the top of the mountain, each breath felt as big as the sky. The last and deepest and oldest of my fears melted away into the bright and holy night. There was nothing to fear, not even the dark. Fear of falling? I had already dispatched with that, with a whip, no less. Fear of failure? It was survivable—to a point. Fear of death? It didn't scare me as much as it used to. Now, it almost seduced, whispering to me on the wind, calling to me from over the edge.

The early-season snow still clinging to the horizontal spots was first to catch the light. Then the lake began to shimmer. The black trees slowly turned dark, dark green, while the sky was an ombré from lavender to mauve to periwinkle.

When I was a kid, my family frequently visited the Queens Museum, which was not in Tuolumne Meadows but Flushing Meadows, whose permanent installation was a scale model of every block and building in the entire city of New York. Planes took off and landed on little wires at both airports, and every ten minutes or so, the whole model cycled through a two-minute night, when tiny lights came on all over the miniature metropolis. You viewed the model from catwalks suspended above it, and my family and I would take turns pointing out our house, our old house, Grandma Ruth's house, Grandma Betty's house, Shea Stadium, the very park where the museum we were in was located. Sometimes, peering down, I imagined that the model was real, that I had a tiny doppelgänger somewhere in this other city that the giant me was viewing from on high, like a god.

When the lights came up on the real Sierra, we had the longest of days ahead to find our way down. We found the trail almost immediately, as if it had been stomped there overnight by helpful elves. The fear and frustration of the cold night and the lost trail burned off with the rising sun, seeming first distant, then illusory, then absurd. It had been here the whole time, and we had only needed a bit more light to see it.

Before I spent every dark minute on the side of Cathedral Peak, I had no concept of trust as anything other than a blind leap of self-obliteration, of following some stranger into the dark, or the middle of the road. I had no sense of what it might mean to trust myself, for that trust to be rooted in self-preservation rather than feeding the wolf of some destructive appetite, no idea that some survivalist Jewish grandmother inside of me could make executive decisions not to take unnecessary risks that would end up showing me sunrises from mountaintops, because it simply felt safer to stay up there, where I was, and take in the view, until the path revealed itself to me.

I wondered if someone more badass would have somehow braved the steep dark, but when I told Fred about it later, he said, "You did the right thing. You got out the Bic."

PART III

HEROES
FOR A DAY

I am content because before me looms the hope of love.
I do not have it; I do not yet have it. . . .

I do worry the end of my days might come
and I will not yet have it. But even then I will be brave

upon my deathbed, and why shouldn't I be?
I held things here, and I felt them.

—Katie Ford, "Psalm 40"

12

Mileage

THROWING MYSELF AT THE ROCKS made me no less hungry for love, but it gave me a desire that could actually be satisfied.

Rocks did not refuse me. We never wanted different things. They only made noise when parts of them broke off and smashed to pieces on the ground, sometimes killing people. They had no emotions, no power to wound or confuse me.

Emotions had no place on the rock. Emotions caused meltdowns. Girlfriends cried, because they were afraid of heights. I wasn't a girlfriend. I wasn't afraid. I never cried. Not up on the wall, not down on the ground.

I never cried in front of anyone, even if they broke my heart. Especially not then.

I'D RETURN TO MY TINY HOME in the Bay between climbing trips only long enough to reap sufficient gas money for the next adventure. My tutoring day job was perfect for the climber-dirtbag lifestyle, and math homework, college essays, and SATs were as reliable as death and taxes.

Life fell into a rhythm, a long loop between the salty Bay and the sharp Sierra. Weekend warrioring, it was called. Different permutations of our local Bay crew would rally up to Yosemite after dark on Friday to sleep next to forest roads for a few hours before we rose in the dark to overcaffeinate ourselves into dehydrated delirium for Saturday's multi-pitch and Sunday's cragging.

The more I climbed, the more I could climb. Quantity and frequency were the keys to not being afraid. "Mileage," it was called. Climbing more made you stronger. Being stronger made you less afraid. Being less afraid helped with the mental game, and theoretically, it was all mental.

By climbing plastic almost every other day and granite almost every other weekend, I got to the point where I could lead all the 5.7s and most of the 5.8s and some of the 5.9s, and follow 5.10 at an unembarrassing pace, which enabled me to climb slightly harder and therefore slightly prouder and more respectable things. Other people got better, faster, but I was finally content to progress at my own pace. I started teaching others, and learning from that.

Summer and I continued our adventures in the Little Lady Leader Learners League. (It felt like a triumph when it was used as a hashtag in a Patagonia ad.) When we summitted Manure Pile Buttress for the first time—no falls, no tears—her other contribution to the successful send was to show me how to take a naked summit photo, making fig leaves out of your shoes, slung around your neck, and your chalk bag, turned around from where it usually sat, at the small of your back, to make a makeshift modesty patch.

That was something else I loved about climbing—how everything was an irreverent joke, just another reason to get naked (or dare someone else to), or roll a doob, or crack a beer, or laugh in the face of death.

Sometimes, when somebody died climbing, all the dirtbags would say was "That's fucked."

Or they would say the dead man had become a raven, and visited them personally, on top of a rock.

I CLIMBED SO CONSTANTLY that I now frequented *two* gyms back home in the Bay, one that was taller and had ropes on its plastic walls, and the bouldering gym, where I still got in for free, even after my friend behind the desk permanently took to the road.

I made a new friend, Ichiro, who also worked behind the desk. Ichiro actually lived at the bouldering gym, in the parking lot, in his minivan. He wasn't the only one with this sort of setup—a well-known El Cap speed climber was said to once have lived in a storage shed that formed one of the natural barriers that described the gym's de facto smoking area, which was furnished with the seats from Ichiro's minivan, removed to make way for the built-in bed.

Ichiro was from the Midwest, his mom Japanese and his dad Dutch. His parents were Moonies, but he'd fled when he found out he wasn't going to be allowed to kiss girls. He'd attended some college, but dropped out to be an adventurer. He was in his early twenties, softspoken yet psyched. He wore Hawaiian shirts with his ever-present glasses, and mostly kept his hair in a ponytail, until he got an impromptu haircut in the smoking area behind the bouldering gym. Like many climbers, he was artistically talented, widely read, and open to all influences. For a time he developed such an affinity for the cast recording of *Chicago* that he played it in its entirety, going both to and from Yosemite.

He'd walked up to me one day in the bouldering gym and said, "I hear you climb trad and you have your own rack." We went to Yosemite that weekend, on which we most agreeably climbed a few moderates. Ichiro was most agreeable.

"I'm good with whatever," Ichiro would say, whether the decision before us was whether to eat, post-gym, at the taco truck or in the Asian mall—or whether to bail from the side of a mountain because of wind, rain, or wildfire, or continue upward despite the elements.

"I'm good with whatever," Ichiro would shrug, just as affable a few hundred feet off the deck.

Or he would say, "I'm chill."

There wasn't anything romantic between me and Ichiro, but I did get my heart broken by José, a recently divorced—or maybe just recently separated—age-appropriate hardman who also climbed at every area gym. The second time we went for pizza and beer at the only place that stayed open after the gym closed, he told me, cheerfully, "I really want to kiss you, but I can't commit, okay?"

He was from Mexico, and his accent made it all sound like one word—*Ican'tcommitokay*, more of a statement than a question.

Was it okay? That he couldn't commit? Right now, the second time we had pizza and beer after the gym closed at 10:00 p.m., the first time he followed me up the winding roads back to my tiny cabin in the redwoods and helped me carry in all my baskets of stuff?

It was okay for exactly one month, during which José texted me at least twice a week, to see which gym I'd be frequenting, where we met and climbed before we went home and hooked up. It was especially okay because José was smart—he was in grad school, for anthropology—and therefore more willing to talk about politics and ideas than the average apolitical California climber. We would talk and talk and talk, in between the sex we had, which was athletic and extremely good, in a basic, obvious, deeply satisfying way, like the pizza and the beer and the long nights at the gym, climbing to exhaustion.

Due to his in-process divorce, José was technically houseless, but in typical climber fashion, it now seemed like his marriage had just been a particularly long bout of couch-surfing. He wore a thumb drive around his neck on a leather cord, like an amulet. He was working on his doctoral dissertation and sometimes asked to use my computer. He would detach the thumb drive amulet from his neck with a click, plug it into the port, and stay up long after I fell asleep in the tiny cabin's loft bed, typing happily and occasionally stepping out on the deck to smoke. In the morning, even if he didn't sleep much, he'd reanimate over coffee, arguing with me loudly and cheerfully, which was why I wanted him to change his mind and decide he *could* commit, because all I wanted was someone to have sex and talk about real things with.

He shamed me into registering to vote in the upcoming midterm elections by giving an impassioned postcoital speech about the power of my American citizenship and how people had died, and, he claimed, he would personally kill, for the privilege of casting a vote in an American election. He said that so many other people were affected by America that it was my responsibility, having been born an American citizen, to try to mitigate the harm in any and every way possible. But by the time November rolled around, he'd decreased his texting frequency to once a week.

I shouldn't have even noticed, because I was supposed to be "chill," and "good with whatever" (my then-therapist called this my "cool girl" persona), but I noticed immediately. I even worked up the nerve to ask him whether he was sleeping with someone else.

"Is that a problem?" he shrugged amiably. "Don't I get to be an almost-forty-years-old divorced man?"

I was infuriated by how endearing I found his slight grammatical error, though it was only a mistake in my native language, not his. I didn't say what I felt, which was that yes, it was a huge problem, if only because it made me want to throw up, and then cry, and then die, and I didn't know how to hide those feelings away and remain sexy and breezy and ready to climb and then fuck and then provide all-night free computer and internet access with complimentary morning coffee at a moment's notice without a single expectation of anything more, even more of the same, now in what was going to be a platoon situation, or perhaps even a rotation. I tried to accept my position for one more week, and then I told him it actually wasn't okay.

I kept my word to vote in the midterms. When I ducked into the cardboard cubicle and leaned over the ballot, I was shocked to see a tear fall onto the governor's name and hover there, its taut surface curved like the lens of a magnifying glass.

José moved in with the other woman he was sleeping with pretty much immediately, and no matter which of the rapidly multiplying number of local gyms I went to on any given day, I saw them together, for years afterward, climbing on hard routes I would never attempt. No matter when I timed my post-climb sauna and shower, she was always in the locker room, a blond afficionado of exclusively thong underwear.

Was it because she was blond? Was it because of the thongs? Was it because she climbed so much harder? Did they talk about politics? Did he laugh at her jokes?

José had said, vaguely and most ironically, that we'd go to Yosemite sometime and climb Commitment, a mega-classic Valley 5.9, but never made further plans. Instead, I went and climbed it with Summer, and she told me about a man who'd broken her heart who wore a yin-yang on a leather cord.

"Spiritual white guy." I nodded sagely. "At least it wasn't a thumb drive with a half-finished doctoral dissertation on it."

It seemed funny again, while we were on the top of the route, and it was all so far away from this rare air, down at the lowly level of the sea.

"LET'S GO TO SQUAMISH," Ichiro said one evening, sitting on the car seats behind the bouldering gym in the smoking spot. "It's chill there."

Squamish was a climbing area in Canada, less than an hour north of Vancouver. It was a sea-level, smaller-scale version of Yosemite, but in a wetter, mossier, fernier forest, with cell phone reception. I agreed, especially since Canada sounded like a logical antidote to Mexico, to which California now felt too close.

After he made the suggestion, Ichiro treated the matter as settled. "Don't forget," he texted that night, "we're going to Squamish!"

A couple of days later, on the outdoor car seats, we pored over a borrowed guidebook, discussing dates. We had to leave on different days and had different driving strategies, but this did not make our pact any less earnest. On his appointed blastoff date, Ichiro texted to announce that he had departed for Canada.

"See you there!" he wrote brightly. "You can't bail now!"

"Don't worry," he texted, twenty-four hours later, from British Columbia. "You can definitely find weed here."

AS I DROVE INTO THE PARKING LOT directly under Squamish's main formation, the Stawamus Chief, I fretted, momentarily, about whether I was in the right place. Just then, in my review mirror, I saw none other than the familiar face of Alex Honnold, climbing's Michael Jordan. If Honnold were here, I figured, it was probably the move.

In Squamish that charmed summer, Honnold himself became my inadvertent wake-up call, striding past the rear window of my Subaru bedroom before the early Canadian dawn. He was always the first one up.

I quickly shared this information with Ichiro, on our first proper climbing day at the Smoke Bluffs, a cragging area not too far from the Chief itself.

"That must be why he's so good," mused Ichiro. "Because he's the *most* psyched."

But when Harold showed up, he quickly dismissed the buzz. "I'm not a climbing groupie," Harold said in his Newcastle accent, and refused to acknowledge the celebrity presence.

After that, Ichiro followed suit. Out cragging another day, I pointed out a soloing Honnold, making his way toward our selected routes. It was Honnold's birthday, and a traditional climbing birthday event was to climb as many pitches as you were years old. Having taken up climbing at the age of thirty-one, I would have had to climb El Cap in a day just to have a shot, a thing only very elite climbers can do. But rather than climb twenty-nine pitches on his twenty-ninth birthday, Honnold was climbing *290*. Because he free soloed, he could climb *down* routes as well as up, and count those pitches toward his total, but it still took him most of a day to climb the 290 pitches. There was a small film crew following him as he completed this task, but to us, it was the background of our own movie.

"Check it out," I nodded at Ichiro, inclining my head toward the generational talent now approaching.

"I'm not a climbing groupie," Ichiro sniffed in Harold's English accent, swiveling his head in the opposite direction.

I racked up to lead yet another gorgeous, protectable, four-star 5.8 that was next to a 5.10 for Ichiro. As I was climbing up my stellar moderate, thoughtfully placing gear at safe distances and dragging the rope up with me, Honnold started soloing up the 5.10 next to me, just a few feet to my right. I paused and watched him for a moment, realizing that I wasn't watching a National Geographic video on the internet, made after the fact of his survival. I was watching Alex Honnold free solo in person, from above, of all vantages, in real time.

He didn't move like I might have expected him to. He gently shook each hold as he placed his hand on it—maybe a habit of soloing, I guessed, checking the hold to see if it were loose, or would break. That was why I used the gear, so even if *I* was perfect—which I certainly wasn't—but even if I could be, the reason I never free soloed was so that if the unexpected happened—if the rock fell from above—then there was some backup besides my own climbing ability. (Though as avid free soloists often pointed out, there was a lot that could happen while climbing from which the rope could not save you. Falling rock could cut the rope, for example, rendering it useless.) Knowing that Honnold could fall at any time but also knowing, or believing, that he never actually would, I understood, unmediated by a screen or a filmmaker, how good—and how truly not scared—he really was.

In the time it took me to assess the size of the spot in the rock where I'd stopped to rest and select a piece from my harness, Honnold, unencumbered and shirtless, climbed up from the ground until he was just below me.

"Hey," said Alex Honnold, nodding politely as he soloed past.

"Hey," I replied, trying to look as casual as he did, with my hands full of all the twisting rope and jangling gear of which he was free.

"Climb-ing group-ie," Ichiro mouthed from the ground as he fed out more rope, so I could inch up the rock at a hundredth the speed of the man who would, in just a few years' time, free solo El Capitan. While Ichiro and I led our moderates in turn, Honnold soloed up most of the routes on the formation. After we pulled the rope from the 5.8 I'd led, Honnold started using it as his downclimb. The route was so easy for him that he down soloed parts of it like it was a staircase, facing forward.

THE ROCK IN SQUAMISH WAS GRANITE, like Yosemite, but known for having better "friction," meaning more rugosity, or surface bumpiness. This advantage, combined with the fact that the Chief sat almost at sea level—overlooking Howe Sound, in fact—meant that the grades of the climbing were "softer"— a 5.7 in Squamish would be much easier than a 5.7 in Yosemite. For me, the sea level part especially mattered, for I seemed to struggle harder than my peers even at more moderate altitudes. I was pretty sure that none of my shtetl ancestors had ever met a

Sherpa. British Columbia's climate was then much wetter than California's drought-parched Sierra, the woods still green and alive. We called it the Hobbit Forest. The boulders were covered in sheets of moss. There were hanging gardens of ferns in the cracks, mini forests of healthy green trees on the ledges, berries on the descent trails.

Between the Hobbit Forest, the Chief itself, the frequent Honnold cameos, the plethora of nearby lakes and creeks to swim in, and the indefinite parking-lot-camping setup, Ichiro and I were sold. We started texting everyone we knew who wasn't already there, rallying them to Squamish.

Jacob, fresh from an unpleasant breakup, flew into Vancouver. Dexter came all the way from California. Jennifer was there, and let us cook and wait out rainstorms in her brand-new Sprinter van. Jacob and I swung leads on a climb called Rock On that was somehow made for us, stuff I could lead alternating with stuff he could lead, so we felt like champions. Harold and Meredith and I went over to a place called Seal Cove, where you rapped down to the ocean from some railroad tracks and then climbed horizontally, hovering above the glass-green sea. All the hardpeople were happy because there were other hardpeople around to do hardpeople things with, like climb the Grand Wall or use Angel's Crest as an approach to check out High Plains Drifter. Even the senseless poetry of the route names was prouder, more Canadian. Two different potential Little Lady Leader Learners shyly approached me and asked if I would ropegun them up moderate things, and maybe they would try to lead. I got to be the one who said, with full confidence, "I'll finish it for you if you can't." In a party of six, Jacob and Ichiro, Harold and I, and Eva and Elliott, two more friends from the Bay, all climbed Angel's Crest, which was one of the Chief's longest routes and took most of a day. The route finished on top of the Chief itself, and one by one, we each emerged from the chimney at the very top until all six of us were together, on top of the world as we knew it. In the evenings, we sat around a couple of picnic tables with a view of both the Chief and the Sound and drank beer and smoked spliffs and talked shit, which was even more heavenly in Canada.

There was, unsurprisingly, a Canadian in Canada. From the eastern part, named Owen.

We knew each other vaguely, had climbed together a summer or two before, for a day or two, in Yosemite. We'd met in an unusually intimate way. When I'd arrived in Camp 4 one summer night at 2:00 a.m. and thrown down my sleeping pad in the line already forming, as if camped out for concert tickets, for when the kiosk opened in the morning, the Canadian was a long amorphous horizontal form in the sleeping bag ahead of me. Sometime around dawn, he'd rolled over, and when I woke up, we were looking into each other's eyes, as if we'd spent the night together on purpose.

When we ran into each other on a Hobbit Forest trail, we pieced this together, and then remembered that back in Yosemite, we had gone over to the Cookie Cliff together and climbed Hardd, with two d's.

"That was the hardest route I'd ever toproped until Hot Rocks, in Joshua Tree last winter!" I exclaimed proudly, as we placed each other.

"About that . . . ," he said slyly. His eyes went sideways, and that was when I realized what was unnerving about him. He had bedroom eyes.

"What about that?" I asked.

"You were taking a really long time to climb it—no offense—and it was really hot at the belay, and I got worried that it was too hard for you and you'd get discouraged, so . . . I built a three-to-one pulley on the anchor to give you—well, me—a mechanical advantage and I . . . kind of hauled you up."

"Like a *haul bag*?" Climbers on multiday climbs on big walls like El Cap used similar pulley systems to drag up all their gear in giant bags made of thick plastic that they had to carry on their backs until they got up on the wall. The bags, sometimes called "pigs," dangled from the portaledges like alien insect eggs beneath the bug-size climbers when you could make them out from the ground.

"No! Not like a haul bag! Like a . . . lovely lady who needs—"

"*Needs!*"

"Not needs—deserves! Deserves! A lovely lady who deserves a little . . . help."

"But why didn't you just *tell* me?"

"I was *going* to, but when you got to the top, you were just so happy!"

"Well, I guess I'm glad you didn't. Based on the belief that I *had* successfully followed Hardd—with two d's—I have since toproped *several* 5.11s!"

"I know, Hot Rocks! Good job!"

"And I *know* no one built a three-to-one pulley on that one, because the toprope was on it all afternoon and I was belayed most patiently from the ground."

"Well, that's even better, because Hot Rocks is 5.11c, and Hardd is only 5.11b, so the 5.11 you *actually* climbed is *harder* than the one that you . . . got hauled up on a three-to-one."

"Oh my God. I'll never live this down."

"I won't tell anyone."

"No, I mean before *myself*."

"Awwww . . . " He mock-frowned.

We'd already hugged in greeting, but now he slung a long arm around me and I caught a whiff of his T-shirt. I was strangely touched that he'd done me the kindness of not interfering with my happiness, though I was also strangely touched that he'd gone to the trouble of building me a three-to-one pulley to give me a mechanical advantage. Also, this new information proved that climbing really *was* mental.

"I'll make it up to you," he said, squeezing me a little. "I'm really, really sorry."

He said it in that Canadian way, "sore-y," instead of the American way, "saw-ry," and for some odd reason—probably the bedroom eyes—it made my stomach flip.

"Wait," I asked. "How did you even know how to build a pulley system?"

"Well, I have climbed El Cap several times," he pointed out, "but I'm also a mechanical engineer."

It was probably the bedroom eyes again, but that also seemed incredibly sexy.

TO MAKE IT UP TO ME, the next day, he took me out on a long linkup connecting mega-classic übermoderates up the Apron of the Chief, let me lead most of it while also offering to lead anything I didn't want to, then complimented my gear placements. This was heteronormative climbing chivalry in its purest form and was the exact type of treatment that male climbers of similar level complained I was privileged to receive "because you're a *girl.*"

Especially compared to his Francophone countrymen, the Anglophone Canadian was super mellow. To make sure he stayed relaxed, he climbed in a pair of thrifted Adidas warmup pants, an especially good find, he remarked, because they were extra long. He was a confident leader and a patient belayer (we were climbing at my level, not his, which was Hardd, with two d's) and through the conversations we had shuffling along ledges and waiting for other parties to clear the routes ahead, we developed a lengthy playlist of media references to share with each other.

When we got to the top of our designated climb for the day, he asked if I wanted to take "the sketchy way down."

"Not especially," I said.

He frowned. "Maybe I shouldn't have introduced it that way. It's not sketchy. It's just *more efficient.*"

After years of James's shenanigans, which often willfully included unnecessary sketch, I was wary of sketch of any kind, though it lurked everywhere, especially among these decade-younger males, but due to Squamish's better friction, Owen's ostensibly sketchy descent was far less sketchy than tiptoeing down Yosemite's slick death slabs. It only took a small amount of rugosity to hold you onto an entire mountain, especially if you were wearing sticky rubber shoes. Things wanted to stick together as much as other forces wanted to pull them apart.

The Canadian walked nonchalantly ahead of me, pausing to fold his body into a kneeling crouch, like a catcher, anywhere he thought I might be scared of walking, unroped, down a steep slab toward what looked like oblivion.

"If you slip, I'll be here, like a doorstop."

"I'm not going to slip," I insisted. "Besides, if I did, I'd probably knock you off like—a ball on a pool table. How much do you even weigh?"

"'Bout a buck-forty," he said, with the sideways bedroom eyes.

"Soaking *wet* maybe," I snorted. "You're a whole foot taller than I am, and you weigh barely ten pounds more!"

"Yeah," he said, giving me the sideways bedroom eyes again, "but you've got *boobs*."

My boobs were bigger than my hands, and often when I considered them, I wondered if they were what Shakespeare called "a pound of flesh." I often wondered how much they weighed. They got smaller, more so and more quickly than any other part of my body, the more I climbed. I wondered if I would get to keep them my whole life or whether they'd become deadly to the rest of me and have to be cleaved from my chest. I wondered if his body would feel light, weighing on mine, if we were to cleave, which meant "stick together" as well as "split apart."

All the bones of his limbs were like geometric vectors when he made his careful moves, climbing or sitting or standing, unfolding and hinging like a camping chair or Swiss Army Knife. I liked the way he moved his body, and I liked his face and the way it changed when he said or thought different things, and I liked the things he said and thought about.

"No wonder you don't need mechanical advantage to climb 5.11. You have the strength-to-weight ratio of a prepubescent gymnast!"

"I climb 5.12, actually."

"How unsurprising."

"You know," he said, beckoning me down another slab of his "sketchy" descent as if I were a tentative cat, before taking his doorstop position like a human cairn, "I have a theory about 5.12."

"What's that?"

"5.12 is the douchiest level. It's the level of climbing that makes people the most douchey."

"How did you discover this? Did you become a douche?"

"Not yet," he said. "But the more I climb 5.12, with the *other* 5.12 climbers, the more I confirm this theory."

The theory, he elaborated, was that if you couldn't climb 5.12, if you only climbed 5.11, it kept your ego in check. Most people who climbed a lot eventually climbed *some* 5.11. Even I had struggled up a few 5.11s, on toprope. If 5.11 was your limit, theorized Owen, then you could live comfortably within your limits. But if you climbed 5.12, he said, that put you in a world with people who climbed 5.13, even 5.14. *Those* people climbed 5.12 routes for their warm-ups. So even if you had finally gotten to the 5.12 level, you would quickly realize that you weren't really that good, only the bottom level of the extremely good, but each level after 5.12 was almost exponentially harder to break through, and most people plateaued at 5.12, and this, he concluded, made you douchey.

THAT NIGHT, I traded the Canadian a Sierra Nevada Pale Ale imported from the States for a hand massage. The hands and fingers of a 5.12 climber are more like tools than appendages. A single finger from which even a skinny person can dangle their body weight is strong.

"Still got that Astro van?" I suddenly remembered, from the time before, in Yosemite.

"Oh yeah," he said. "Built a bed for it in the parking lot of a Home Depot."

"Wow," I said. "Impressive."

"I'd invite you to check it out, but I wasn't expecting company, and it's a bit of a mess."

"No worries," I said. "I keep the Suby pretty tidy."

"I'd check that out sometime," he said, almost politely, doing something positively chiropractic to my wrists.

"No shoes in the house," I said, as we crawled through the hatch.

But he was so tall that his feet did not fit inside, even when he went diagonal. We worked it out during the awake part, but to sleep, he had to bend his knees and tuck them into the backs of mine. Canada was so *nice*.

During the week we spent together, dirtbag-courting in the parking lot, we never spent the night in his van.

"*Your* place is much *nicer*," he said, after we returned to the scenic parking lot from separate adventures the next evening. He brought over his camping chair and placed it next to my Suby, taking my hand and beginning to gently crack the bones.

"You know," he said, later, as we lay in the back of the Suby, "I've got vague plans in California next month."

This, among our tribe, was a very high level of vague future commitment.

I had not actually expected the Canadian to come south, when he messaged to say that while he had been delayed by a forest fire raging in or near Yosemite, his vague California plans might theoretically soon be coalescing, if conditions allowed. "California is definitely happening," he wrote, though by the unwritten rules of flaky California planning, that could mean anything. So I was pleasantly surprised when, true to his word, he arrived on the penultimate day of the next month, a week after my thirty-fifth birthday. He drove all day from Oregon until I heard his Astro van come to rest outside my door.

I tried to affect what I remembered as his general attitude of chill, but when I opened the gate and hugged him, I could feel his heart beating as fast as mine. Then he did something even more exciting—he kissed me in greeting. James would never have done such a thing. He would have made me wait until late into the night before I would even find out if the nauseating pendulum of what Gen Z would later term our "situationship" was swinging toward "with benefits" or "just friends" on any given night or climbing trip.

The Canadian carried some essentials into the teeny-tiny cabin and put them away in little spots he found, like he was planning to stay a while. He told me he'd downloaded every season of the Canadian television show he'd told me about in Squamish, and we could watch it together.

"Tomorrow night," he said, wrapping his arms around me. Even "tomorrow"—especially in his Canadian accent, which put the word "more" into it—sounded like more of a future than I was accustomed to anticipating.

His feet dangled off the edge of my loft bed, too, unless he tucked his knees in back of mine. He didn't really fit, but it was like he did. It was like how I hadn't really climbed the 5.11, but it was like I had.

He said he wanted to meet my brother, so I introduced him. He asked if there was anyone around he could hang out with who was his age, so I made us a date at the bouldering gym with Ichiro.

While I was taking a smoke break in the smoking spot, the Canadian came and joined me, even though he didn't smoke. He sat down next to me and held my chalky hand. Ichiro drifted out, to get more aggressive shoes from his van to try a harder boulder problem inside.

"This is where we planned our trip," Ichiro said. "To Squamish."

"Good trip," said the Canadian. "Good move." He squeezed my hand and went back inside the gym to try his boulder problem again.

I offered the joint to Ichiro. Though he usually refused, this time he didn't.

"I like your boyfriend," said Ichiro. "He seems chill."

"He's not my boyfriend," I said. "We're just hanging out. It's chill." I changed the subject. "He climbs hard. You guys should be friends. He can teach you to big wall."

"Is this, like, a *playdate*?" asked Ichiro.

"Not a playdate." I laughed. "Just hanging out. Just chilling."

WE WENT ON ANOTHER CLIMBING TRIP the next weekend, to Tahoe, and carefully made a grocery list together, divided it up, and shopped simultaneously at two different supermarkets. On the weekdays between our climbing trips, we started planning our meals earlier in the day, so one or the other of us could prep the meals while the other worked, tutoring (me), or doing digital nomad nerd computer things (him), or he was out running errands, a major climber activity during rare stints in urban areas, shamelessly returning well-used items no longer needed to REI or Walmart. We even started planning our meals for later in the week. Like real people did. In real relationships. It was just like having a real—person, but knowing that one day, in the not-too-distant future, he would take everything he owned and leave.

No one had come to my home and stayed more than one night at a time since Robbie, now five years before. I hadn't even so much as cooked a meal with anyone I'd been sleeping with since then. Every lover or experience or situationship I'd had in California had either been a lost weekend of no more than four days that might repeat itself in six to twelve months, depending on whether the other party got a real girlfriend or went back to his old one, or a three-week to three-month period of hooking up with the same guy in response to what was essentially the climber version of the "You up?" text, the even more succinct "Gym?"

WE WATCHED SEVERAL EPISODES of our Canadian show every night and got through so many that we had to download more seasons. We watched whole movies, sometimes in two parts, with sex in the middle. I was working on an essay, and I read it to him and he made a good suggestion. Then I submitted it, so he would know I was serious about something I was actually good at. (It later got published, and even a notable mention in *The Best American Essays* the following year. It was about a different, pre-climbing, noncommittal man.)

When I mentioned that one of the kids I was tutoring was doing logarithms, he asked if I knew that the way that our cams worked could actually be illustrated by something called the logarithmic spiral. I said that was above my pay grade, as a tutor of high school math, but he said it was easy and he would explain it to me, using a cam. We sat on my couch, which was really half a couch, to fit under the loft bed in the tiny cabin, and he held up a real cam and then drew things with a pencil and used formulas, and it all made perfect sense. He was nice and smart and made sense to me, and I liked talking and having sex with him. I was starting to realize that these facts—or were they feelings?—would soon lead to suffering.

I was constantly being shamed by my married friends, particularly Leila, for sleeping with the too-young climbers.

"They're just wasting your time," she'd said sharply, over drinks, on my most recent New York visit, and to my own surprise, I'd burst into tears.

"I didn't mean to make you cry," she'd said, in a strangely singsong voice that made it sound more like she had.

I felt ashamed, like I was having the wrong feelings.

I could never be sure if I was saying or doing the right thing, when it came to matters more complicated than which route to climb, or which piece of gear to place where. Then, I knew that if I had done the wrong thing, I might die, and if I were alive, I must have done something—everything—right.

I WAS DEVELOPING SOME KIND OF . . . FEELINGS, probably also the wrong ones. Maybe he had them, too. Or maybe he didn't have anywhere to park his van and make his toast until he found his next vertical objective and an appropriate partner for it. Or maybe he wanted to put me in his rotation, and I would be his California girlfriend, or whatever, some girl in California who was "chill" (except she wasn't, technically, a girl, and she was only pretending to be chill), and he would also have one in Colorado, or Alberta, or Alaska, or the Cirque of the Unclimbables. He had his remote computer digital nomad job, so he wasn't without income, so I didn't have to worry it was like Robbie. It definitely wasn't like Robbie. Because he was Canadian, and because he was nice. I didn't even have to worry that this was like José, because this guy had his own computer.

At the exact moment I identified the feeling I was having, it turned into something else. It was when we got back from the Tahoe weekend and for the second weekend in a row, I had someone with whom to unpack the car, and it went more than twice as fast as schlepping alone.

As we got ready for bed, tired from climbing and full from our road burgers, I realized that what I was feeling was *happy*. But the instant the word floated into my mind, I felt a pit of fear in my stomach worse than any sketchy climbing moment. It was all completely temporary, it would not last, he would not stay, he was too young. The clock was ticking, I could feel it, and though I was the one accused of having the "biological clock" (also the name of a route, in Joshua Tree, that I had climbed, with James, adjacent to the ominously named I Forgot to Have Babies), it was he who controlled the wasting time. The more I enjoyed this, the more I settled in, the sooner he would leave. There was one thing you could do that was even worse than letting someone insane treat you like shit, and that was letting someone nice make you happy, when you knew they wouldn't stay.

During the third week, he did not mention a climbing trip for us that upcoming weekend. The vague climbing plans in Yosemite might soon materialize. He had to stay open.

Perhaps my tone betrayed me. Perhaps the coolest thing, as always, would have been to say nothing at all. But I was trying to be cool, and maybe even deliberately vague, when I said, "I'll miss you when you go."

"I can't marry you and give you babies," he replied, almost reflexively.

I didn't know what to say, so I said, "You should go."

It was dark. I meant in the morning. It was an awkward night. We had sad sex. I wasn't happy anymore. It felt more like sex with James, not physically, but psychically. Like I was abandoning myself to feel the abandon, only to find the abandon had abandoned me, just as the man soon would. Because we had been doing everything together, the sex just felt like one more thing. Because climbing together and talking was so nice, the sex part wasn't even the only thing. That was part of what had made it feel more real—that there were other things besides climbing. But that didn't mean anything. It was just part of hanging out and being chill and even my best friend thought that some of the happiest feelings I'd allowed myself to have in years were all a waste of time.

HE PUT ALL THE STUFF IN HIS VAN. He seemed kind of shocked to be leaving. I hadn't meant to kick him out of my house, I'd just been stung to have been turned down for a marriage proposal I hadn't even made. I was so mad at myself, for not knowing how to be chill and good with whatever, for wanting and needing and expecting and feeling what I did.

"I'll . . . let you know if anything changes?" he said, raising an eyebrow.

"Okay," I said. "Sure." All I could think about was not crying.

I felt like I had committed some kind of error. It had been wrong to have the feelings, or wrong to give them voice.

We hugged. "I'm sore-y, Emily," he said, Canadianly.

"No worries," I said. "It's all good."

I went back into the tiny house before he got in his van. I went into the bathroom, which had no windows, and was lined with some strange, green, unclimbable stone. I shut the door and turned on the fan, got down on the floor, and folded my knees to my chest. I waited until I heard his van start up and drive away before I let out my wail.

13

The Tower

IGNITING THE COFFEE, I could see the tower looming above, a single finger raised to the starlit sky.

We were only going to climb the North Chimney, at 5.9, the easiest way up the tower. The route climbed up the inside through an empty, hollow space. Doing research before the trip, I'd come upon a video of a professional climber free soloing up the tower's hardest route, the 5.11 North Face. When she got to the top, she put on a parachute and jumped off.

I was always doing the least extreme version of this seemingly extreme activity, by using a rope, by climbing 5.9 instead of 5.11, by climbing dry rock instead of ice and snow, by not taking up any of the myriad related gravity sports involving speed or acceleration, demanding you cheat death in a different way. While other climbers spent their rest days biking or running up and down whole mountains, or backcountry skiing in avalanche territory, or even jumping from the very cliffs they climbed, I always took the easiest route into verticality, and came down only in the most controlled of descents.

"You're a very conservative climber," Jacob once observed.

"It's my one conservatism," I agreed. "My one moderacy." It was because climbing itself was already so radical—and because I was so truly mediocre at it, and in this realm, skill and talent really did protect you from death. Besides, it was only a hobby, just for fun. I wasn't a professional, or trying to be one—though I often thought that if I died or got fucked-up, then I'd truly look like a fucking amateur.

All of this stuff sometimes seemed like a religion, a spectrum of devotion that ran from people who mostly did it on holidays to people who did it every weekend to people who did it every day, building their whole lives around it and giving their whole lives to it, like true believers do.

CASTLETON TOWER IN CASTLE VALLEY, Utah, was a perfectly rectangular four-hundred-foot-tall prism of red rock atop a thousand-foot cone of dust, dirt, and talus (piled-up baseball- to basketball-size boulders). It was almost the exact height of the Monarch, my grandparents' forty-five-story condo on the Upper East Side of Manhattan.

The Monarch's beige brick was paler than Castleton Tower's Mars-red sandstone. As we trudged up the dust cone, I imagined a doorman, waiting at the base of our climb and wearing the flat-topped hat of the imaginary military that holds open doors and hails taxis for the wealthiest New Yorkers, the people Fred always described as "rich fuckers" as their Los Angeles counterparts descended on Joshua Tree like locusts, in ever-increasing droves. Growing up, the doormen in my grandparents' condo would recognize me as I strode through the revolving door, waving me through with one white-gloved hand as they lifted a corded phone from its cradle with the other, telling my grandmother, whom they called "Mrs. Diamond," "Your granddaughter is on the way up."

To climb the desert cracks, we had all made fingerless white gloves out of athletic tape. Tape gloves were more necessary on sandstone than on granite. The same pro climber whom I'd watched fly off the tower in the video also maintained a comprehensive blog with instructions for a specific taping method we dutifully imitated. It satisfied me that my white gloves had a purpose, when the doormen's had been just for show.

As we approached the base of the tower, I was still adjusting to the reality that my grandparents were no longer high above the Upper East Side on the thirty-first floor of the Monarch, where they had always been waiting behind the door of an apartment that smelled like matzo ball soup year-round. Instead, now they were lying side by side underground in a Long Island cemetery. My grandfather had been gone for almost seven years, since the winter of Robbie, and my grandmother had died the previous Thanksgiving, while I was climbing in Joshua Tree with no phone reception. The scratches on my hands from the trip were still bleeding two days later when I picked up the moist, dark dirt by her grave and threw it down on the pine box where she lay.

I didn't inherit my grandmother's huge, strong hands, but sometimes, when I held on to the rock, I thought about how viselike her grip had been. She had a way of encircling my entire upper arm, sometimes for help crossing the street, and other times to trauma-dump, alluding to some shadowy thing that had happened to her in a small, dark room, somewhere in the Bronx, long before I was born. I'd always thought of her grasp as a death grip, but when I started to use my own hands to do what Fred called "hold on," I came to think of it more like a life grip. My grandmother had always talked even more about life and joy and pleasure and freedom than whatever peril lurked in her memory.

THE UTAH CANYONLAND WILDERNESS where Castle Valley and all its desert towers were located was outside a small town that was far from the city in a state full of white Christian religious fanatics. With its red dirt, relentlessly polite Mormons, flat, square mesas, and rectangular towers, it felt as far from the jagged steel and concrete edges of the five boroughs as one could possibly get. Already at some elevation and still going up, I felt like I was finally at a safe and appropriate distance from the transgenerational trauma of the Jewish people—though the beach where my grandfather had landed in the Allied Advance had the same name as this strange, red state.

IT WAS ME, JACOB, CLARK, AND ERIN, a childhood friend of Jacob's who'd joined us in Joshua Tree that New Year's and turned out to be a natural-born crusher. She'd grown up weekending in the mountains and had no fear of heights, cold, speed, danger or even, seemingly, death. She and I had been on a trip, just to the two of us, to Joshua Tree that spring during which she'd had a raging head cold that affected neither her climbing nor her mood. She was steady and contained in a way that was foreign to me. Most human beings I'd met in my life up to that point trended toward unpredictable, if not explosive.

Jacob had moved to Utah for grad school, so Clark, Erin, and I drove out from the Bay in one long, twelve-hour day. On the subsequent four-hour drive from Salt Lake to Moab, we saw a whole freshly-killed moose in the back of a pickup truck at the first gas station we stopped at. At the next one, I flashed some Mormon missionaries while the rest of the crew waited in the idling Subaru.

When I found out that Mormon teens were routinely subjected to interrogations by their middle-aged ward bishops about their nascent sexual thoughts, I made it my own mission to give these young missionaries something to properly confess. (Though it was my private fear that a Mormon missionary might see my bare breasts and *not* have a sexual thought, or one worth confessing to the ward bishop.) Surely, I reasoned, if that wasn't some kind of prosecutable harassment, it could be a mitzvah, or some form of community service. Climbing brought me into closer contact with a surprising number of Christian fundamentalists, and I saw it is as my duty to deprogram the few who hadn't already deprogrammed themselves.

The sky brightened as we made our way up the dust cone, atop which the tower sat like a monument to nothing. A ribbon of mist floated between the tabletop of a distant mesa and the sparse trees dotted the valley floor below.

To distract myself from my burning lungs, I wondered how many Jews like me had climbed this sandstone tower in this Mormon state. All the other towers in Castle Valley had names like the Nuns, the Priest, the Rectory, or Sister Superior, though I couldn't see what Catholicism had to do with the ancient red rocks the white settler Mormons had stolen from whosoever land this really was. I thought, fleetingly, of how I had read about the Mormon Church converting the souls of dead Jews to their alien religion without consent and said a quick prayer to reclaim my grandmother's recently departed soul from their weird, windowless temple, just in case they were still doing it, in violation of our lawsuit. Because her childhood trauma made her afraid of small spaces and darkness, my grandmother had begged me for my whole life to make sure she was buried at sea, "with a window, so I can look at the fish." But when my grandfather died first, she changed her mind and decided to be buried next to him. At his funeral, she tried to jump in the grave.

"Sammy," she wailed, sitting in a wheelchair next to the perfectly rectangular hole, "I have to see you one more time . . . "

She slowly tipped forward, until my uncle put his arm out and shouted, "No, Ma!"

You knew someone loved you if they tried to jump into your grave from a wheelchair. Or maybe they just thought they couldn't live without you. But that wasn't how partnership worked in the vertical. You weren't tied together for all eternity, only the time it took to climb a mountain, or a tower, or just a pile of rocks. Or until death parted you—though, unless the rope got cut, you'd still be tied together, even then. You were only bound by free choice and shared desire, to stand on the same small spot in space.

ERIN HAD AGREED to do the scariest part of our route, which wasn't, supposedly, *that* scary. She was going to make the one hard move in the one tricky part, the one part where you weren't supposed to fall, because Erin wouldn't fall. She never did. Sometimes, when I felt like the runt of the litter, I consoled myself that many of my climbing buddies were decade-younger former competitive athletes *and* California natives, and that I was doing all right for a nerd from New York approaching her cougar years with no prior extreme-sport experience save frequent attendance at punk shows.

The four of us would climb the tower in two parties of two. The boys would climb Kor-Ingalls, the most famous route on the tower, while Erin and I climbed the North Chimney. The two routes shared a final pitch, and so we'd meet at the top and tie our ropes together to rappel down faster. Then we'd get burritos and drive four hours back to Salt Lake City so we could drive twelve hours home to the Bay the next day.

If James were here, he would call this a "mission," a term with meanings both military and religious. The Mormons' mission was to convert people to their personal beliefs about God and underpants while ensuring that all sexuality was policed by men who believed themselves to be priests or gods, while a not insignificant minority of them molested children. Our mission was to get up and down the rock tower in time to get burritos.

There were no more trees above the base of the cone. Everything—this tower, the other towers, the big dust cones they sat on, the mesa that formed one of the valley's walls—everything was made of red rock, red dust, or empty space.

When I arrived at the top of the cone and the base of the tower, the others were napping in the sun with their shirts off, their pre-taped hands curled in their white gloves on their bellies. Jacob opened one eye when I dropped my pack next to his. I took off my shirt and lay back on the warm rock.

"Perfect temps," muttered Jacob.

"Sending temps," I replied.

I could never sleep unless it was dark, so I looked around. The tower loomed straight above, giving me reverse vertigo. Up close, its faces were far from flat. It caught the sun on facets, dents, and dishes formed by parts that had broken off and fallen down over thousands and millions of years, grinding into the dust beneath our feet. From where we were lying, we could see two of its four faces—the ones we would climb—meeting at an edge.

Such a foreign place this was, so far from the dark, moist dirt of the East, where I was from and my ancestors were now buried, so different from the gray Sierra granite, in the color and consistency of its finer, redder dust that worked its way into the gear and the whorls of your ears. The Hebrew word for the afterlife, "Sheol," meant simply "the dust," and this was one of the only things—maybe the only thing—about the Jewish religion that had ever felt right to me.

The part that had never felt right was the part about following the patriarchs' rules. The people who did it like their lives depended on it acted like following the rules, even ones that told you to do terrible things, was good. But I found all the rules and laws and rituals in the ancient books written by the dead patriarchs disgustingly sexist, if not frankly perverted—fanatical rabbis checking your underwear every month to make sure your period was over before they gave you permission to fuck (Leviticus 15:19); fundamentalists in Brooklyn covered head to toe, from bad wig to New Balance, in tight bodysuits for prudish "modesty," while the men and boys felt the sun and wind on their hair and skin. Or the laws these zealots fervently worshipped and blindly obeyed were so vilely violent they turned my stomach—cutting babies' genitals as soon as they were born; the macabre Passover celebration that rebranded God's mass murder of Egypt's children our great liberation. Progressive rabbis' patently white feminist attempts to reform or queer this twisted bullshit only made it worse. And then there was the genocidal violence of Zionism, its tentacles in every temple, and what it had wrought, in the desert so far from here that these murderous madmen bizarrely claimed was our homeland, when I already had a perfectly good one back in Flushing, New York.

Thinking of the patriarchy and frank sexual violence that defined both the Jewish and Mormon religions at their very roots and rotten cores, I began to wonder if the traditions were really so different. They both worshipped a cruel and toxic masculine power as godlike, no matter what it did to the bodies of children.

My grandmother had hated religion, because her own father had been as religious as he was abusive. During the Depression, he gave the family's little money to the synagogue, leaving them without enough food to eat. He verbally and physically abused his wife and four daughters, and that was hardly the worst of his deeds. My mother described him, old, deaf, and davening (rocking back and forth in devotion to his patriarchal rape God), banging on the table and shouting when he realized no one was listening to his muttered prayers to the God who was neither good nor great enough to stop him from being a wife-beating child molester.

My grandfather hated religion, too, had no use for it, and no time, for he read voraciously about history and current events. He'd called me on my dorm room landline, sophomore year of college, the only time we ever spoke in a call he initiated. He'd heard, correctly, through the family grapevine, that I'd been so taken with my Religious Existentialism class that I was considering applying to divinity school to do a PhD in a discipline I was planning on calling "God and Death."

"Emily," he said, "this is your grandfather, and I am just calling to remind you that in this family, we don't believe in God."

On the day after his own bar mitzvah, my father had burned all the religious texts in the family barbecue. As for myself, I'd spent every second of every bar mitzvah, Shabbat service, or Passover seder I'd ever attended wishing I were somewhere wild instead, or imagining I could burst into flames and take the whole charade with me. I knew there was something else to trust and believe in, besides the perverted rules of a false and awful God I didn't trust any more than the wild-eyed, scraggly-bearded zealots who claimed to serve him by severing skin from babies' bodies, or forcing women and girls to cover all of theirs. I knew there was an omniscient, omnipresent source or force that could never be contained in a musty book or a room full of people muttering in its dead and ancient language, telling some terrible story for the ten-thousandth time.

God was not in the books those dead perverts had written, over which these halitotic scragglebeards now muttered and moaned. God was not in the windowless temple, nor the ward bishop's sex confessional, nor the baby-cutter's slicing knife. God, if God were anything or anywhere, was in the changing colors of the sky and the changing corners of the stone, in the friction that held you on and the gravity that conspired with the grease of your sweat to pull you off and down to your death. This force of love had no wish to judge or punish you, and any man who claimed to speak to or for God had to be lying, for anyone who had ever been beyond a single white man's wilderness boundary knew that whatever was out there spoke to you directly, from inside your immortal soul.

IT WAS TIME. The first pitches were empty. We jumped to our feet and put on our shirts and dumped the ropes and the clanking racks from our packs, stashing the bags at the base, closest to the trail, to retrieve on our way back down.

Clark and I, who would lead first, began clipping the gear to our harnesses. I listened to the sounds of the carabiners opening and closing, the gear gently settling on its loops. I wasn't afraid, exactly, but I had never done this before. Climbed a tower at all. Climbed much on sandstone, which was weaker than granite. You couldn't trust the gear the same way, and that made me nervous. Sandstone was naturally smoother than granite, but worse, naturally softer. The rock could break. The cams could pop. It was always best not to fall, but now there were more reasons not to. Sandstone was sketchier, harder to trust.

We finally separated as Clark and Jacob walked around to climb their route. Erin and I came to the base, and she began to flake out the rope. She had one cam on her harness, the big purple number 5 she would use on the second pitch, and I had all the rest. Our gear was all mixed up together, along with whole racks of borrowed gear we'd brought out from the Bay, so we'd have as much as we could stand to carry, and more than we used back home, so we could place extra gear, in case some of it popped out of the strange soft sandstone, if we even fell at all.

The first pitch of our route was made of double cracks, or two parallel cracks, side by side, about as far apart as the width of a person, in a corner against which you could press your back or hip or butt.

"Your style." Jacob had grinned, before he disappeared around the corner with Clark. "Three-D."

He'd noticed that I liked to climb things I could stick my whole body into, which we called "three-dimensional climbing." It was because I felt safe that way, almost crawling my whole body into the rock. The body-sized spaces were cozy and comforting, and, as in situations during which I pressed my body against another living person's, I liked having as much contact as possible. Unlike the dark rooms and dark memories of my grandmother's shadowy childhood, there was always a way out of the small spaces—sometimes called "squeeze chimneys"—

222

and the way out was always *up*. You'd wriggle through a slot or a hole and get reborn on top of a mountain.

Jacob's reminder was just the kind word I needed. I picked up the sharp end of the rope, draped ceremoniously at eye level, and tied myself in.

Erin had already tied herself to the other end of the rope. She showed me her knot, and I showed her mine. She clicked the locker on her belay biner to indicate its lockedness.

I gulped and wiggled my eyebrows. "Here goes," I said.

"You got this," she said.

"Going up," I said, like I was the doorman in the elevator, and put my white-gloved hand into the dusty red crack.

On this tower, instead of an elevator or even a stairway, there were cracks in sandstone. The jams were so good that I could almost walk up without interrupting the rhythm of my breath. I had been climbing long enough and frequently enough that I wasn't scared at all anymore, once I was climbing, and dissolved instead into a flowing, floating calm. Sometimes I pretended I was scuba diving, and let the ebb and flow of my own exaggerated inhales and exhales hypnotize me. I thought of my grandmother, who had been a swimmer. She'd swim across the whole lake at the house they'd bought in upstate New York, her arms tracing arcs, her face turning sideways as she breathed. "That slow crawl," my cousin had texted in remembrance, one of the only others to have witnessed and then inherited it. I swam up stone the way she slow-crawled across the lake, breathing and splashing, using her body even as it slowly journeyed back to the dust. This desert was the opposite of water, so far from the sea.

My grandmother wasn't afraid of the water, and I was not afraid of heights. She had been afraid of the dark, which I wasn't anymore, not after my epic on the side of the mountain, a long dark night of the soul broken by a transcendent dawn. She was afraid to sleep alone, and didn't have to, not for a single night, from 1945 until 2008. I was afraid I'd sleep alone forever, but I felt less alone in the embrace of the rock. The rocks seemed a safer place to be than a family. Rocks didn't transmit their trauma through the genetic directions that fashioned your very flesh. They just gave you a beating, from which you came back stronger. The rocks drew just a little blood, from time to time, fresh and red, to remind you that you were alive.

"Protect your beautiful self," my grandmother used to say, from all kinds of perils unspoken and implied. It had made me angry, this constant warning, made me want to endanger myself out of defiance. But my grandmother wasn't my grandma anymore, she was an ancestor, a soul, maybe even a free spirit. Now my life was all that was left as proof of hers. Her own survival had been the gift, had delivered me to my own length of carved-out time.

At the belay, I finally faced the world beyond the wall. Sometimes, when people said they couldn't believe I didn't get scared of the height, I shrugged and told them, "I just never look down!" But once safely clipped to metal bolts with two redundant nylon slings scientifically determined to each be capable of holding a falling pickup truck, I was never scared, especially after I saw so many others ascend without ropes, or fly down with parachutes, or suits with nylon wings. While I was lashed to the walls, ignoring the height was the last thing I wanted to do. It was the height I craved, the view it afforded, the space it made, between me and everything else.

Once I had Erin on belay and she'd started up, I moved the rope through my hands and took in the view. Red dust, red walls, red mesas, blue sky. The tower sat so high on the cone and so high in the high, red desert that even from one pitch up, I could see what I privately called "mountains beyond mountains."

This land was so incredibly beautiful. It really was a shame about all the crazy Christians, and all the horrible things they'd done. And the

Jews. They'd done horrible things, too, just not here. But despite the funny Catholic names of the formations, and the occasional reminders that next to Nevada there lay a hard-right Christian desert theocracy, there were no other signs of religion or even humanity here. Only maybe God, in all the empty space.

Looking out, for miles and miles and mountains beyond mountains, I saw no life on Mars. I finally felt adequately alone, untethered, free of the weight of the past, the stories I'd heard, the fears that weren't mine, the worry that came from nowhere and was stricter than God. I felt safer up here than I did on the ground, safer than I did around most people.

I heard the ravens before I saw them, heard their wings. They came from over my right shoulder. With their wings spread wide, they were much bigger than they looked from down on the ground. There were two, dead even with my belay, swirling in spirals. I made out their heads and beaks and black eyes, the serrated pattern of their wingtips. As they rode the thermals, the sun turned their feathers iridescent. The rich black gave up its contained rainbow, turning brown, then purple, then black again, but now aglow.

As I watched them reel and tumble like pilots or gymnasts, I realized I had what the ravens had: freedom. Not freedom *from* my body, as in death, but freedom through and in it, in what it could do, and where it could take me. Once, tripping with Leila in some faraway place, I'd looked at her earnestly and said, "Our bodies are just vehicles for our souls to have experiences," and we'd repeated this incantation, like girls playing at witchcraft, for the rest of the night, and then for years after.

I could almost hear it in the whisper of the ravens' wings, could feel the breeze they created on my cheek through the air they disturbed with their flight. All the stories, of Abraham and Isaac and Moses and Jesus and Mary and Joseph Smith, of the big daddies and their doomed sons and the anguished mothers and the ruined whores—those were only in our minds, in scary books and windowless rooms filled with the chanting of muttering madmen. And all the trauma, in the ancient deserts and the old country and in dark rooms at night, long before I was born—that was only in our bodies. All that the patriarchy did in the name of their false God, they did to our bodies alone. Our souls fly free as ravens.

I wondered if the weight of the past were lighter up here, like the weight of the atmosphere was. I felt something I'd never felt before, flowing to me from my grandmother, though her body was six feet under in familiar but faraway dirt. Or I'd felt it my whole life, but never this purely. It was love. The love that came with the gift of my body, plucked from the ether by these mortal, now-dead Jews. Now that my grandmother's body was gone, her trauma was gone. Her fear was gone. All that was left was infinite love, the kind that comes from the dust and moves through human bodies and then goes back to the dust.

Then the ravens were gone, like they had only been there to greet me, at the doorway of the tower, where the route began to wind its way inside, and I was alone again in my perch, tucked into this cozy little nook so high in the sky that my only companions were birds.

The climbers who also jumped off of things and flew down believed that their dead friends were ravens. A very famous one had died, around the time my grandmother also had, she at more than twice his young age. On this very climbing trip, we'd passed around a climbing magazine full of elegies to him. Now his friends claimed he visited them, where they jumped, as a bird.

ERIN'S HEAD APPEARED, her hair black as a raven's wing, and then the rest of her.

"Nice lead," she said, clipping into the anchor.

We sorted the gear, and I switched the belay from toprope to lead. The next pitch went inside the tower, which was not solid but labyrinthine with rock rooms and echo chambers and tunnels and passages. While the first pitch had been "exposed," outside on the wall, the next one climbed inside the chimney, the hollow space inside the block-shaped tower for which the route was named. Erin rose with the ease of smoke, inching up with all the clinking gear on her harness. She had a way of climbing chimneys that was especially secure and graceful, her feet planted on opposite walls, taking sure, confident steps in a delicate vertical walk. I once asked her how she made the harder moves I couldn't bring myself to make, on lead, at least, and she'd frowned quizzically and said, "Trust."

I had no idea what she meant by that—trust whom? Trust what? The universe? Other people? The rock? *Yourself?*

I couldn't entirely see her make the hard move, but she didn't even say "Watch me," meaning prepare to catch her, by holding the rope tight, if she fell, so the scary part must have been inconsequential to her. Then I felt the tugs on the rope that meant I was on belay.

When I came to the tricky spot with the toprope taut above me, the purple number 5 cam was like a secret, tucked into the crack behind the "useless bolt." Not long after I found it, I joined Erin at her belay and said, "Nice lead."

We linked the last two pitches, meaning I led them both in one long, single rope length. Until the very end, when I popped out just below the roof of this naturally occurring apartment building, I was inside the tower, dragging the rope up natural staircases and over ledges and through whole interior rooms with skylights and portals. The tower's interior reminded me of old warehouses where I'd trespassed with punk friends, breaking the glass of abandoned garbage trucks with rusted crowbars, adding destruction to ruin. Or a high, dry shipwreck, like some I had dived on scuba trips with my family. The tower was on an opposite journey, a naturally occurring thing now changing under the grasping hands of man. The tower was not a ruin, nor a monument. It was just another conveniently shaped hunk of stone.

I had never felt so safe and secure in any real building as I did winding my way through the tower via a twisted natural ladder shaped like a half helix of DNA, held by the earth even as I climbed high above it.

As I moved toward the light, I heard Jacob's and Clark's familiar voices. Though I couldn't see them, they could somehow see me, and they started calling my name into a sunbeam that was guiding me toward it like the window in a cathedral.

"We're up here!" they shouted. "On the summit! Come join us!"

I stepped outside the stone building onto a final bit of face—climbing straight up a flat wall like you do in the gym—that would lead to the summit. I don't know what possessed me, for I have never done this before or since, but I had seen the pro climber who jumped off the tower listening to music on headphones while she soloed. Standing comfortably on a small ledge, I got out my phone and queued up my psych playlist. "Some Nights" by Fun., with its marching drums, came on. I tucked the phone safely in my sports bra and let it blast me as I topped out Castleton Tower with a soundtrack. It was epic beyond epic. Mountains beyond mountains.

It was the drums I liked best, in this song and others. They were the only thing loud enough to drown out the sound of my own beating heart, the internal drumbeat that sent me on the upward march. The pounding of my heart and the slow waves of my breath, a pulsing of life and blood amid desert dust and endless sky.

In a few more moves, I pulled myself onto the summit, and there were Clark and Jacob, standing on the flat square of the tower's rooftop as if it were a magic carpet. Erin followed, and soon we were all taking summit photos, hanging out and giggling like teenagers who had gotten away with something.

For the first time, on the summit, I wasn't thinking about death, or the void, or the gravity that would accelerate my fall if I jumped, bringing the ground close like a hungry lover, rushing up to meet and claim me. I was thinking about how the empty sky was everything that mattered, and how empty it was of everything that didn't. If only everyone else could see what we saw, they would realize it wasn't about jobs or buildings or civilization or God or religion or maybe even family. It was about rocks and sky and ravens and stone towers and friends you could trust. Nothing more and nothing else. Only when I was on the very top, and could see to the horizon in every direction, could I be sure I was safe and free as a bird.

Jacob and I rappelled down first, to go return a borrowed cam to its owner at a gear store in town before her own climbing plans early the next morning. We were back at the base of the tower in no time, starting down the cone. My bones and joints were not yet tired, I felt like I could climb or walk forever. We loped down the steep path until we were back at the campground that was just one Porta Potty with a wooden fence around it, where our day had begun with coffee before dawn.

"Let's get some coffee," Jacob said now, at sunset, starting the car. "Long drive ahead."

"Did you see the ravens?" he asked.

"Of course," I said.

"Did you hear them?"

I nodded, and Jacob smiled at me, that sweet and secret smile that made me think maybe we were related, somehow, brother and sister from another mother or mister, or Jedi, or something. I smiled back, looking out at the desert's dying light, and we drove on in a rare and most companionable silence.

It felt just as good to be here, on the ground, as it had felt on top of the tower mere hours ago. My climbing friends were the only ones who understood so much about me with so few words. I was glad we were friends, not lovers or blood. We moved so freely through the world, seeing things only we saw, and sharing things only we knew, tied together in our solitude.

14

The Warrior Will Do
What She Must

I can do it with a broken heart.

—Taylor Swift

I WOULD NEVER HAVE GONE to South Dakota if not for Kyle Rott. I ran into him, in the El Cap Meadow, on a springtime trip to Yosemite Valley. I told him I was driving to Minnesota to go on a canoeing expedition, and he said I had to go climbing in South Dakota.

"You'll love the Needles," he said. "Not the California Needles, the ones in the Black Hills. Let me know when you're getting near there, I'll put you in touch with my friends."

I drove all the way to Minnesota and went canoeing for a week in the Boundary Waters Canoe Area, a series of hundreds of interconnected lakes on the border between northern Minnesota and Canada. A mining company was trying to destroy the pristine wilderness by turning all the water in it to sulfuric acid, supposedly to profit from the extraction of a few pennies' worth of copper. The Patagonia clothing company was supporting a group of anti-mining environmentalists with its nonprofit do-gooder arm, funding a short film about a pair of explorers—local canoe and dogsled guides—who were living in the wilderness for a year (with weekly food and laundry drops from the environmental nonprofit in town). One of the filmmakers was a social media climbing friend. We'd never roped up (he climbed 5.12), but, as they said in the Hidden Valley Campground in Joshua Tree, I'd been to his fire. I'd admired a photo of the lake wilderness on his grid, and he'd suggested I come along and write about the efforts to save it from destruction. I looked at the map and saw all the climbing areas I could hit between Berkeley and Minnesota, and promised to meet the photographers in the Grand Marais municipal campground on the fifteenth of June.

In the Boundary Waters, I was bitten so thoroughly by bugs that I scratched myself bloody inside my tent each night, then rose at dawn to help the photographers get money shots of the explorers paddling through mists that were hopefully unequivocally beautiful enough to save the waters from ruin. Canoeing, as a mode of exploration, involved "portaging," or carrying the canoe on your head, on the slippery, muddy trails between the lakes, plus everything else, all wrapped neatly in waxed duck canvas bags that looked like props from a Wes Anderson movie and were sold in myriad outlets in town. I tried to portage the canoe exactly once and almost dropped the unwieldly and expensive Kevlar on some sharp rocks. But I was very taken with Minnesota—the ginormous trees, the pristine water, the high-latitude summer sun, the way the locals unassumingly said "Oh ya" to affirm that they'd done something major.

After five days embedded with the canoeists on their expedition, I spent five more sleeping in SubyRuby in the parking lot behind the environmental organization's office in the gateway town to the canoe wilderness, dutifully reporting a sweeping piece on the entire mining issue and its various local and international players that was never published. (I eventually wrote a brief lyric essay about the trip for the Patagonia blog.) I visited the mining company's local office, where there were pictures of the unpolluted wilderness framed on its walls, a counter-point to the environmentalists' wall-size blowups of the sickening col-ors of the acidified, post-mine waterways the corporation had already destroyed on other continents. I interviewed people with pro-mining signs in their yards, who assured me, while blowing decidedly non-organic cigarette smoke directly into my face, that the mine, which was, in actuality, to be manned almost entirely by remote-controlled robots, would "bring back jobs for the boys." Their WE SUPPORT MINING signs were stabbed in their lawns next to the ones proudly advertising their support for Trump. The sheer quantity of such signs I'd seen on the drive from Berkeley to Minnesota had already convinced me he'd be president come fall.

I started heading back West. Harold wasn't too far over the border, in Canada's Midwest equivalent, and he met me to climb on Lake Su-perior and check out Bob Dylan's house in Hibbing. It was just a house like any other house. I talked Harold into driving a mere five more hours south to climb the Devils Tower in Wyoming, but we'd have to wait out the last week of June, when, according to the National Park website, local Indigenous tribes "requested" that climbers "voluntarily" refrain from climbing the tower, their place of worship.

Harold, a veteran of many epic drives, showed me a choice Walmart parking lot in Bismarck, North Dakota, where I could sleep in my car while I labored on my longform piece about the anti-mining movement, trying to make a submission deadline to a fancy environmental maga-zine. (Sleeping in RVs—and by dirtbag-logic extension, vans, minivans, station wagons, sedans, and two-door sports cars, all of which climbers did, was, at the time, widely permitted in most Walmart parking lots, and they got our business in the morning at the in-store Starbucks when those of us lacking en suite vehicle bathrooms came in to use theirs.) But Harold got called back to work in Canada at the last minute and hung a sharp right northward, so I had no particular climbing buddies or plans between the Continental Divide and the Pacific Ocean—except for Clark, who'd said that when I got back to California, we'd climb Fairview Dome together, in Tuolumne Meadows.

I spent the last days of June sleeping in the Walmart parking lot in the back of SubyRuby, where it was only darkish from 10:00 p.m. until 5:00 a.m. I was at the fancy coffeeshop in town by the time it opened at six, where the recent oil boom had financed a block-sized replica of the Brooklyn hipster bohemia I had enjoyed during the previous decade, from morning lavender latte to craft cocktail nightcap.

On the final day of the month, I submitted the fruits of several days of furious lavender-latte-fueled writing to a slew of indifferent editors—and noticed a voicemail in my phone. It was from Kyle.

"Hey, Emily," he said, in his thoughtful mountain drawl. "I saw on the interwebs that you were in North Dakota, so you must be getting pretty close to Black Hills. I called some of my friends in Custer and told them to expect you. They'll show you their bivy once you get there. If you need a place to stay on the way, I called my mom, she's in Sioux Falls, but there's also another bivy on the way if you're coming in late." Kyle launched into a careful description of the bivy's exact location, a series of turns I hastily typed into an iPhone note. He mentioned the Crazy Horse monument as a landmark. "I also sent you a kind of secret guidebook we made ourselves, it's kind of a local thing, so don't share it around. I'm so psyched for you. You're gonna love the Black Hills. Wish I could climb there with you. Look me up when you come through Montana, though."

In my direct messages was a link to a Dropbox. In the Dropbox was a PDF. It was a multipage document with hand-drawn topos (route maps) and brief route descriptions.

I texted the nongendered names whose numbers Kyle had texted me, Harper and Dakota.

"We've been expecting you," one of them replied. They sounded

male, as they didn't use any exclamation points or punctuation whatso-
ever. They guided in the mornings, they said, and I should meet them at
their trailer parked by the lake in the state park at two.

INTERESTING, I THOUGHT. The Black Hills. Crazy Horse. People named
Dakota.

Commencing a six-hour drive across desolate plains toward what
Kyle had called the Fish Pond Bivy, I saw no people for hours, only fields
and fences and occasional livestock. I saw a football field in the middle
of nowhere. When I pulled over to pee on the side of the road, the plains
were so still that I could hear my own pulse inside my body, as I only
ever had on the most silent of nights. I didn't have to fear some psycho
because the world was so flat I could see every living and nonliving
thing straight to the horizon in every direction. The land was mercifully
empty of Trump signs. I could scream and no one would hear. I had
never felt so utterly alone. I got back into the car and burst into inexplicable tears, trying to figure out why I was crying.

It was *America*, I decided. I'd never been alone with her before. Just
the land, without its colonizers, though I was technically one of them,
too. It wasn't mine—none of it was ours—but it felt like mine. Not the
blood-soaked flag I spit at whenever I saw it, nor the dead white men's
lies and all the bodies they'd buried in the stolen soil, but my country,
whatever it was, to whatever degree it had ever existed, as anything I
could ever think of as home.

Kyle's bivy directions were spot-on, and I rolled into a gravel pullout just after midnight. There was one other car there, dark and quiet.
Hopefully not a psycho, though I was too tired to care. It was a hot
night, but I rolled up all the windows and locked all the doors, unfolded
my pocketknife, placed it under my open hand, and fell asleep in this
new and spacious state.

HARPER AND DAKOTA were sitting at a wrought iron café table outside a trailer with the name of their guiding service on it, parked next to a man-made lake ringed by shorter versions of Joshua Tree-shaped rocks. They were both indeed male, both smoking American Spirit cigarettes and wearing their sunglasses on strings.

Dakota offered to belay me on a moderate so I could get the lay of the land. We went around the lake and climbed a classic crack called Classic Crack, then met up with the climbing guiding service summer intern at a needle of granite of the sort for which the climbing area was named. The kid led the route, which was called Cerberus, and I followed him up, and then we did something called the "Needles rappel," wherein, instead of threading the rope through two rings anchored permanently into the top of the rock in order to rappel back to the ground, we simply folded the rope over the very pinnacle of the spire we had just climbed—it fit into a little groove worn in over the years—and rappelled down opposite sides, each body a counterweight to the other.

As we replaced the borrowed rope in its plastic bin in the guide trailer, Dakota and Harper agreed that since Kyle had vouched for me, it was okay to show me their secret bivy, the Nude Beach.

At the Nude Beach, a few more (clothed) climbers were preparing dinner or enjoying beers. One, Katie, worked very early in the morning helping to inflate hot-air balloons that carried tourists over Mount Rushmore. Another, Nathaniel, had just driven up from the city, or from the nearest populated area with the word "city" in its name.

"I don't have a partner for tomorrow," Nathaniel announced to the general bivy.

Dakota nodded in my direction. "She can climb," he said, with gruff approval that puffed my chest with pride.

I had run it out a little (left more space between pieces of gear), on purpose, on our one climb, because I'd been climbing a lot and felt strong and bold, and so Dakota would think I was brave. The Needles were granite, same as Joshua Tree and Yosemite and Squamish, and though everything else about the area felt wholly unfamiliar, the rock itself felt like home.

"Ever done a Needles rappel?" asked Nathaniel from the city.

"Oh ya," I said, imitating the Minnesotans' Midwestern understatement. "First one, today."

"I've got a rope and a rack," said Nathaniel.

"Let's use your rope," I said, "and my rack."

I TOLD NATHANIEL I didn't get up very early and that I had to have my coffee first. When I woke up, the bivy was empty of guides and balloonists, and Nathaniel was looking impatient in a camping chair next to his own, newer Subaru. We brought both cars back to a lot near the guide trailer and took Nathaniel's car to a different parking lot, driving through two kissing rocks he told me were called the Needle's Eye. There was a tea bag in the coffee mug in his cupholder. He'd acquired an ulcer, he said, though he was only twenty-seven. He chewed tobacco, like a baseball player, spitting the juice into a plastic bottle he kept in a different, more base-level cup holder, and also smoked the same brand of cigarettes as Harper and Dakota, turquoise American Spirits. Despite the many cultural differences between the red states and the blue ones, the one I never got over was the sight of climbers smoking cigarettes that came in packs. I didn't presume that any of these local climbers were quite as fascistic as much of the rest of their deep red state—though I did soon find out that most of their rest-day activities involved firearms, in addition to alcohol and tobacco. But if there were any non-fascists in these particular hills, they were probably the climbers with their Subarus and even their Birkenstocks, which Nathaniel was wearing.

I told Nathaniel I was a notoriously slow hiker and he said, no problem, if I fell too far behind, he'd just stop and have a cigarette. He asked if I wanted to lead anything, and I said anything protectable under 5.10. He said I might like the International Chimney on Cathedral Spire Three. The silhouette of the Cathedral Spires was on the area's unofficial commemorative climbing T-shirt, and they were numbered One through Nine. They were a short hike into the Black Hills that Nathaniel seemed to know by heart. He explained that the Black Hills were so named because to the Lakota people of the area, the hills, covered in tall pines and spruce trees, had appeared black in contrast with the surrounding pale prairie. He loved the pines so much he had a lodgepole pine tattoo, he added. He had climbed all nine of the spires, he said, and it could be done in a day, but today we'd just climb Two and Three. One through Four were the best, and Three was where the International Chimney was.

"THERE'S ROSE QUARTZ IN HERE!" I shouted down to Nathaniel from the top of the International Chimney. "Giant crystals of rose quartz!"

He didn't quite hear me, so I repeated myself on the summit as he set up the rappel.

"All the quartz crystals in the granite!" I said. "They're *rose* quartz!"

"You seem pretty excited about that," he said.

"Oh ya," I replied. "It radiates love!"

"Ya, right," he said. "Maybe in California."

I watched the rope moving through his hands while he told me about his father dying. His long fingers were like the spires of the Needles themselves—articulate and specific. His face was made of planes, angular in some places and square in others. He was such a stranger to me that I forgot what he looked like between meetings at belays. He had a slight, stubbly, unintentional-looking mustache. His eyes were very blue. We talked all day, whenever we were near enough to hear each other, and he never said I talked too much, nor lacked for something interesting to say to me.

INDEPENDENCE DAY was a major holiday among the climbing community of the Black Hills. First, we went to a drugstore in town and bought giant vinyl floats. We took them down to the lake in the state park and floated around and paddled up to rocks and jumped off them. Later, the locals explained, there would be some kind of party, at someplace called the Burnout Turnout.

The local gang was like a miniature version of the much larger climbing communities around Yosemite, Joshua Tree, or Squamish. There was a slightly older couple who owned a house with some land where dirtbags were always welcome to camp and use the bathroom and firepit. (I was later proudly informed that the house hosted the regional level of the US Air Guitar Championships.) There were the itinerant guides, like Harper and Dakota, who came every summer and slept at the Nude Beach and departed each winter to climb ice. There was the even-more-itinerant young crusher, the kid who'd led Cerberus the day before and been the counterweight of my first Needles rappel. There was the entire leadership of the Black Hills Climbing Coalition, which met every Tuesday at the brewery. Nathaniel was the president.

THE KID WHO'D LED CERBERUS the previous day settled a bet with Dakota by doing a naked free solo of a preordained route. Someone asked Nathaniel if he'd taken me up Moonlight Rib, and when he said we'd done Spires Two and Three instead, it was decided that taking Kyle's friend up Moonlight Rib would be an official part of the festivities.

The climb was frequently free soloed, they said, because it was easy to climb but hard to protect, but we could use a rope if I insisted. (I did.) Nathaniel free soloed up to the bolted anchor on top, and I followed behind, up one hundred feet of easy climbing. Harper from the day before soloed up an opposite rock, and when he yelled at us to look at him for a photo, which he called "footie," we both flipped the bird. Sometimes, when I look at that picture, I think that is the happiest moment of my whole life. I'm standing comfortably on giant holds, grinning with pure delight and just a hint of unchecked aggression, my right middle finger pointing straight to the summit maybe twenty feet above. On the summit, only Nathaniel's sunglasses, forehead, and forearm are visible, a line of sinew starkly drawn even through the lumpy pixels of a bygone digital resolution, as his left middle finger points to the sky.

After we rapped down, the locals performed a bizarre and spirited ritual that involved them zip-lining, shirtless, between two parking lot spires, with beers in their hands, while reciting parts of the Declaration of Independence from memory. Then we went to the Burnout Turnout and drank beer until it finally got dark and more fireworks than I'd ever seen in my all previous blue-state life exploded over the Black Hills. After the fireworks, as if by tacit agreement, Nathaniel followed me back to my Subaru, and what happened next was even better than Fourth of July fireworks in a place where people really, truly love America.

I SPENT THE NEXT THREE WEEKS shacked up with Nathaniel in Rapid City, South Dakota, climbing on Mount Rushmore and in the Black Hills and at the Devils Tower, and the rest of the summer roaming the Mountain Time Zone, meeting Nathaniel for a weekend in one part of Wyoming and some friends for another weekend in another part of Wyoming before finding Kyle in Montana on my way home to California to climb Fairview Dome with Clark in Tuolumne Meadows, which we did.

The South Dakotan and I spent three torrid weeks together before he'd said matter-of-factly that the idea of us having a real relationship was absurd. It had seemed marginally more viable than the Canadian incident—if only in my mind—for a few half-baked reasons. Our age difference had been less scandalous, though Nathaniel was still younger (nearly all the single male climbers were in their twenties; any man who wanted a relationship and was in his thirties, like I was, could have one, or several). Like the Canadian, the South Dakotan was a mechanical engineer, which meant he was smart. He read books and talked about them, had ideas about politics. He got my jokes and was funny. All the things I cared about—sex and climbing and conversation—felt amazing to do together. We'd even cooked. And shopped. And organized the car together. (We were both Virgos.)

During one of our many endless conversations, I made a self-deprecating remark about how I probably talked too much, because it was something my meaner lovers or more toxic friends had always picked on about me, but Nathaniel smiled.

"I like the things you say," he said. "Sometimes, when I'm listening to you talk, I'm listening, but I'm thinking about what I can say next, to make you say even more interesting things."

The sex was like that, too. So was the climbing. The only thing that hadn't felt right about it to me was his reticence. It was getting old, feeling a genuine connection develop between me and another person and watching them snuff it out just as the flame was beginning to catch. Leila and the rest of the adulting adults said things about managing my expectations that confused me further. How was I supposed to feel things other than what I felt, or want things other than what I wanted?

We'd watched the Olympics together in a brewery. We'd spent a night down a forest road, awake in an epic thunderstorm. We'd summitted the Devils Tower twice in one day and rappelled down in the rain. He'd taken me to every thin-hands crack from 5.7 to 5.9 within a fifty-mile radius and led any 5.10 that might be required to access it. I'd told him the saddest things that had happened to me recently, or that happened to me when I was a kid, and he'd hugged me, or squeezed my hand, if he were driving. We texted all day.

Unlike the Canadian, the South Dakotan hadn't had the decency to just ghost when the non-relationship situationship quasi-non-love-affair bubble burst. The pressure I'd applied—or maybe just excitement I'd expressed—for him to plan a fall climbing trip to California was too much. After he announced that he could not have "a relationship," he'd texted and called relentlessly, telling me how much he wanted to be friends, which was even worse than the heartbreak.

I did not want to be friends.

I WAS GONE FOR ALMOST THREE MONTHS, seeing the North Country and Bob Dylan's house and the Mountain Time Zone and the Trump signs, getting my hopes up and my heart broken, and climbing in five new states. When I got home to Berkeley, I arrived in a new place.

I'd gotten the boot from my beloved tiny cabin in the hills (it was, technically, a mother-in-law unit, and my landlord acquired a mother-in-law to go with his new wife and second family), but I'd landed on my feet. The beacon of a single, frantic social media post had somehow reached Ichiro.

"You know," he said, "I don't usually pay much attention to postings about houses, since I don't live in one myself, but you seemed kind of stressed, and then I remembered that Aidan was leaving the houseboat, and I thought, *Weinstein would like that houseboat. It's chill.*"

It was chill. It was a one-room apartment only slightly bigger than the cabin, with real plumbing and a real toilet and a real kitchen. The only difference was that my new tiny home was floating. Instead of a view of the bay from the hills, it had a view of the hills from the bay.

People kept asking me where I'd found the cabin (Craigslist), and now the houseboat (Facebook). I repeated my refrain: "Lucky in rental real estate, unlucky in love."

I hadn't spent much time in my new home in the marina before I'd left on my nearly cross-country trip, but it was worth it already for the great blue heron sightings.

The houseboat had a big, heavy front door, just like a real house, even though the studio apartment was one single room, only four or five times as wide as the door. The door opened to almost graze the foot of my bed with only a few inches of clearance. The bed took up half of the one-room apartment, which itself took up half of the houseboat, where I lived, alone.

I'd been home some weeks already—since Labor Day, and it was now early October. It was the dark before dawn, the lung time. I was in the deepest sleep, in the darkest night, when something went bump. The boat was moving, but it did that, sometimes.

It wasn't a boat but, technically, a "floating home," a house perched on a barge, with rotting decking outside. It was big and stable enough not to rock with the wind, but the unmistakable weight of a human footstep could make it swing away from the dock, or list from side to side. I felt the intruders before I heard them, moving the house with their footsteps.

I thought it was a dream, rolled over, tried to slip back to sleep.

Louder, now. And faster. Thunks. Footfalls. Someone was on the boat.

I was just coming to full consciousness when the doorknob rattled. Then I heard it twist, and the door begin to creak open as time slowed down, like those elongated seconds of car crashes and big climbing falls.

If anyone ever tries to hurt you, my dad told me, when I was little, over and over, *kick 'em in the nuts, poke 'em in the eyes, and scream as loud as you can.* Then, he added, *Go for the jugular.*

Someone was coming into my house, into my room, at the foot of my bed, in the middle of the night. I was naked, alone, and half blind. I fumbled for my glasses and did not find them, so I rose from my bed to meet the threat, screaming as loud as I could.

I rushed toward the door, and the shape coming through it. The pitch of my own scream was a gurgle, a gargle in my throat. I remembered the sound from my brother's toddler tantrums, ricocheting through the family car. A roar, an ululation. My eardrums vibrated from within. I wasn't lunging so much as flying, screaming as loud as I could.

I pushed. I shoved. I slammed the door shut.

I braced my full weight against it and heard a voice speaking from my palm.

"Nine-one-one," said my phone, which I seemed to be holding. "What is your emergency?"

I LOST MY VOICE FROM THE SCREAMING. The following night I went to an Ani DiFranco concert I'd long been anticipating with a friend and couldn't sing along, though I knew every word. I could only make the shapes with my mouth. My voice was gone. I had used it to scare whoever had scared me away.

Later that same morning, my landlady called a locksmith, who came over and installed a dead bolt. Why hadn't I had a dead bolt before? It was so obvious, so New York. It was protection. I wouldn't climb without a rope, so why was I sleeping without a lock? What had I been thinking? I had let so many of the wrong men in, on purpose, and then just left the door open for my worst fear, a stranger.

I ordered, from Amazon, a palm-size air horn, some purse-size, military-grade pepper spray, and a Louisville Slugger baseball bat. I consulted a chart, to select the correct size for my height, then sized down an inch because the houseboat ceilings were only seven feet. I propped the bat next to the bed and put the air horn and the pepper spray and a pocketknife in a little basket next to it, and showed it off to visitors. I called it my "home invasion basket."

I got into bed the first night with this ridiculous arsenal spread out around me, thinking that what I really needed, and really wanted, was not an air horn and pepper spray and a Louisville Slugger in the correct size for my height, but not to be alone in the night anymore.

How would I fall and stay asleep, alone in this bed, indefinitely? But now, finally, I knew I didn't have to be afraid. I had always wondered what I would do if my worst fear came true, if a man came to my door, if a man came into my room, while I slept, in the middle of the night, and I had to defend myself. Now I knew. I would rise, roaring, alight with adrenaline, and rush him, prepared to poke him in the eyes and kick him in the nuts and go for the jugular.

That wasn't all I had been prepared to do, I realized, fondling my Amazon arsenal. In the frenzy of my terror I'd been prepared to neutralize the threat. *Go for the jugular.*

I looked around the one-room apartment, at the light leaking in from the other boats and streetlights, and spoke into the silence already broken by wind and water and halyards clanging against the masts of ships.

"I'll kill you, motherfucker," I threatened the dark.

I lay down and pulled up the covers, then reached for the Louisville Slugger and practiced maneuvering it out from behind the bed in one swift motion, jumping to my feet, bringing the bat to my right shoulder, back elbow up, as I had since Little League.

Keep your eye on the ball, my dad had coached, with Wiffle bats and Wiffle balls and then baseballs, always real baseballs. Eye on the ball. Follow through.

I imagined the sound it would make, connecting with a human skull.

"I'll brain you," I told the invisible intruder, for good measure.

And with that promise, I laid down my arms, and said a silent prayer of thanks to all the crushers who had hung the ropes on the hard pitches. Even if they *couldn't marry me and give me babies*, even if they *didn't want to be in a committed relationship*, even if they were more afraid of intimacy than free soloing, even if they couldn't find it in their hearts to accompany me into the dark night of the soul, or accompany me into more than a few of them, they had helped make me fierce enough to face it on my own.

And I fell asleep, and I slept, in my own bed, alone.

THE HIDDEN VALLEY campground felt different, after the 2016 election. I went to Joshua Tree for Thanksgiving hoping to hide from it all, but the nihilism pervading the country seeped into the Hidden Valley. The idyll was broken, if it had ever existed. I was in a bad mood for political, personal, and existential reasons.

It was in this bad mood, on a cold and windy day, that I decided to climb a route that was just a little too hard, even though I wasn't that psyched. I was looking for escape from my own mind, something that would absorb me so totally that I wouldn't feel feelings.

Harold had done it first. He'd climbed a 5.11 that didn't have very many stars—meaning it was hard to climb, but not especially fun, and taken the first-ever whippers I'd ever seen him take, ever, apologizing, Britishly, for every one. But this one-star 5.11 was near the classic Pope's Crack (5.9), which had lots of stars, so it was supposed to be fun. Harold talked me into it, promised he'd finish it for me if I had to lower off.

I just didn't have it that day, probably because I needed to climb more than I wanted to. Maybe it wasn't good to need anything from this strange pursuit, but better just give to it, when you had something to give.

I blew my onsight by hanging on an early piece of gear, a cowardly thing to do. Then I hung on the next piece, an even more cowardly thing. Now I was apologizing to Harold, not even for falling, but just for hanging.

My hands were too small to fill up the whole crack, so they kept slipping, even when I made them into fists, so they were already bloody, even though I was only halfway to the top. I wanted to give up, to lower off, to let Harold finish the route instead. But I couldn't let myself. I was determined to get something from this rock, something I couldn't get from people.

The next part of the climb was also hard. It was a traverse, which meant climbing sideways. It was "heady," which meant both *scary* and *not a good idea to fall*. I'd managed to place a piece of protection, but as I learned, in Tuolumne, from climbing sideways-backward with Fred and Flora, the gear doesn't protect you as well, going sideways. If I let go, or fell off, I'd go flying—sideways.

Swinging sideways was the same as falling down, if you hit something. I'd read that in an old issue of *Climbing* magazine, in the sauna at the gym, what felt like a long time ago. It was called a pendulum. Now, I had created one. My body was the projectile. I was a human wrecking ball.

Did I want to wreck, shatter, go splat? I did not, could not, would not—even if I wanted to. My body wanted to live too much. My body was holding on for dear life.

I couldn't make anyone want me, couldn't make them love me, couldn't make them choose me, but I could love and choose myself. I could choose to live, over and over and over again, choose not to give in to my fear that I'd fall and go splat, become strawberry jam, that I'd die before I could ever be loved.

"You want it too much," someone had once said to me, about sex or love, though I now can't remember which. I'd been afraid of how much

I wanted what I wanted—love, sex, babies, to write a book—even before I'd been told it was too much, or impossible. Now I was even more afraid to show or tell anyone what I wanted.

I'd always wanted it all, that was and remained true. But how much was too much to want something that meant everything? How could I ever make it mean less?

The only way to make it all mean less, or preferably nothing, was to go above. Above the ground, or above the gear, to *go above your nerve*, as my namesake Emily Dickinson wrote, alone in her room in her white dress, never having adventures, unless you count fervently corresponding with other people's husbands, which I can sadly report from personal experience is a tiresome hobby for a woman in her prime.

The most quotable lines of the poem were the first ones:

> *If your Nerve, deny you—*
> *Go above your Nerve—*

But I liked the next ones even better:

> *He can lean against the Grave,*
> *If he fear to swerve—*

And the last ones even better:

> *If your Soul seesaw—*
> *Lift the Flesh door—*
> *The Poltroon wants Oxygen—*
> *Nothing more—*

I'd had to look up "poltroon" when I first saw the word. It was an archaic or literary term that meant not just a coward but an *utter* coward. Even the coward wanted to breathe, to *get that good oxygen*, like Fred always said, reminding you that the breath alone could keep you alive and make you brave.

So I did it. I let my body save my life because my body wanted to live. And feeling how much my body wanted to live made whatever part of me that wasn't my body want to live, too. Even if it hurt.

How had Emily Dickinson known, without throwing herself, stoned, at walls of stone, over and over, for years? How had my namesake known, if she never left her room, that there was a coward locked inside you, gasping for air, and all they wanted was the same thing we all needed, in order to live? Even an utter coward wanted nothing more than breath.

Charging up the final bit of crack to the top, I heard the sound of my own breath again, more mechanical than oceanic, like a ventilator, like some machine was breathing for me; it was that deliberate and regular. It was the machine of my own body, which was not a machine at all. It was made of human, mortal, living flesh as surely as the mountain was made of stone.

That was why I wanted love. Because I was not a rock, nor an island, nor a machine. I wanted love because I was human and mortal and made of flesh and blood.

The rocks had not taken my longing for love away. Even the mountains were not big enough to contain my longing. They only gave me the strength to keep trying to answer it.

The rocks had asked so much of me I hadn't thought I had to give. In my blind desire to climb them, I had given more than I'd known I had. But now I wanted something I couldn't get from a mountain. And I would have to be even more brave.

My soul had seesawed, teetering and tottering, wheeling and reeling, but I'd found a way to open a door in my body and feed it. To give even the cowardly parts of myself the air every living thing and burning desire deserved. In giving the scared parts air, I'd fanned the flames of my heart's desires. The coward might want oxygen, but so, too, did the fire.

I was always climbing away some broken heart. It didn't fix the broken heart, but it made me strong enough to bear it. It made me capable of living in the world with burning and often unsatisfied desire, that only burned hotter when it got some *good oxygen*.

I'd thought that if I could stop caring whether I lived or died, maybe I could stop caring whether I was loved. But now it occurred to me that if I could bear to keep living, then maybe I could be loved. I could climb toward what the poet Katie Ford called "the hope of love." She described the hope of love as "looming" before her—like a crux pitch, or a headwall.

All this time, I'd thought it was my past, or my pain, or my fear that loomed so large. I had not imagined that it could possibly be my hope.

LEILA AND I had come up with a new saying, postelection, on a scratchy phone call while she wrangled her toddlers and I drove alone on some dark road. *The warrior will do what she must.*

I knew what I must do. I would fix my eyes on the summit of my heart's desires. I would throw myself at my wildest dreams the way I had thrown myself at all the walls—and hearts—of stone. I would crawl inside the rocks, but I would not hide there. I would scrape and scrap until I stood on top and it all made sense, if only for a moment. I would let what climbing had taught me make me brave in other ways, help me face fears even greater than falling.

I'd found safety in the broken rock yet again, found places where I fit, found a way out of danger and limbo, a way to let my fear pass through me so I could keep climbing toward my own looming hope.

You could not climb with a broken bone, but you could climb with a broken heart. You could come to know its ache as proof of life—growth, even. When muscles ached, it was because their torn parts were mending, knitting themselves anew with stronger strands and ropes of living stuff.

Even my fleeting wishes for death were proof I was alive. Even when my heart hurt so bad I wanted to die, I held on. I kept climbing. I wanted to live.

EPILOGUE

'D MISSED GLENN'S DAUGHTER'S WEDDING because I was rafting the Grand Canyon with a friend of my brother's. When I came off the Colorado River, I had a message from Glenn telling me to meet him and Fred in the Needles of California, a remote climbing area in the southern Sierra Nevada.

"It'll be on your way home from Arizona," Glenn wrote, helpfully providing directions to an illegal camping spot where he would already be without service by the time I got the message. I followed the directions deeper and deeper into the woods, where the paved roads turned to dirt, the two lanes into one, all the way to the end, where the unmistakable trucks and vans were circled, right where he'd said they would be.

The California Needles were granite peaks poking out of pine forests already smoldering, in some places, from lightning strikes, which was not uncommon in Sierra summertime before the climate crisis reached its fever pitch, and has only become increasingly so. The rock formations all had witchcraft names—the Magician, the Sorcerer, the Witch, the Warlock, the Wizard, the Charlatan, the Necromancer, and even the Djinn, which, according to the downloaded dictionary in my airplane-moded Kindle, was described as "in Arabian and Muslim mythology, an intelligent spirit of lower rank than the angels, able to appear in human and animal forms and to possess humans."

You had to hike three miles past a fire lookout tower to get to the notch between the main formations, where there was an idyllic meadow with grass as green as Astroturf, protected from the sun by the tall rocks' cool shade. The granite was almost white but covered in some kind of lichen that ranged in color from Day-Glo yellow to safety orange to neon green, making the rocks look like they had been haphazardly highlighted by an overly enthusiastic god. The giant domes made the mountains beyond look like molehills. It was also part of the Needles' mystique that at any moment, you could be buzzed by a fighter jet from a nearby military base.

The day after I arrived, we climbed Igor Unchained, so named, explained Fred, for a rattling sound or motion made by the climbing that reminded the first ascensionist of the character from *Frankenstein*. All I remember of that afternoon was the now-familiar experience of being short of breath, while following the constant tugs on the rope from Glenn or Fred up above.

The view from the wall was so spectacular that I'd stopped several times, just to look. Six of the eight formations were all clumped together. From one angle, they looked like shark's fins, or a stegosaurus's back, from another, like the peaks on hand-whipped cream, covered in rainbow sprinkles of bright lichen. All afternoon, I'd stare at them, trying to catch my breath, until the rope said, silently, *c'mon, c'mon*.

When we got back to camp, Fred concluded that now that I was acclimatized, tomorrow we should go climb White Punks on Dope, over on Voodoo Dome, located around a bend in the road that snaked through the formations. The route was mega-mega-classic. Five stars. Considered by many, Fred quoted from the guidebook, to be "the best moderate route in Southern California."

We moved our camp from the forest to a pullout across the highway from the approach trail to the route, where we had a clear view of the formation. In the long mid-July sunset, which was intensified by the haze of the nearby wildfire, Voodoo Dome looked like it could be part of exactly the kind of "religion characterized by sorcery and spirit possession," that was, according to the Kindle dictionary, the definition of the word "voodoo." The sunset filtering through the fire smoke made the white rock fingers look as if they were being lit by colorful stage lights.

It was just me, Glenn, and Fred in the pullout below Voodoo Dome. True to Fred's prediction, not a single car passed our spot next to the highway. Glenn fed his dog, Muggles, his raw meat meal right on the yellow line. We made a big dinner to fuel the climb the next day and ate it in camping chairs with cupholders for our beers. Even though Glenn and Fred assured me that the route name was just the title of a seventies punk song by some band called the Tubes, the racialized language unnerved me, so I laid out my Black Lives Matter T-shirt for a little extra performance allyship that no one but a couple of other white punks on dope would see.

"On the day Obama was inaugurated"—Glenn shrugged, "we climbed Black President."

"Alpine start tomorrow!" Fred joked. In Joshua Tree, where most of the routes were a single rope length, it was perfectly acceptable to set out for most climbing days at noon, after a nice slow morning of coffee and doobs and a big breakfast and more doobs. But we were in the mountains now, and tomorrow we would be doing six pitches (rope lengths) of climbing, so even though it was midsummer and there was plenty of light, we would have to move faster if we didn't want to get benighted, like I had been a few years ago. We did have to wake up early, but not, like, in the dark or anything.

"We're trying to enjoy ourselves here," Fred said as we bedded down for the night in our cars in their dirt pullouts on the side of an empty highway. "It's just for fun."

THE NEXT MORNING, we hit the approach trail just before daybreak. Glenn and Fred, though decades older, were both much fitter and faster, and took off ahead of me, with Muggles at their heels. The whole way up to the base of the climb, I'd find them waiting for me, passing the last of a no doubt once-giant doob. They'd give me the still-burning roach and take off again, and I'd take my rest and catch my breath, a single white female punk on dope. We repeated this process all the way up the approach trail. They never let me get lost, making sure to stop at any forks or iffy, overgrown spots where the trail wasn't clear.

The dirt trail turned to broken rock where the pine forest ran into the base of the wall. Muggles kept us company until all three of us were off the ground. Then Glenn told him, "Go home! Back to the van!" and Muggles started down the approach trail like he had important business.

I thought I could have led the first pitch, since it was a crack the size of my hands, but the next four made me very grateful to be in the company of a bona fide Stonemaster and one of his bolder students. The route was mainly a face climb, meaning you climbed it by holding on to dents and edges and nubs on the rock's face, and there was also a lot of slab climbing, where there weren't even nubs, just rock sloped just enough in your favor that you could stay on it with the physics of the friction caused by your own weight on your own rubber soles.

Glenn led the most classic parts and Fred led the trickiest parts.

While each of them led, the other two of us would take turns belaying, chatting idly, or just sitting in companionable silence.

At the top of the third pitch, the halfway mark, we stopped for lunch. We'd made sandwiches that morning, but Fred had a surprise. He'd carried sliced homegrown tomatoes from his and Flora's garden, kept in a Tupperware because otherwise, Fred said, they'd make the sandwiches soggy.

Before the final pitch, we rested for a moment on the big ledge, getting the ropes all ready. To climb with three people, you needed two ropes. I'd trail the extra one up behind me, then bring them both up at the same time.

"Ms. Weinstein," said Fred, handing me the rack. The guidebook hadn't said anything about the last pitch except that it was a beautiful splitter, so I was only a little nervous. I was always at least a little nervous.

"Summit pitch," said Glenn. "Saved the best for last." We silently exchanged the display of his brake hand, my knot.

"Make it good," Fred said.

Though I wrote with my left hand, I always reached into the unknown with my right. It felt like a magic trick, stretching the arm out of the socket, reaching up, up, up into the crack, finding *that good jam*, feeling it lock in, *locker*, and then tiptoeing my feet into a crack and leaving the ground, appearing to levitate, though really, it was an illusion; the secret was flesh locked in rock.

I began leading us to the top, swimming up the stone, settling into my scuba diver breath, to *get that good oxygen* coveted by coward and hero alike. Glenn's and Fred's words of encouragement faded into pleasant, idle chatter as I climbed out of earshot.

I knew they would never let me deck. I knew I would be safe with them, as long as I *made it good*. They weren't my fathers or brothers or lovers. They were my teachers and my heroes, my friends and my chosen family. My people. Just as much my people, if not more so, than the Jewish people or the American people. There was no danger hidden in their love, maybe because there was so much danger in the sport itself. I trusted them, more than I'd ever trusted anybody.

"Tell your parents they don't have to worry," Fred said, once. "We *got* you."

They did. They had me. They meant it.

Climbing just above them while Glenn held the rope, I was deeply in the zone, almost in a trance. A beautiful splitter could make you move in its own secret rhythm. The chop-chop of the hand jams, the tiptoe of the following feet, the regulated, regulating breath, the pause to place the gear, the satisfaction of picking the right piece, right away. The click of the carabiner as you clipped the rope, and therefore yourself, to the wall. Attached.

I never looked down, only far, far out. It supposedly kept you from being seasick, to look at the horizon. After a sailor had told me that, I used it in the mountains, too. Or I ignored the view and the peril and height it implied and faced the wall, looking for all the small things there were in this world to hold on to. *You'd be surprised how much your body wants to live.*

The top of a dome wasn't like the top of a cliff, where you might huck yourself awkwardly from the vertical back to the flat. On top of a dome, the climbing turns into walking as the curve flattens out under your feet.

I was standing on top, on two feet, safe again. I had landed back on flat ground, a tiny patch of it, thousands of feet above the sea I could almost make out just around the bend of the earth's curvature. I had arrived here using little more than the air all around me (plus the mid-climb ham sandwich) to ascend and rise, against the force that was always trying to pull me down, only wanting to keep me close, and tethered to the earth. Now, alone on the summit, I could see what the dome had been blocking from view.

Mountains beyond mountains again. There was the rock I was standing on, which wasn't white at all, but every shade of gray. Beyond that, a hillside covered in dense green forest with only a few bits of bald granite visible here and there. In the deeper distance, another gray wall rose, hinting at peaks that might be climbable, or might not, or one day would be, by someone yet unborn. None looked as proud or as bewitching as these few granite needles among the pine ones. And beyond that mountain, more mountains, crisscrossing like paper cutouts, one after another after another, getting bluer as they faded into what Rebecca Solnit called "the blue of distance."

I was too far away for Glenn and Fred to hear me if I yelled "off belay," but they'd know they were on belay when the rope went tight, and besides, they could solo it anyway. So I looked out, at all creation, contained only by the bright blue sky, the clouds turning colors as the ancient forests combusted into devastated ash. You could almost feel yourself under the sky's invisible, ever-changing, imaginary dome, atop this rock dome named for a religion characterized by sorcery and spirit possession.

It had worked. The voodoo. The sorcery. I'd been possessed by demons, but I had come to possess myself. Belong to myself. Belong.

Upward, ever upward—*Excelsior. Eureka.* I had found it. It was the will to live. Or the willingness. I'd thought what I wanted was the summit, but now that I was here, I realized I wanted it all—the journey, the fear, the pain, the suffering, the danger, the risk, the uncertainty, the unknown and unknowable. Those, too, along with the top, and the view. I still had a chance, to try, to "get after it"—whatever it was I wanted, and I finally knew what that was. To write a book and fall in love and be a mother, all things I might fail to achieve but would nonetheless try.

It had always been exactly that, but now I finally had the will to pursue my heart's desires, and not just hold on for survival.

The fighter jets never came, so I stood on the summit and let out a roar that only a human being could make, out of breath alone. Glenn heard it, and sent back a single monkey call.

I built an anchor to bring up my followers, my teachers. I could barely reel in the slack fast enough as they both came running up on the ropes I'd hung. When he came into view over the lip of the very top, Glenn stopped to chalk his hands and shook something at me.

"The small stuff!" he said. "We forgot to give you the small stuff!"

"Oh." I shrugged. "I just placed a nut."

"I cleaned it," Fred said. "It was good."

I GOT SEPARATED ON THE DESCENT, and lost sight of all the cairns. The last thing anyone had said to me was "Down." The way the dome was descended was by running down it, like a kid running fearlessly down a steep hill.

Down, I thought, running, slipping, sliding, falling. *Down.*

The dome's rocky slabs gave way to dirt. Ditches and ravines. I tried to sort of ski down one, grabbing a tree and then another, like poles. One branch snapped, and I picked up speed. I watched a pointy stick carve a line into my forearm, which began to bleed. I licked it, long since out of food and water and thankful for the wet and salt. I tried to watch for poison oak. I ran and jumped and sidestepped and stumbled, down, down, down. When I was nearly there, I finally found my footing. When I was a kid, I ran down every hill as fast as I could, and was never afraid. You had to stop moving your legs on purpose. You had to just let them run.

Then I saw the road. Then I stepped on it.

We had climbed up and over the whole dome, so now which way

were our cars? I picked a way. I smelled the smoke before I rounded the bend. They were sitting in their camping chairs, in the middle of the road, beers cracked.

"This is the second doob," said Glenn. "You missed the first one."

"I got lost," I said.

"No, you didn't," said Fred. "You got down."

"Wait," said Glenn. "Don't sit yet." He came over and poured the contents of a water jug over my head, like I had just hit the game-winning homer. Dirt and dust ran down my body to form a mud puddle at my feet.

There was a cold beer sweating in the cupholder. I popped its top with a lighter and they passed me the doob.

Fred pointed with the neck of his beer at the summit of the route we'd just climbed. "We went up there," he grinned.

"Did we?" I wondered aloud. It never seemed real, afterward, but for the blood, and the scars, and the aches—and the stillness.

After we ate, and the sun went down, Fred's stereo was blasting the usual eclectic mix, now Bowie.

"That's us," he said. "'Heroes for a day.'"

He went out to the middle of the empty highway and stood right on the yellow line, his arms spread wide, and looked up at the stars. I walked a few feet down the line, and did the same.

"Heroes for a day," I whispered to the night.

I wasn't lying on the yellow line waiting to be roadkill, like I had been all those years ago. I was standing on it, upright and vertical, like only a human being can.

In memory of Kyle Allen Rott

1987–2023

ACKNOWLEDGMENTS

VERY SPECIAL THANKS to my friend, confidant, and consigliere, Franz Nicolay, who always believed; to Megan Nicolay, without whom I could never have done it; and to Laurel Braitman, who told me that I would be mad if I didn't write this book. Deepest gratitude to my bashert agent, Rayhané Sanders, and bashert editor, Veronica Alvarado, for their hearts, minds, and loving attention. Thank you to the poet Mary Austin Speaker, for her keen eye and design wisdom.

Great gratitude to Pam Houston and Emily Rapp Black, early readers of this work and great teachers of literature. Many thanks to The Headlands Center for the Arts, Caldera Arts, the Roundhouse Foundation, and PLAYA Summer Lake, and especially to the art angels Holly Blake, Elizabeth Ervin Quinn, and Maesie Speer. I'm incredibly grateful to the whole team at Simon Element and Simon & Schuster, especially to Maria Espinosa, Laura Levatino, and Jessie McNeil, who worked so very hard to make this book so very beautiful.

Thank you to my high school English teacher and school newspaper adviser, George Blain Bocarde, who told me I had ink in my veins, which gave me the idea that I could bleed on the page; to Lewis R. Gordon and Anthony Bogues, my first professors of existentialism, philosophy, and truly radical thought and action; and to Alison Osius, for a wonderful editorial experience at the tragically out-of-print *Rock and Ice*.

ACKNOWLEDGMENTS

I am most grateful to the climbing community, and to everyone with whom I've ever shared a rope or a fire, especially Mike Lechlinski and Mari Gingery, John Gruey, Dean Fidelman, Lori Butz, Jean Radle, Allyson Gunsallus, Lindsey Beal, Ralph Burden, John Crook, Patrick Cole Watson, Cole Hoard, Matt Berke and Amelia Wallace, Kye Klamser, Josie McKee, Lauren Austin, Ayla Mae Wild, Lauren Thatch, Elaine Chang, Tanya Rutherford, Cedric and Susannah Bien-Gund, Andy and Charlotte Schriner, and Carissa Schmidt and Nathaniel Schiesher, all of whom have been such kind supporters of my literary strivings, as well as such fine companions in conversation and mountain adventure. I am grateful to my dear friends Erica and Marnie Webb; my dear healers Dr. Erika Dalheim, Dr. Johanna Lelke, and Thais Diehl, my poet hairstylist Pamela Heal, and all of my dock neighbors past and present, whose font consultations, champagne celebrations, and unintentional community are without parallel, especially Bo Farnham, Shosh Roselinsky, Iñaki Garat, Josh Jacobs, Tanner Burke, Justin Kommit, Gianna Ancich, Ann Cromley, Armando Tobriner, Janet Cobb, Stefani Berger, Lucy Phenix, Kay Frame, Helen Canin, and Dr. Sarah Hart-Hess. I am grateful to Helen Christensen, for the room of my own with a view where I wrote this book. Thank you to my fellow Buck's Rockers, Science Olympians, and Infernites.

Most special thanks to the many beloved friends and family who have unfailingly supported me in staying this course and realizing this dream, especially my aunt Ellen Weinstein, who showed me the way to be a professional artist, my uncle Ian Weinstein and aunt Monica Rickenberg, for their sweet encouragement, and my *first* first cousin Julia Lovisa Diamond. Infinite gratitude and love to my amazing parents, Ann and Carl Weinstein, without whom none of this would have been possible.

ABOUT THE AUTHOR

EMILY MEG WEINSTEIN was born in New York and raised in Queens and Long Island. She lives, writes, and teaches on a houseboat in the San Francisco Bay, roams in her second home, the Free Ford Freestar, and roots for the New York Mets.